ON THE WIND'S WAY

ON THE
WIND'S WAY

by William Snaith

G. P. Putnam's Sons, New York

For my wife, Betty, whose company on board softens the edge of the most arduous voyage and whose thoughtful and knowledgeable planning when we set off without her has contributed as much to our safety, comfort, and enjoyment as that of any crew member on board. It has been our custom to salute her version of the well-found yacht at least once during midvoyage. With grateful memories, I do so once again.

ON THE WIND'S WAY

EVERY man should have a point on the scale from which to measure the events of his life, something constant and unchanging against which to reckon his highs and lows, something larger than a batting average and more meaningful than 1000 on the Dow-Jones. I've been lucky enough to sail across the ocean several times and there found a datum of a sort. The North Atlantic is constant enough; Lord knows, it is a steadfast adversary. Its changes are all of a piece, each voyage across meting out its own share of adventure. It can be hard or easy, yet either way it adds up to an unchanging experience. When one constant is a sailboat and the other the sea, improvements to equipment, tricks newly learned to thwart the sea's forays, fade in the presence of that immutable force. Sailing the ocean is a lively adventure for me, that and something more, for each time I have gone the experience has been a high peak in human affirmation.

The sea has not changed since "In the beginning" when as the first task on that mighty third day, it was divided from the dry places. It is the dry places that have changed. Verily, brother, they have changed.

You may turn a deafened ear and half-shut eye to those who cry purple doom, who envision total alienation, of living in fear and trembling, of anguish and despair, of going on meaninglessly in a bleak and anonymous landscape (all this and inflation, too). Yet even with this turning away from total doom there comes a time in the still of a dark night when an insistent voice stops saying, "I can't believe I ate the whole thing," and imprudently asks, "Why am I here?" "Where am I going?" It is then that one needs affirmation and datums. The first defends one against the disquiet from within. The second acts as a certified scale, a measuring stick by which to assess the relentless changes creeping in, almost indiscernibly from day to day. Without a datum or control it is difficult to measure drift. Man is a curious creature; his life functions are slow in responding to evolutionary change, but in response to social change he is a highly mobile unit. Worse, he can, like a chameleon, take on the drab coloration around him, perhaps without being aware of the change.

The memory of a sea voyage may not be the strongest weapon to defend one against the enemy within and without, but its recall can light up the dark of that certain still night and leave pleasure in its wake. Time may be absolute or relative; it is also the function of man's memory. The joys of memory telescope time, just as the joy in listening to the music of J. S. Bach compresses the three hundred years since it was written. The stories of sea voyages from the *Odyssey* through *Hakluyt* and into today retain immediacy and freshness because they took place on the never-changing sea, and each one goes to the secret core of a man's joy. It is a pleasure found not only in the tale of adventures but in the certitude that here on the sea, a man can reaffirm his human animal self, by the power of his arms, his will, and his skill in a direct encounter with a huge and impersonal element and do so in close company with chosen companions.

There is a great joy in the knowledge that this magic still goes on, can still be found. It will continue as long as there is an unspoiled nature to contest and love. Voyages in small sailboats are still made where one can be in the presence, however briefly, of the infinite and of the eternal mysteries. This is the story of one such voyage—a race from Bermuda to Sweden.

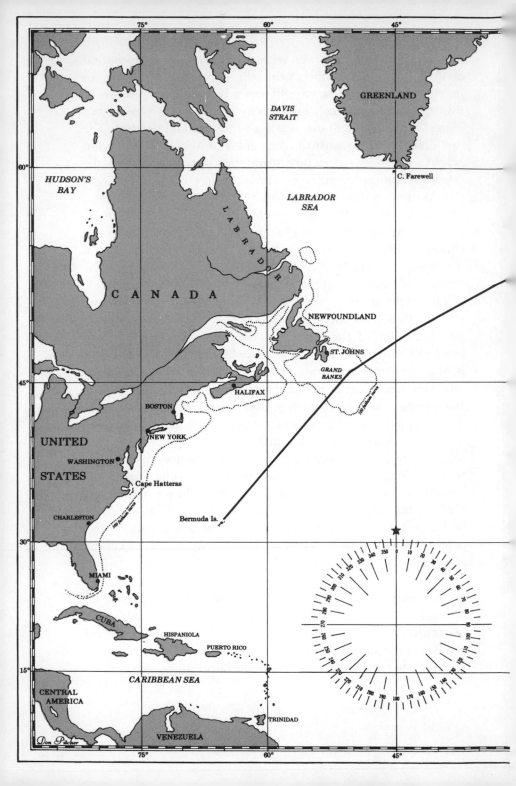

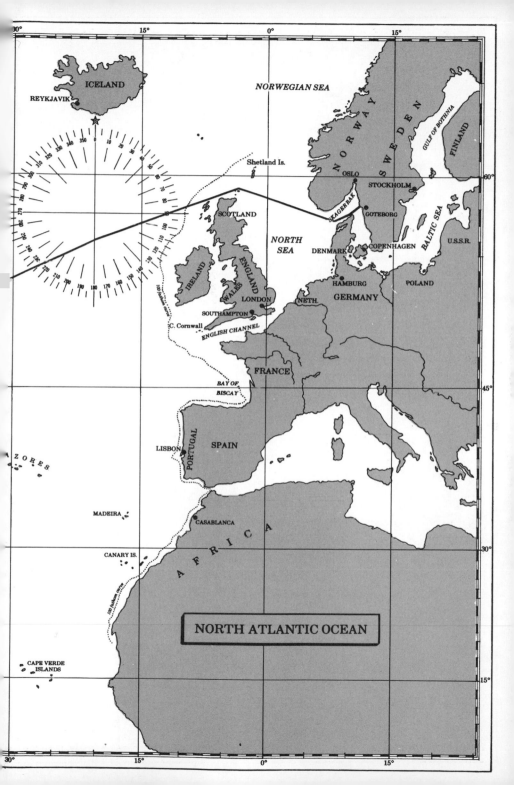

1

WE are coming on the Grand Banks, east of Newfoundland, having had troubled sailing for several days. Outwardly the passage is going well, but we know differently. We have had an accident and are perilously low on drinking water. One tank, the large one, lost all of its water. The other had been leaking badly, but miraculously, since the wind drew aft to the quarter, that leak has either stopped or slowed down. The tanks are located midship under the transom berths, and despite removal of major amounts of costly woodwork, we cannot discover what happened or why. We are simply faced with a dismal fact and future. We have less than twenty gallons left in one tank (which may start leaking again) and about twenty gallons distributed in plastic containers.

Bucky Reardon, who had sailed summers as a hand with me ever since college, brought the disaster to my attention a few days ago, the first night out as a matter of fact, saying, "Captain, you better take a look at this." The moment he spoke I knew we were in for trouble. He was using his disaster voice, a cross between the messenger bringing the news from Thermopylae and the yearly reading from the Book of the Dead—the same voice with which he tells me that the head is broken down or that a torn centerboard is hanging alongside like a wounded shark. (These are not imagined incidents: He has had occasion to announce both such calamities in the midst of races. He has probably been elected to do so by the rest of the crew because of his acknowledged good standing with his God and with me.)

I went below to find the cabin sole taken up and a good deal of water in the bilge. If a voice can suggest a hesitant shrug, his sounded like that, saying, "I don't know, Cap, you better taste it." Despite my self-advertised reputation for discernment in things liquid, it was quite obvious that I was not being asked to pass on a vintage. This one would never pass the Pure Food and Drug Administration much less the Chevaliers du Tastevin. It was highly flavored with engine lubricating oil with just a dash of rusty beer can and not of a good year, but, with all that, unmistakably fresh with little salt in its base. Suddenly, the baffling happenings of the past several days, if not clear, were partially explained.

The logistics of the race to Sweden for the King's Gold Cup were complicated. First we sailed the Cruising Club of America's race from Newport, Rhode Island, to the finish line off St. David's Head Light in Bermuda, some 650 miles away across the Gulf Stream. This race is an important and heavily vied for classic in its own right. At Bermuda we were to outfit and start a new race to Marstrand in Sweden, about 3,500, perhaps stormy, miles away. The night before the finish of the Bermuda Race the fleet encountered a short-lived, vicious tropical storm. *Figaro* must have torn her tanks then.

(Weeks later, when the tanks were examined in a shipyard, the pattern of the disaster could be pieced together. In all probability, as the boat tossed about in the storm, the rush of water surging up and down in the tanks tore the baffle plates loose, whose function, alas, is to damp the rush and protect the tank. The plates were riveted and, when torn loose, permitted the water to run out of the gaping rivet holes. In one tank these holes were near the bottom. That tank lost nearly all of its water. The holes were halfway up the side of the other tank. But we did not know all this at the time of discovery. Being believers, we took it as another wicked stroke of the fates.)

Figaro has a nagging leak, not a big one, but persistent. Even the most perfect need some touch of clay to defend them against hubris. It is probably through a stuffing box. She, therefore, is no stranger to water in her bilge. In a shoal centerboarder, even a pail of water loose in her shallow bilge wreaks havoc, getting into drawers and lockers. There is nothing more disheartening on a cold wet night, when you are looking toward dry underwear and shirt before turning in, to find your clothes in the drawer nestled in a pool of water of their own. Because of this weakness in her list of charms, we pumped her regularly and were slow to recognize any increased flow. As a matter of fact, we tried to brush such intelligence aside. But now the discovery of the leaks clarified the strange goings-on in Bermuda.

After finishing in Bermuda, and in the early stages of preparation for the race to Sweden, to begin a week later, we found our tanks low on water. Hamilton Harbor in late June is hot and humid, a sunny bright sauna bath. Water is an imperative. When you are faced with far-reaching and frightening problems, your first choice is to erase the awful portents and pass the blame on the carelessness of your helpmates. It is an easier prospect to contemplate. Besides, one should never pass up the opportunity to reinforce one's authority. In stern tones I accused the men of bathing on board and of other unmanly and unseamanlike practices. Brushing aside their protestations, I carefully explained that this particular year Bermuda was experiencing difficulty in the matter of water. Since the blight hit the cedars, high thermals held the clouds in a teasing halo offshore. (I know of few inhabitants who wanted or deserved a halo less.) This discouraging phenomenon made the rain fall in an agonizing ring around the scented isles. The waters were being given back to the waters. The islanders were helpless in the face of a frustrating phenomenon slowly turning them into first cousins of Sisyphus. This contingency had to be met by direct measures, for they knew which side of the bread held their butter. Brides may be one man's delight or another's trial, but they are meat and drink to Bermuda. The young brides, being introduced into the heady world of matrimony in the pleasure dome of Bermuda, need inordinate amounts of water to keep themselves fresh and lovely for their clean-cut ardent young husbands. The more heat generated by the climate and the inner fires set roaring by legality and propinquity, the greater the frequency of showers. The more salt added to the so-called fresh shower water, the more often the *bain-douche* is turned on. Fresh and clean brides are the lifeblood of Bermuda's economy and are as dear to them as any Transylvanian virgin to Dracula. Whatever else, the hotels must resound with the joyfully innocent shrieks of these maidens that were. Therefore, water was being grudgingly doled out to yachts at prices approaching *vin ordinaire* or Coca-Cola.

In order to insure a supply of water, we filled our tanks early, before the begging mob descended. The afternoon before the start we took *Figaro* down channel to St. George to be near the starting line. On the way around through the channel from Hamilton we sounded the tanks again and found them low. The life-style in Bermuda during the week from the ending of one race to the start of the new one is as sybaritic as the Anglo-Saxon ethic will allow; nevertheless, it still plays havoc with one's response to adversity. The shore-side indulgences, while not equal to Ancient Rome in its decadence, leave one subject to the same vacillation and irresolution in the face of threat and misfortune. So again the lectures and accusations and recriminations from me instead of finding out why. As we were coming into St. George, while I berated the crew, Bucky spotted the Coast Guard cutter, our starting vessel. We came alongside her at the pier. There is a quality in Irishmen which enables them to find one another in the midst of the crowd, a sort of *sang de peau* which passes through the air, performing a magic on the emigrés from the Green Island which blossoms either into a donnybrook or blood brotherhood.

Luckily, the one Bucky found on board the cutter was a

kindred spirit. He passed us a freshwater line in defiance of regulations and the austere majesty of the United States. We felt no guilt. It was only water and we were taxpayers.

The discovery of the cause for the loss of water weeks later when we were back on the beach did not help us that first night out. That night, ignorant of the cause of the trouble and in the democratic spirit beloved by our Republic, we held a long council of war discussing our options:

(1) Abandon the race and go back to Bermuda, less than twenty-four hours away.

(2) Abandon the race and sail back to the States, about four days away.

(3) Continue the race and delay a decision until near a point of no return, say near Nova Scotia or Newfoundland, and reconsider our options then.

If men had the gift of prophecy would there be so many casual acts of commitment? Would the saber that moved the Light Brigade forward have arched through the sunlight with such flashing grace? Would Custer have considered Little Bighorn just another piece of frontier real estate? Would Ahab have turned Starbuck's warning away so easily? We too are ungifted with the arts of prophecy, but we did know our water was seeping away and we had weeks to go. Did we weigh our choices carefully? Did we reach for reasonable, if disappointing, conclusions? Hell no! We are sporting bloods all, caught up in that ridiculous syndrome "The race goes on." So we went on.

We are here, drawing nearer Newfoundland, less than forty gallons of water aboard for eight men, no guarantee against further loss and with at least two weeks of sailing still ahead —one-third gallon per day per man, for all needs—drinking, cooking, etc. With great self-control, we could make do with that, but what if we were becalmed for a week (unlikely) or, worse, dismasted (horrors). The final decision is to be made. It is not one to be taken lightly. The crew in their trusting innocence have in effect left the decision to me. They are being bravely stupid or stupidly dense about our plight. They are taking the tradition of "the Captain makes the decisions" too seriously. I am a Sunday painterish Lord Jim blessed with no more wisdom and prescience than any man who can afford a 46-foot yawl. And as for any gift of prophecy, if I were to open a chicken I would not even be able to look at the entrails with equanimity much less read them.

If only they knew how I could use a sign! Any reasonable amount of doubt or warnings of caution, however reluctantly expressed, would help me reach a conclusion; even an agreement with a degree of hesitation in the voice would have an enormous impact on the nature of my decision. But how do they act in this moment of critical decision? Half of them have gone to sleep and the other half are on watch, thinking only of getting into a berth themselves. I am below, awake, suffering the same long night of tears which must have been Pizarro's lot just before he burned his boats. But then Pizarro was a hard case, a bravo. Could I be any less brave than my crew? The tradition of the sea does not take kindly to men who quit; it enshrines only men who say, "Don't give up the ship" or "I haven't begun to fight." Yet I am almost overwhelmed by the idea of going out improperly prepared, awed by the sheer size and the power lurking in the unchanging sea.

I have regressed to an older time, when the sea was a hiding place for monsters and death was served out carelessly, unthinkingly, in an unfeeling lottery. Dare we go on? Dare I ask my friends to go with me? We are running out of time. They will want an answer.

It is night. *Figaro*'s cabin is invaded by the sea's mysterium and the undercurrent of threat, but she is uninvolved with fallible human credulities and frailties. She carries steadily eastward, her cabin a single luminous island in a vast heaving darkness. Tonight the cabin does not serve as completely in its usual capacity as a retreat and shelter. The area of assurance has narrowed. I am staring, almost vacantly, at the pilot chart laid out in front of me, searching perhaps for some secret sign, one not immediately visible. Somewhere buried in it is the hope of revelation, a moving finger writing an answer to my urgent need for guidance. The chart stares back as vacantly; there is a feeling of arrested time, as though I am under the influence of a hallucinogen.

A shaded, low burning oil lamp, fastened to the forward bulkhead, swings in its gimbals. Its light extends in softly diminishing intensity to the terminator line where shadows and uncertainty begin. In its pendular swing, the area of illumination pushes into the soft-edged shadows. As the border of light advances into the berth, the huddled bulk of a sleeping member of the off-watch appears. He is Monk Farnham, our navigator. Up until now I have been aware of his presence through his gentle snoring. The light swings away and he disappears again, but the decision cannot be as easily wiped aside.

The shifting penumbra picks out objects, the highlight gleam of the stylus on the drum barograph, a sharp accent which leaps from the background with the pinpoint intensity of a light from a distant shore. The ink line under the stylus is poised at 29.50 in a division of areas marked as changeable on a small bellows barometer. The light moves on to the brushed steel knurling of the radio knobs and other reflecting surfaces, bringing them briefly to life. Like certain ideas, these things spring into being as they are transiently illuminated, then, dulled by the shadows, fade.

There outside our thin palisade is the sea, devoid of memory, unaware and unfeeling of the weight and presence of any man or machine, dealing out savagery or serenity from either hand as in a lottery and wholly indifferent to the plight of any mariner, ancient or modern. The sea! Last of the mysteries within the earth's mantle; an untamed element, earth's last frontier as well as the first mother. Possibly the last skulking haunt of discarded gods. How does one presume to challenge such an adversary in the middle of an adventure which is not

7

going well and whose outcome is not only unclear but whose auguries are bad?

My staring catalepsy is broken. I am aware of a nervous reaction. I had placed my hand palm down and fingers spread, on the lower part of the chart as I stared at the area near where we sail. Unconsciously, perhaps in an attempt to concentrate thinking, as one does in pacing, I had been stamping the eraser end of a pencil up and down between my fingers. The pencil moved up and down between the fingers in an orderly progression, like staves on a sheet of music inscribing a wail. I am reminded of a time I did this very thing, on a dare, with an ice pick. For the life of me I cannot remember why I took up the dare. Perhaps to prove to myself that I was brave or that I had icy control. There must be a flaw in character to respond to such a dare, an exercise in bravado. Should such a man be entrusted with a decision affecting the lives of other men? But this is only a pencil and I am being very careful.

I drop the pencil and get up from the table to have a look at the night. Poking my head through the companionway, I see Knud at the wheel. The other members of the watch are forward, on lookout and tending gear. Knud's rainhood is tied under his chin; his face wet with fog is strangely underlit by the red glow coming from the binnacle. He looks like a vision from the nether regions. All of the wrong planes are illuminated. His face is all red highlighting and deeply shadowed planes, like an experiment in chiaroscuro by Correggio or Caravaggio. He speaks gently enough: "All's well here, Skipper, she marches along." I acknowledge his desire to cheer me and look around.

As the boats heels I see the gray crest of a wave abruptly loom, as it rushes into the pale light coming from the open hatch, and as suddenly disappear, as it is absorbed into the encircling blackness. No stars show; their cold glint which normally establishes a top for this void is hidden. The rush of the wind provides a clamorous counterpoint to the racking silence of nighttime vulnerability.

In spite of everything one knows and has learned,

tonight—here in the cabin—the world has shrunk. It has taken on the dimension of our problems, as though we have been thrust back to an older time. The world was once flat, offering choices of physical and moral courage to a Columbus, a Galileo, whose charts showed the earth as a limited space surrounded by horrors and hobgoblins. It took a high order of courage to think of the earth as a minor place in the universe, to think of it as something other than as God's appointed rendezvous for his best-laid plans. Once the point has been made, it became easier to further diminish it and its gods to that of a bush-league planet hanging in a minor corner of an already huge and perhaps still-expanding universe. That's how they tell it now. All this is possible. Tonight it is equally possible to think of the earth as a threatening enigma, with a super-power in charge, who regulates and rules through horned and finned legates and vicars and who punishes or rewards with equal disregard. It is possible that the edge of the sea swarms with sea serpents, dragons, and discarded gods blowing conch shells, sounding the knell exactly as drawn by old geographers. All of these old boys couldn't have been off their rockers! The visible world is reduced to a narrow quadrant bristling with threats. For the moment these are restrained to an angry encirclement; the thin wooden walls of *Figaro* are our fortress. But the threat from the outer darkness can turn to trouble without warning. Dare we add the scarcity of water as another hazard to this already chancy environment? This is a harsh arena which recognizes no neutral corner or My Lord of Queensberry rules.

I look again at the pilot chart for the North Atlantic. It is covered with wind roses giving the percentage of winds by directions and force for each month. It speaks of gales. Gales mean trouble—wind, rain—rain is water. Do you suppose we could catch enough of it? The chart is only an average; it is not a guarantee of rain. But the wish is father to the thought. Do I dare trust us to an average and can we catch enough water if the average performs? I do have a rain catcher aboard, made

9

for some such impossible situation as this. It is not the sort of decision one makes on such vague hope. We'd best sleep on it. Strangely we do.

2

IT is hard to stay gloomy aboard *Figaro,* although events conspire to peg our spirits at the nadir. It is not too farfetched to imagine she exudes happiness, an invisible elixir distilling from her woodwork, making short work of the glums. She's just the opposite of the craggy manors that lady writers of Gothic novels discover on Cornish cliffs or isolated moors in Devon or Transylvania. Whereas these haunted bits of architecture inject their inhabitants with broody gloom, *Figaro* does what she can to chase the blues. Besides, I really don't believe the average man has the stomach for protracted gloom unless he be one who looks for it around every corner like Schopenhauer or wallows in it like Hamlet. Most of us would incline toward hedonism or one of its jolly subdivisions. Unhappily the events of life intrude and no matter how we stuff the mattress with down, a few nails from the fakir's cot show up in our bed of pleasure.

In response, therefore, to *Figaro*'s magic elixir and my own brighter instincts, I awoke after the long and lonely night of wondering and reached eagerly for lightheartedness. From my first waking moment, I felt sure the right decision would be made. That conviction persists despite a look out of the companionway. We are in the murky first ring of a watery purgatory. Somewhere nearby is Virgil waiting to guide us deeper or else the Flying Dutchman ready to rattle his chains. We must elude them both.

Figaro sails in an eerie environment, a world of curdled gray mist. At times the coils of curd thicken and a deeper murk settles around her. Suddenly the layers thin and the boat sails in a strangely pale crepuscular light. Each droplet in this thinner mist hangs separately against the washed-out yellow eye of the sun; a scummy cataract of varying density veils its burning stare. The chalky green face of the ocean is seen in a short radius around the boat, its heaving surface broken by small tumbling crests. The waves come out of the mist suddenly, invisible until they are almost on the boat and then as quickly disappear ahead; a rush of energy, hurrying toward an undisclosed rendezvous. Only the bow wave roils the even pattern of the oncoming seas as it falls back diagonally across their path. The churned air imprisoned in foaming bubbles breaks out and hisses in rage as the bubbles clutch fruitlessly at the hull slipping by. Then with a last crackle, no longer sounding angry, like the ultimate gush of gas escaping from stirred champagne or of Alka-Seltzer, the wave expires quietly into the mist leaving a wake discernible to no one but the two Mother Carey's chickens who have decided to be companions to this voyage. The bow plunges steadily on as though it, and not we, knows where we are going. It is not precisely the morning for hornpipes and chanteys.

As the morning moves on the weather looks as though it will break clear, even a suspicion of frosty blue tints the muddy blanket overhead. But then the boat enters another area of heavy fog, the sea disappears, all but the bubbles. The bow can no longer be seen, but its wave is still heard in tempo with the rise and fall as it plunges on somewhere ahead. *Figaro* carries on steadfastly, unshaken by the lack of visibility. I cannot say as much for myself; blind Polyphemus at the mouth of the cave, wondering from which corner the assailant will come.

My son MacLeod stands at the wheel. His watch captain, Bobby Symonette, sits under the dodger smoking a Montecristo No. 1, the size which lasts longer. An unfailing rule on all my *Figaros* gives the man smoking a good cigar the right to enjoy it under the dodger (except in the case of alarums and excursions). I think it a crime against civilized behavior to let a cigar burn like a torch, hot and hard in the wind. The fact of my liking cigars must have a great deal to do with this sensitivity. Cleody, on the other hand, who does not smoke cigars feels the rule to be outrageous, especially in view of the fact that Bobby can make the enjoyment of a cigar last more than one hour. To Cleody's mind this is one hell of a long time to devote to civilities while other men stand out in the wet and cold. In spite of his voiced protest, he steers cheerfully.

I am not the one to thwart the authority of the man in charge, especially in a rule of my own making, so I sit down alongside Bobby and accept a cigar. After carefully lighting up, I ask, "Do you think we can count on catching enough rain water on the way across to piece out our supply?"

"It's a thought. We've never gone across when we did not have our share of rain. We might as well put it to use."

"I am thinking that way. If we wash in seawater, don't shave, boil as many things as we can in half seawater, except for coffee and soup, we could make it across with water to spare. If we catch rain in addition, we will have built-in insurance."

Monk, from a position in the galley aft, says, "It sounds good to me."

During the lunch break, at the change of watch, the first time we are all together, I broach the idea to the whole crew. I tell them about the rain catcher made for just such a contingency. It is especially fitted to the boat, a suspended fabric bathtublike gismo lying in the waterway, the tops fastened between the rail and the hand grabs on the cabin top. It is fitted with a spout at the bottom so we can pour off into containers. Knud Reimers, the other watch captain, is a Swedish citizen. He likes the idea of coming home in a sailboat. It is the true Viking (he pronounces it "wicking") return; the only honorable return is to stand up in a boat or be prone on a shield. Once the older and, by inference, wiser men are agreed, the young unhesitatingly go along with the idea. They put their faith in us; we have placed ours in the boat. She has become more than a thing; she is entrusted with our lives. We are committed.

Everyone goes enthusiastically topside to see how the rain catcher fits. We dig it out of its bag. A shock-odor of creosote hits us in the nose, so strong that were it not for the damp sea air our eyes would smart. The cloth is fiberglass. It must still be curing. The smell is so strong we decide to leave it on deck spread out on the cabin housetop to let it air. We are convinced that now having awakened the chemical beast, if we dared put it back in the bag, it would creep in the night.

We are surrounded by fog. The rain catcher and ourselves are soon as wet as if we had been dipped.

Figaro never falters through all this. She plunges along as though she did not have grievously wounded tanks in her vitals and as if the souls on board did not secrete little quaverings of their own. Seeing or not, oblivious of the threat of oncoming or overtaking vessels, she sails on. Occasionally, an out of sync wave catches her bow and a shattering of spray shoots diagonally across her deck. Shaking off the water through her freeing ports, she picks up her rhythm as though nothing happened. She's one hell of a boat. How can anything bad happen to you when you are in her!

That's a good question, friend, a real measure of the mythic trust one puts in a creature-thing. Anyway that's what it is all about and how it stands. We are physically sound, perhaps a bit bruised in spirit, and committed to some two weeks of racing in the open Atlantic. While the crew do not show it, there must be an underlying unease, like that running through an army that has crossed a Rubicon by forced march and wonders if its baggage train will catch up. We have placed our reliance in one another and in the boat. If ever a boat is capable of putting out magic, we could sure as hell use some of it now.

A sport is something special in order to offset an image, which, to the uninitiated, must appear to be an idiot's delight.

For those not hooked on ocean racing, yachtsmen must seem to be a web-footed, secular subsection of the Penitentes, a strange order of devotees, each man serving as his own Torquemada and his own subject for trial by water. He allows himself to be torn from his normal habitat and defenses; his usual bodily functions, habits, and schedules are upset and in a restlessly rocking shelter at that.

This little vessel, the repository of our faith, in whose fortitude we believe, despite her seeping innards, is the only heroine in an otherwise all-male cast and blessed with a man's name at that—Figaro. Like all beauties who quicken subjective response, she can be given dimensions. Instead of the standard breasts, beam and buttocks we count her vital statistics as 46-foot overall, 32 feet 6 inches on the water line with a beam of 12 feet. She is a centerboarder and a yawl. Designed by Olin Stephens of Sparkman & Stephens and built in eighteen long months by Joel Johnson, a fine craftsman in Black Rock, Connecticut, in itself a muddy backwater which somehow finds its way into Long Island Sound. She is double planked with Honduras mahogany over ⅜ inch Oregon spruce. Her keelson is white oak, a massive timber, personally selected by Joel. He used a hand adze to achieve the finished shape. It was a great sight to see Joel standing astride the balk and taking off long slivers and short as accurately and fine as with a plane. One rarely sees that sort of skill and craftsmanship anymore. Just to see it is a privilege. Unhappily the balk lay too long in the building shed during the protracted building period while wonders took place above. It checked badly, being very green in the beginning, and did not dry well. Right after launching, we had trouble with the nagging leaks until another craftsman stopped them. Now the water comes in only at the stuffing box and that too will be cured. Orginally, Figaro drew 4 feet 6 inches with her board up. With her bronze board down, she drew another 3 feet 6 inches. I changed her draft and ballast for this race, but that story deserves a separate telling later on.

Her layout is quite conventional, with her galley aft. The

main saloon is handsome. It is paneled in Brazilian rosewood; the forward bulkhead paneling frames an open fireplace with a white overmantle. This is shaped like a truncated obelisk. It is of white formica into which nautical decorations in imitation of scrimshaw were cut. As part of the decorations I included a line from Samuel Pepys' *Diary*, "My Lords in discourse discovered a great deal of love to this Ship." Even in her building days, I sensed she would be that kind of boat. I did these engravings myself and have the calluses to prove it. Oval escutcheons on which gimbaled oil lamps are mounted are done in the same technique.

This saloon holds four berths, two regular uppers and two in-extension transoms under which are the wounded and bleeding water tanks. A cabin forward is separated from the saloon by the head on the port side and two hanging lockers across the passageway to port. The roller coaster movement of this forward cabin is exaggerated when the boat is banging into a head sea. When we are at sea, its use is normally reserved for the ship's acknowledged "Iron Guts."

But a boat should be more than a sterling example of the boat-builder's art and man's desire to embellish her with decorations. Obviously, she means a special thing to the man who sails her. She has the ability to surcharge each event with a special aura, a release of spirit, a feeling of safety, and a sense of fellowship.

Consider a single instance when the boat becomes the only secure center of your suddenly changed world—a North Atlantic storm (there is a 75 percent chance of encountering one in a crossing). The usual cyclone system, not a cyclone but the pattern associated with a low-pressure area, lasts an average of two to three days in its coming and going, during which unhappy time a thought threatens to overwhelm all other ideas. It is the question buried in one's mind or expressed to a companion alongside, "How the hell did I get myself into this?" Like as not, the storm will leave bone-tiring repairs in its wake. Yet, if the boat and company are proper, it somehow adds up to a rewarding experience.

Not the least of the various magics which take place is the bond created between a man and the boat in which he sails. It is not necessarily that between a man and a thing. After a time at sea a boat becomes more than a clever assemblage of insensible matter. I think of a boat as a creature thing. For me she is infused with a persona, hovering on the edge of animation. It should not be difficult to understand how a yacht can become imbued with anima and personality. After all, it is a shelter and shield, however frail, and each yacht develops attributes and characteristics peculiar to herself in the way she meets the conditions and hazards of a passage. She can be cranky or sea-kindly, but in the end the man and boat are made partners in the presence of the antagonist, the sea. To one degree or another this bond is shared by all who sail in her and is not the sole privilege of the man who pays her yard bills, although somewhere within the Judeo-Christian ethic the idea persists that the degree of love is directly related to the amount of oneself and of one's wealth given. However painful this way to or from love may seem, especially to a man paying alimony, or yard bills, there is no doubt whatever that the bond between the boat and the owner-skipper increases when the burden of a decision which involves his faith in the boat is placed upon him.

Even while the man who sails in her responds to her anima, this creature-thing somehow becomes adapted to his bent and temperament though cherishing idiosyncrasies of her own. Chameleonlike she takes on the coloration of her owner's needs. Each man uses his boat in his own way to fill certain wants. There are as many roads to Nirvana as boats and men. Nowhere does this show up as precisely as in choosing a name for the darling of his heart. Linguistics and semantics have become important analytical tools in philosophy and behavioral sciences. The choice of a boat's name is the semantic key to his dream, a revealing decision; the clues to his attitude are as clear as the strewn shreds in a paper chase.

The names fall into easily identifiable categories. As an instance, *Mother's Mink* and *String of Pearls* betray certain uxorious guilt feelings. *Press on Regardless, September Song, Last Chance,* speak of the quiet perturbation in the face of onrushing years. *Atomic, Hurricane, Leopard* (usually found on racers) vie with the names chosen for automobiles by automakers in the hunt for virility symbols and a wish-fulfilling longing to identify with tearing power and force. Of quite another order is the desire to relate to the beauty and poetry of the sea. One could let go in Mailerian hyperbole or choose a stanza from a Masefield poem which would dramatically fill a transom and provide inspiring reading for those behind. But timidity, inhibitions, and age-old models intrude. A popular device whereby to capture the sea's magic is to choose a name with the prefix "sea." The waters abound with *Sea Winds, Sea Stars, Sea Witches,* etc. It is my presumption that there are as many names starting with *"Sea"* in *Lloyd's* Register of Yachts, as listings of Martinez in the Madrid phone book, or in the Manhattan directory, for that matter.

In another reaching out for identity with beauty, we encounter *Aphrodites, Apollos,* and *Circes,* and for those who wish on a star, there is an *Orion, Vega,* or *Arcturus.*

A whole other order of boat names belongs to the dedicated family men. Their boat transoms carry conjunctive family names such as *Joanted* or hyphenated as in *Mar-jac-lou.* It is the bridegroom's last epithalamic song or else a sneaky way to involve the whole family in a sport for which they have little stomach and less enthusiasm.

I do not intend to denigrate any man's choice of name for his ark of dreams but rather to confirm the notion that there is a boat for all seasons in men.

I have made a brief résumé of the origins of boat names because it now falls on me to reveal how I chose the name for my own heart's delight. I have known privilege, joy, rage, and frustration as the owner of a string of boats called *Figaro 1* through *Figaro 5.* On the face of it, this redundant choice paints me as an unimaginative clod or one with dynastic dreams. I must profess, "It is not so." My first boat bore the name *Cleody-Skipper,* named for my two eldest sons, MacLeod and Shepperd (Skipper). With the birth of our third son, Jonathan (Jocko), reason returned. The addition of one more child-inspired suffix seemed an empty game. I came to see the shortcomings of the practice. The first seizure on acquiring a new boat is poetic, an anodyne perhaps for signing the check. But my new boat had a smallish transom, incapable of carrying a reasonable stanza in Coast Guard-approved letter size. I did own a beloved dog named Figaro. Immediately one is repelled. What manner of man would exalt a dog over his children or give a dog's name to a thing of beauty like a sailboat (even if the dog is lit by a beauty of his own and if the genus name is that of God spelled backward). It is a tangled tale requiring some explanation. The secret lies in the answer to the question—how did my dog get his name?

A phenomenon that I recognize but can never quite explain is the fact that I instinctively find myself thinking at cross purposes to any establishment with which I have contact, be it institutional, political, social, or esthetic. As an instance: I am emotionally and actively dedicated to contemporary art. I am the head of a leading design firm. For several years running, my paintings had been hung in the Whitney Museum Annual of American Paintings (a practice now discontinued). I was protected from what was happening around me for a time by my recognition of two older polarities of genius—Picasso and Klee. But one day, looking past these two, I wrote a critically polemic book bemoaning certain onrushing antihuman trends. In this I took my stand alongside Ortega y Gasset and other distinguished voices against the spoilers of the human spirit. But, unlike them, I fell from institutional grace.

In another instance, as a minority liberal ideologue in a tory stronghold, I served for several years as Democratic Party Chairman in my town but finally gave way to the fact that I had little admiration or stomach for politics and for several of my party's candidates (and even less for others).

In these various ways, I find myself closer to the quaking edge than the quivering epicenter of a whole order of establishments. It is not by plan—it just turns out that way. It is obvious that being a temperate rebel, never having learned either to make my peace or take to the outer barricades, I have wound up in a mild limbo with undefined geographical borders. There is no home for such.

There may be something in all of the foregoing which harks back to my never-waning admiration for Beaumarchais' antic scamp Figaro—not just for the embellishments added by Mozart and Rossini, but for the character himself.

It is him, the essence of that character, for whom my dog was named and whom my various *Figaros* honored—a lively scamp thumbing his nose at the establishment around him, left, right, and center.

This explanation for my repetitious selection should be enough, but even while recognizing the dangers of "He doth protest too much," there is a very sound, if entirely different, reason for the reiteration. We live in a confused and overly-communicated-to world, wandering at a loss in the midst of a traumatic identity crisis. We are witness to the loss of self in the lonely crowd. It is comforting in all this to hold on to a sense of continuity, a something that belongs to you and to which you belong. It may be minimal, but nevertheless it is reassuring to be part of a continuing stream, even if it is only the name for boats. This should not be confused with the hollowness of dynastic dreams or substitute clutchings for immortality. Choices like this begin and end with you. This minimal symbol of continuity may be a poor thing, but while it lasts it is all your own.

Having thus introduced you into one of the pothering muddles that confound and confuse a yachtsman's heart and mind, I can speak glowingly of my joy, rage, frustration, in the ownership of my *Figaros* all in one breath. It is because my normally happy involvement with boats is complete. It is my form of Zen. Beginning with the passive enjoyment of the beauty of Sail to the active excitements of competition and through this latter into the theory and self-inflicted practice of do-it-yourself yacht design, I have been enthralled by boats in their many aspects. Through boats I have made lasting friendships with men who sail with me and whom I sail against.

A boat designed to cock-a-snook must be saucy, pert, and nimble on her heels. *Figaro* is all of that and more. She is reliable and gives off confidence that she will take you out and bring you back safely.

3

WE should have known this particular argosy would be loaded with grief. If we had not been so hyped up by the idea of racing across the Atlantic once more, our built-in early warning system would have been operational and flashed the red light. But the excitement and adrenals running at high pressure jammed and tuned out all psychic antennae and receptors. ("What then! What if you knew?" one can ask— Gone anyway, I guess.) Well, it might have made a difference. At least we would not have treated all adverse situations casually, like an annoying fly, something to be brushed aside or swatted down. It wasn't just the disappearance of freshwater. We should have seen the signs from the start we made on one of Bermuda's prime cruddy days.

Bermuda weather generally performs as advertised, just like the pictures in the travel folders. It's all there—the pink house, its white roof sparkling against a cerulean sky, the lovely long-legged nubile bride propped against a bicycle, the fatuous grin on the stalwart young husband clad in plaid shorts, knee-length hose, and an electric white, button-down shirt, and over all the sunny-bright weather. Bermuda weather is a clockwork phenomenon. Someone gets up every morning, winds up the Bermuda High and sets it spinning benignly overhead. From it pours sunshine and other good things. Under its glowing beneficence everything becomes transformed into a pleasure dome. Scruffy lawns look like English cricket pitches, school-teachers from East Cowslip take on the fascinating features of starlets playing out the role of debutante of the year, and the ocean shimmers like the biggest and friendliest heated swimming pool in the world.

The weather always acts that way except when you are making a landfall or on the day one hoists the blue Peter in signal for the departure or at least until one noses out of the long channel from Hamilton sheltered behind the reefs. Once outside, the wind is adverse, the heavens growl warnings, and the sea kicks up such a fuss at the Mills Breaker Buoy and at Kitchen Shoals that even the hardiest stomach is threatened with a major wringing out. Caliban is still alive and well and sticking it to you on the scented isles.

That is how it came on during the morning hours of Thursday, June 30, when we, charged-up and desensitized by the trumpery image of ourselves as the last of the seaborne adventurers, set out to wrest the Gold Cup offered by the King of Sweden from all of the other eighteen ocean-ranging hotspurs entered against us. The day began inauspiciously and deteriorated from there. A desultory thin rain falling from low-hanging clouds made us just as wet as if we were in one of the driving variety. Rain water in any circumstance has the galling property of finding its way past all shields and bindings, down your neck or up your sleeve to sensitive regions inside. This rain in its timid fall did not have the strength to flatten the sea which rolled in without nobility, grandeur, or threat. The waves were just lumpy, irregular, and acutely uncomfortable. They established no regular rhythm. From time to time a piece of cloud in guise of a mist would tear off its main body of dirty opalescence and descend over the face of the starting area, more like the vaporous mottlings from Dr. Jekyll's laboratory than fog. It would plunge us into early isolation, obliterating one vessel from view of the other.

The committee, during this low-visibility prelude, hoisted a postponement flag and kept us jilling about the area of the starting boat under main and power, not the best way to provide a steady platform. Presumably this was done to pick a time when the starting area would be clear enough for them to see and control the whole line. That may have been the case. Privately, I thought the committee incapable of normal vision even under ideal conditions that day. They had been the heaviest celebrants at the farewell parties. The lucky bastards knew they had nothing to do after the start but crawl into bed under the lee of a plump rump, the greatest warming pan ever devised, and sleep it off. But over and beyond normal incapacities, they had brought dozens and dozens of visitors to the starting area to view a spectacle billed as A GREAT OCEAN RACE. To have this go off in low visibility is against all rules and traditions of Tourism, a tradition relentlessly pursued ever since the arrival and setting up of shop by Prospero, late Duke of Milan, who welcomed all visitors to his sometime tempestuous shores.

The wind blowing from 120° at about six knots did not supply enough punch to hold *Figaro*, wearing nothing but her mainsail, steady in that lump of sea. She rolled about. Our stomachs were getting an early initiation, the first trying out after an all-too-happy spell ashore. The contestant boats milled about aimlessly, reaching up and down, moving in seemingly irregular patterns, one boat following another like the pigeons in the Piazza San Marco hunting for bypassed kernels of corn.

We did not waste all of that milling-about time. We were able to sail close to the destroyer escort serving as starting boat and identify our wives, at least those who had come to Bermuda, while they in turn got a close-up look at us. At the rate they were rolling on their spectator ship we were hard put to determine whether they were trembling more for us than we for them. We waved madly and threw kisses with the abandon of beauty queens driven in an open car around a football stadium at half-time.

To our impatient eyes, the visibility seemed to be improving;

the race should start soon. At long last the notion got through to the committee as well, or else the rolling about had begun to stir up their unfriendly juices. In that chilling mist one should not discount the anticipation of cuddling under the covers in a stable bedstead. For whichever reason, they lowered the post-ponement pennant and fired the warning gun. With that, all hell and Genoas broke out and the boats began charging about as though this were the signal for the start of a 25-mile race around the buoys instead of the start of a 3,500-mile ocean race. It is all part of the racing syndrome—this headlong desire to clip fractions of seconds at the start, when minutes adding up into hours will be lost during the passage and the loss perhaps not even recognized in the rueful accounting at the race's end. It is a sad time, that accounting, when one discovers that victory has been successfully eluded once more and the two-edged knife of regret and the thought of how it might have been, slowly turns in the gut.

Our stopwatch was right on tick with the prep signal, and we hit the line with the starting cannon. Monk counted out the final seconds with a calm I am sure no one felt—"5–4 –3–2–Gun." At the wheel and feeling great at the split-second accuracy of our start, I was on the point of extending congratulations all around for the great precision and execution in the last minutes of maneuvering when suddenly a recall signal sounded from the race committee. Someone was over early, the poor bastard. This signal always sends quaking shivers cascading from the pit of the stomach to just below the knees. But we were OK here at the extreme end of the line, farthest from the race committee boat and hidden behind a cloud of starting sail—they couldn't mean us. Hell, they couldn't even see us. Looking up the line, we saw *Palawan* turn back to restart. That was that. I sighed with relief and was at the point of congratulating the crew once again for being so well placed, with our wind free and charging along, when Ed Raymond, on another boat, broke the dream. He called over, *"Figaro,* you were over."

I was on the point of replying, "Up yours, we were," or

something equally mollifying when our own Bobby Symonette, the Simple Island Boy, who had been sitting on the bow pulpit calling the trim of the sail and gauging our position in the line, said, "I think he's right."

When your own men lose the faith, there's nothing left to do but retire and hope to fight another day. So I called "Gybe O" and wheeled back for another start. We lost three minutes recrossing the line. It is surprising how far ahead your competition can get in that much time. To anyone but a tail-end Charlie, the spread of so many boats stretched out over the horizon is an inspiring sight. I can imagine the challenge to gallantry that must have inspired Nelson's captains and men when they saw the sails of the French fleet stretched before them. But I did not feel the challenge so much as disgust. In spite of occasionally mouthing slogans like, "The man who isn't over early at least once a season or who does not touch bottom in trying to slip by inside, is not really trying," I take each such event as an error on the part of the chart makers or as a plot against my pursuit of happiness.

In this instance, I remained true to form. "Goddamn it, we were right on the line at the gun, besides those blind bastards couldn't see us unless they had closed-circuit television. We were hidden behind every boat in the fleet."

My crew consoled me. "You're Goddamn right—forget it. We have a race to run."

I simmered down. I should have known right then and there that this was to be a bad trip, but I kept shoving the intruding truth off. Pollyanna and Mr. Micawber keep rising to the surface in every ordinary man unless he is a self-condemned loser. Therefore, the whole truth did not come into focus until 1730 that afternoon when Bucky came to me, fresh from the bowels of the boat, and invited me to taste the bilge. Then it burst over me like a bag of water thrown from the second story. After we had measured the tanks to find 8⅞ inches of water in the starboard tank and 10⅛ inches in the port we began to recognize an unfolding disaster for what it was. We could think of no positive recourse to action. We were too far from shore to find a temple in which to make suitable sacrifices, so we settled for plugging along, secretly hoping that if we paid it no attention it would go away. We had no estimate or rate of the leak.

At 2000 when the tanks were sounded again, we found the starboard tank almost dry and the port tank down to 8½ inches. Of the two, we now knew the starboard containers to be in the worst shape. So we emptied the last of its water—about eleven gallons—into the port tank and for the first time talked about abandoning the race.

At 2200 we began to fill all available containers with water from the port tank and stowed them around the ship and then, fresh out of ideas as to how to further solve our dilemma, the deck watch returned to duty and the off watch betook themselves to their berths and pleasant dreams, and I to the first of several long nights of tears, my mind a steaming caldron filled with such stuff as boiled up by three hags of the blasted heath. I was roiling with despair, self-condemnation, and silly plans. Suddenly, our situation became clear to me just as the awesome implication must have unfolded for Custer when he finally began to count all those Indians.

On Friday morning, the first of July, as befitting the imperial commander-in-chief for whom the month is named, we decided to press on regardless to within striking range of the Canadian Maritime Provinces. As with the renowned Julius, the die was cast, a Rubicon crossed. In an earlier book, I have discussed the superstitions surrounding decisions and starts of voyages made on Friday. I am fated, it seems, to make my throws against the fates on that day of the week. Long ago a ghost was given up on a sere and sun-scorched hill and a black pall hung over the world. Since then Friday has been an ominous day in all Western places. Only in the urban concrete desert does anyone think of saying TGIF. My crew are seemingly undaunted by our circumstances, the decision, or the day.

It is too late for warning signals. We're for it. On and on into the fog goes our brave company.

Few experiences match that of sailing in a thick, deep impenetrable fog. You are encapsulated in a huge feathery shroud, wondering what is ahead. But the boat, unencumbered by ideas of the unseen, charges along as though the path were secure, not bristling with concealed threats. The Grand Bank waters are busy and at times hazardous. An area of low-powered steamer lanes as well as a busy fishing ground, it is also a region where at this time of the year one can run into ice. These are not necessarily big icebergs; just small bergy bits as the Newfies call them, small for the *Titanic* but enough to hole a small boat. We are in a region of fog, created in part by the confluence of the warm Gulf Stream and the frigid Labrador Current. The whole area is about 400 miles wide, and on our route we have no alternative but to sail through part of it. There is no positive protection for the almost invisible small boat from being run down in the fog, except to pump the foghorn. You can't stand there endlessly pulling and pushing the plunger in the tube—it is an invitation to idiocy. The noise is infinitely more degenerating than the threat. The sound envelopes you within feathery walls—moans from a soul abandoned by Charon, lost in a watery limbo. In order to conform to the law, the horn must be sounded. We sound it, but at intervals scarcely conforming to the rules of the sea. Once it seems an answering wail comes from ahead, muffled, hard to tell how far distant. Our intervals become law-abiding. Breathing almost suspended, we listen for an engine or the rush of a bow wave. There's that sound again! We breathe again. The flat belief that nothing will happen to us returns. It makes such a voyage possible. Our intervals on the horn stretch out again.

At times it seems clearer overhead, although the horizon is less promising. Monk, ever the optimist, will try for a noon sight. If he can catch the sun on the hang or near that moment, we can fix our position. Local noon is a half hour away. The chances are ten to one against his getting a sight this noon, but he's up there waiting and watching.

The bodies below are squirming around in their blanket cocoons. *Figaro*'s movement is not her usual unalloyed joy. No record run is in the making. The air is light and mucid and is vaguely tainted with an odor like that in a steam room gone cold, in which someone had tipped over the remains of a cardboard container of clam juice. The wind blows from dead aft, and, while not seeming so at the start, after being in it for a while, one realizes that it is very cold. The accompanying swell is on the quarter and is either the slop in remembrance of things past or the herald of nasty things to come.

We are carrying the lightweight, blue-top spinnaker which gyrates from side to side like a go-go dancer's behind and is not half as fetching. Perhaps a go-go dancer is the wrong image to convey, since there is not enough spastic twitch and jerk. A hula dancer comes closer, the head and one foot are fixed, but the middle, like the sheet clew, weaves all over the seascape. Go-go or hula dancer, it rolls from side to side as the mast swings in the swell, subjecting the spinnaker to a racking survival test which in turn accentuates the roll of the boat and reduces life below to a moderate state of durance vile. The sleepers are prone and passive as are those in the half-world between sleep and waking. The latter are trying to dull themselves to the onrushing reality that soon they must face an even unpleasanter world than this rolling rack. They struggle hard to hold on to the edge of the dream.

At sea, removed from the warm, stable comforts of the connubial bed, one suddenly discovers that sleep is an athletic activity requiring physical coordination and muscular control. As in all gymnastics there are varying styles. One kind can be called the belly floppers. They sleep facedown, sprawled like a free-fall parachutist before pulling the rip cord. In these sailing conditions the limbs are spread to provide a four-point landing system. Those sleepers who are irrevocably dedicated to back and side repose are getting the shaft, rolling about like dugout canoes shorn of their outriggers or a hot dog under a short order cook's spatula. The experienced with uncommitted styles have learned to adjust. Bobby, the Simple Island Boy, is a builder of intricate nests. He has woven a bower lined with a blanket and spare clothes which wedges and shields his body from excessive movement and unhappy contact with the outer perimeters. It may take him five minutes to become disentangled and another seven minutes to explain the intricacies and workings of his soft machine to the alternate user of the bunk. It must work very well—he looks moderately rested.

I wish my sleep could have the seemingly untrammeled quality of Bobby's. But so many concerns assail me once I am in bed. As the Captain Courageous of this argosy, the boat, in my mind's eye, is variously sinking, being dismasted, or, worse, *LOSING A RACE!*

The last is a grinding disorder of the mind. From time to time the notion persists that a competitor is living it up with a private rail-down breeze in another part of the ocean. The idea becomes so real that it requires all of your common sense to keep from tacking over to go wind-hunting. Alas, when you finish the race, then what a screech of pain howls through the secret hollows of your being; you find the wild imaginings were all too true. While you spent the night like Jacob and the Angel, wrestling with your instinct, the undeserving bastard *(The Winner)* without the irresolutions of thinking it through but simply by the luck of being there, held a rail-down breeze for the whole night and through half the next day. In some manner your psychic antennae received a number of signals which, when fed into your private computer of instinct, came out with the right answer. Naturally, your common sense rejected it. Why, oh why, is your logic and reason so often thwarted, so that lucky bastards who just happen to be there walk off with the silver? You are left at the end with playing the role of a stalwart sea dog. You can't even howl aloud to ease the

31

pain. You can't tell anyone about your unfollowed instinct for fear of being called a horse's ass. In such situations, everyone you talk to is blessed with 20–20 hindsight. There is nothing left for you except to twist the hara-kiri knife a little deeper while you hoist another rum punch, clicking glasses with another stalwart loser alongside. You drink a toast to the next time when you both will know better.

There are certain malefactions of the captain's trade which rise to wreck his sleep. There are others he shares with his companions, for, alas, he is a male animal as well, inheritor of all the sins, failings, and urgencies that human flesh is heir to. Depending entirely on how long he has been at sea, what level of fire burns, how well the flame is banked, he may share with the crew a vision of cloven-footed Pan crouching and gibbering across the cabin. The leering one parades a covey of temptresses past fervid eyes. Once this vision takes hold there is nothing left to do but shut your eyes and look at the pictures projected on the inside of your eyelids, prayer having lost its efficacy for holding the devil at bay, what with the fall of the abbeys, the emptying of hermit caves, and the elimination of purdah.

In contrast to the worldly burdens which accompany me to the sack, are those of our company who still retain the look of innocence, of untrammeled youth. Steve of the open countenance, facing life directly, seems also to be facing it in his sleep or himself being stared out of coutenance. He is spread-eagled on his back, his head rolling from side to side with the changing angle of the boat. It is an unwitting, if ultimately sorrowful gesture, as though some unhappy vision of the future is being rejected. He is imploring the all-powerful cause of his unhappiness to bring a halt to whatever is happening. Make it stop! Go away!

The all-powerful takes no notice, but we try. The go-go spinnaker is snubbed with a choker sheet. Some of its excesses are slowed but not enough to bring any real joy. Perhaps the watch on deck has taken such late notice of the miserable sleeping conditions because it will soon be their turn in the rack, and God helps those who help themselves.

I call the off-watch with a rousing solo, an *a cappella* selection from the cantata "Sleepers Awake," which I think not only beautiful but apt. As always any attempt to keep the cultural level of this voyage up to the mark is greeted with complaint. I am disheartened. J. S. Bach in his very special heaven must be saddened. It is disheartening for one who believes in the uplifting and healing properties of art to find such a level of response from grumpy, disheveled auditors. They quench all thoughts of evangelism as they stagger about in their baggy-kneed long johns. In their unfeeling response, they are more concerned with niggling plaints of being done out of five more minutes of sleep. These are difficult companions at times, but my very own.

4

WITH the exception of Steve Matson, I have known and sailed with each of the crew members for years. Their qualities are a source of continuing pleasure. For slim reasons I am in position of command, but whether I am worthy or unworthy, they give me their full trust. They are believing and loyal to me and to the boat, sleeping soundly, seemingly untroubled, while my stomach does flip-flops as I suffer the slings and arrows that my part-time captain's flesh inherits. My only claim to authority over them is that "I own the ball." That's how some players get to be quarterback. Come to think of it, I represent the last stand of capitalism; I control the means of production. But capitalist or not, and if I am filled with wonder at their loyalty to me, I am more than grateful for the company of such paladins. The decision to go on no longer quavers with uncertainty. We always hope that once the shore lines are cast off, uncertainty drops over the horizon with the land. Instead, we are committed to a long line of uncertainty stretching tenuously across the Atlantic. The crew at least is not one of the uncertain elements.

Before we sail there are always a number of decisions to make. Generally, decisions create more doubts than they clarify. Not the least of the quandaries is the matter of crew. Unlike the raffish sweepings of the Portsmouth and Plymouth waterfronts who willy-nilly gloried with Hawkins, Drake, and

Nelson, modern ocean racers are gentlemen sailors who must meet rigorous standards.

1. *In the matter of race committee certification:* A crew must have demonstrable experience. If a ship is lost and everyone drowns, the papers will be filled with public wailings. The committees will be properly sad, of course, but, worse, it might endanger the sport. The drowning must, therefore, be on your own head. The committee cannot be placed in a position of blame as being lax and frivolous in certifying a boat ready to race.

2. *In the matter of crew's approval of one another:* To be locked up in a small, unprivate, jostling space capsule with strange people for several weeks is like being placed in a culture breeding flask in a laboratory. Any small infection is bound to wax, swell, and break out in epidemic proportions. The ideal crew member is a rare creature indeed. He has the coolness, courage, and derring-fo of James Bond; the inventiveness and mechanical skills of Tom Swift; the agility and strength of an Olympic decathlon winner; and the winning ways and affableness of a graduate *summa cum laude* of the Dale Carnegie Institute of charm. He has a fund of new stories, is a good listener, and is as neat in his cabin habits as Mr. Clean.

You start with these requirements and settle for what you get. But you must be close. His crewmates must enjoy the pleasure of his company. Else who needs it? Do you go through all that palaver in convincing a wife and sweetheart that an absence of three and a half weeks will have salubrious effects on your idyll? Do you lay your career on the line convincing the boss that you can be absent for an amount of time beyond your regular vacation without injury to the flow of work and without giving him the idea that he might do without you altogether? And you do all this just to find yourself cooped-up with a jerk in a small nuthouse for a seeming eternity. Forget it, brother, don't call me next time, I'll call you.

3. *In the matter of reassuring the captain-owner:* A crew should be skillful enough to reassure the captain in the secret fastness of his heart. The captain must know that when all hell breaks

loose and he doesn't know what it's all about, someone aboard does and what's more will do something about it.

Few Sunday captains are equipped to make such personnel decisions, although training in decision making is built into our democratic society. It is the curse of a goal-oriented society; all parents apparently wish to bequeath this symbol of power and achievement to their children. If one accepts the earlier postulate that a decision gives rise to new doubts and uncertainty, then by syllogism it follows that in wanting their children to be decision makers, most parents wish a life of incipient ulcers, insomnia, and other unpleasant things on their spawn. One can only wait for that great day when the computer takes over and we can abandon our hesitations to the care of a corroded transistor.

It is not as farfetched an idea as appears at first blush. The pattern goes something like this. From his earliest years, before he says anything more than Da-Da, his training begins. Hard, unfriendly objects are thrust into his dimpled hands. He promptly puts them into his mouth. He is really required to put the square block into the square hole, the round into the round, etc. Should he be unlucky enough, however, to hole out in under 102 seconds, grog is served all around, and he is doomed.

From this point life becomes untenable to the Huck Finn within. He was been marked for command. Up until now no harm has been done. If he cannot make it past this stage, he has at least been trained for jigsaw puzzles or as a punch-card operator.

Should he pass, however, and miraculously escape long hair, love beads, hand-embroidered jeans, and other upspringing traps and enticements, his training continues until the final evaluation for his placement within the infrastructure. Through all his he never quite loses his uncertainty, but it is disguised by a certain tribal euphoria and medicine man fetishes.

His self-confidence is kept high by modern chemistry which rids his shoulders of dandruff; his breath is kissable; and dry perspirants leave no telltale underarm damp to betray his inner turmoil. He is cool, man, cool, already showing the outward marks of a great captain.

If this achiever passes into the world of captains, his real unhappiness begins. There are no more yes and no tests with clear answers in the back of the book, no more props to assurance. That kind of change is too sudden. Our man would be slavering about like one of Pavlov's creatures waiting for the food to come but for the fact that our social machinery is not stupid. If that were the case, we would have blown ourselves up before this. The social contract recognizes that it cannot always be run by uncertain captains. So it devises boards and committees to split up the culpabilities or, better yet, table the motion and make no decision at all. But there comes a time when one man must decide—as in choosing a crew.

Despite his training and the decision-bolstering devices, a captain-owner really is unprepared to make choices among men who offer themselves or must be wooed. Some men are better racers than he is—a fact difficult to acknowledge and still keep the voice of command from ending on a rising inflection. Then there are the other kind who should not be permitted to go to sea without their keepers, men whose shallow abilities are disguised through glowing affidavits by association. "I sailed on *Ondine* last year," one says, and immediately you have visions of a stalwart standing at the wheel with a star to steer her by. Instead, it turned out, he manned the port, running backstay, not being trusted elsewhere.

I have had minimal early training in the arts of command, having failed miserably with my square and round blocks and was therefore abandoned at the outset to the lesser cadres. I turned out to be a late bloomer, but no machinery existed in my day to bring this latent promise out. In my stumbling progress, I fell into yacht ownership, and in spite of the clear prerogatives that go with that estate, I share many of the same hesitations as my *beau ideal*, Horatio, Lord Hornblower. Like him, I keep my hesitations under an icy calm, except of course when I begin to holler and yell. Because of this underrunning uncertainty I am loath to switch around in the matter of crew, seeking for the bubble, quintessence. When I find a man who is capable, who knows what he is doing, does not feel demeaned by a turn in the galley, and above all is a delight to be with and who can tell stories, I bind him to me with bands of iron. All the men aboard are old friends. I am happy to call my young son MacLeod an old friend. We have all sailed the ocean together and know one another's ways. If I knowingly had to pick a crew with whom to be dismasted at sea in a boat equipped with leaking tanks, I could choose none better than these.

(My fingers are crossed. I hope this mention of dismasting remains an abstract. It is sheer carelessness to talk this way.)

This crew meets all the standards enumerated earlier, as well as certain further requirements of my own. There is the matter of age. In certain circles an average crew age above the midtwenties is considered over the hill, ready for the glue factory. In order for me to average out, I would need to take along my grandson, Colman. Besides, I don't always hold with the certain circles. I think them overly influenced by around the buoy racing—one all-out afternoon and then to the hot showers. Ocean racing is made up of many bad afternoons, ugly mornings, and hard nights. It calls for the long slog in conditions which, endured in other circumstances, would be considered as a sampling of the Grand Inquisitor's best. I find that the young tend to burn out early. They need more sleep and do not know how to husband their strength.

There is the hoary farmer's story of the bright young bull and his sage old companion at stud that makes the point succinctly. Says the young bull, noticing a break in the fence leading to the panting, virginal young heifers, "Let's rush down there and ravish us one of them cuties apiece." The old bull, first lifting a lid over a rheumy eye, then with a slight twitch of his muzzle, drawls, "Let's walk down and do the lot."

I am glad to see that the National Aeronautics and Space Administration subscribes to the same thesis (not necessarily in their approach to heifers, but in the choice of astronauts). These men are past the first flush of youth, settled and responsible. Besides, I am a classicist, drawing models from the past, equating age and wisdom, youth and ardency. There are three stages of excellence from Achilles to Odysseus to Nestor. Some men are always young or old. Catullus never could be old nor Juvenal young.

Toward this goal of excellence my crew is a balance of energy and wisdom. Four men are over thirty, four under thirty. I use thirty as the equator. This is a time which holds peculiar attitudes toward age. For that matter, at the time of this race the four younger men were all students. In any case, my method makes for balanced watches, loaded with wisdom and wiles on the one hand, and piss and vinegar on the other. It is as follows:

Starboard Watch	*Port Watch*
Knud Reimers, watch captain	Bobby Symonette, watch captain
James "Bucky" Reardon, A.B.	MacLeod (Cleody) Snaith, A.B.
Bruce Burgess, A.B.	Steve Matson, A.B.

Standing Out

William Snaith, Skipper	Moulton "Monk" Farnham, navigator

5

SINCE I make such a to-do about the crew, you should know something about them. A crew is a group of distinct individuals. On land they may be isolated integers living private lives—family men, members of the PTA in good standing, or rampaging bachelors. Each man is hidden from view, busy with his own life. On a small boat all physical and some emotional privacies disappear. Each person is an indivisible part of the whole. Subtract one and the quality of a voyage changes. It is the return of tribal man, his vital force important to the group. He has emerged from the shadows of urban anonymity.

It is therefore important to know them. But how do you tell about a man. Once, during a long, lazy voyage, I read a delightful book called *Brief Lives* by a John Aubrey, late gentleman-commoner, Trinity College, Oxford. He wrote his lives sometime during the reign of Charles II. They are a miracle of compression and, to my mind, a marvelous set of biographies. You might not find out very much about a man, but when Aubrey is through you never forget him. For instance, this is all he has to say about a mysterious John Holywood. *"Dr. Pell is positive that his name is Holybushe."* So much and no more, a real hanger. Who is Holywood and who the hell is Dr. Pell? Is mere accuracy the crux of Aubrey's interest or the size of the wood?

Dr. William Harvey, whom we venerate as discoverer of the

blood's circulation, practiced an old and captivating form of homeopathy when his own blood cooled. Aubrey reports, *"He kepte a pretty young wench to wayte on him which I guess he made use of for warmthe sake as King David did."*

On the otner hand, Sir Walter Raleigh kept his cool to the end. Sir Walter *"took a pipe of tobacco a little before he went to the scaffold, which some formall persons were scandalized at."*

Interlarded in the lives, one finds bits of advice. One such medical bit almost sounds as though it would work. For a toothache, *"Take a new nail and make the gums bleede with it and then drive it into an oak."*

He serves his personal histories with all meat and no bread filling. There are few dates or other biographical baggage and no emotional involvements on the part of the biographer.

But I cannot escape involvement; that is the last thing in the world that I could do. Each of these men is special to me. While not endowed with the history of the remarkable Tudor, Roundhead, and Restoration personages in Aubrey's *Lives,* they are my friends and companions to this voyage.

And so without benefit of research, dates, or recourse to honors lists, here they are:

Knud Reimers

Knud is an old friend, a naval architect and yacht designer of note. He lives and practices in Stockholm. He sailed with me in the 1954 Bermuda Race in *Figaro II* and in the Southern Ocean Racing Conference (or Circuit) during the winter of 1956 in *Figaro III* in her first year out. He is a gentle and endearing man, full of fun, a marvelous cook, has a fund of stories which he tells with a beguiling accent, and to crown all this, he is a great helmsman. His even temperament does much to head off troublings in our paradise. Interpersonal relationships have become more complicated since they took on this encyclopedic name. Even on a boat as sweet as ours and given so balanced and decent a crew, it is inevitable that when eight men live closely together in cramped quarters under trying conditions, a few hard edges show. He has the gift of dulling that edge or turning it aside.

Many of his stories are based in Scandinavian folklore, although when I see and hear him, he reminds me more of a clean-shaven Druid than a bold, bad Viking. It was Knud who told me, after a proper amount of cogitation, that *Figaro III* was built of lucky wood. In this thesis, she was formed from a tree which had been inhabited by a good spirit, a sort of tenancy which we are told still goes on in the unseen world around us. It is a phenomenon continuing from the days when the Oak of Morven stood at the center of the universe. The tree forming *Figaro* had obviously been cut at the proper time of the year and, by some lucky happenstance, by ritually pure instruments and hands. I believed him then and believe him now. She was never less than a thing of joy. When *Figaro III* was sold because of my insatiable hunger for more speed, it was a day of sadness for our whole family. I think of her kindly still and enjoy seeing her on the rare occasions we meet, although she now sails against me.

Only a man like Knud can tell me such a thing in the middle of a gray afternoon some 1,000 miles offshore. He is at the wheel. There are two of us in the cockpit. He is skillfully sailing my boat downwind under a parachute spinnaker, placing her at the proper point of each wavecrest so she will take maximum advantage of each tobogganlike rush. It is exhilarating sailing, spiced with peril. If she should broach! But she feels so safe and sure in his competent hands that the others are flaked out or huddled below. Only such a man can tell you this magical secret in a calm and matter-of-fact voice and have you accept it as the revealed truth.

Monk Farnham

Monk, an old friend and shipmate, has sailed with me for donkey's years, generally as navigator. They threw the mold away after he was shaped; he is a vintage man. Now ensconced, happily for both of them, as editor of the magazine *Boating*, at the time of this race he was chomping his way through jobs which deserved neither his talents nor his energies.

Not the least of his endowments is the gift of tongues—not the glossolalia of the ranter or the ability to carry on a seduction in Serbo-Croatian (although I'll bet he could make one hell of a pass at it)—but he can speak directly to the gods of wind and wave, and what's more make them listen. Even more amazingly, when they have been particularly disgraceful in their prankishness or obstinacy, he has threatened them and, wonder of wonders, made his threat stand. We marvel at his aplomb, standing boldly at the rail, shaking a fist at the face of the sea. He is at his scathing best, but we hesitatingly remind him that any vengeance wreaked on him will lamentably take us along. To no avail, we are cowed by his courage and vehemence when he is in a spell of incantation. He carries us along, our fear and trembling hiding behind his fervor.

He has gentler gifts beyond this mad streak of secularism. His memory bank of chanteys and poems, pure and porno, is prodigious. Like one of the fabled two-gun men of the West, he can let go from either side, scenic or obscenic. It is a matter of tone and mood to fit the occasion. But you do not invite a man on a long sea-voyage only to make your intentions and displeasures clear to Poseidon's suborders or to sing of the seduction of the sweet lass from Chichester. He must be hand-useful as well. Monk is a fine seaman, skilled navigator, and a maven of the arts of the sea. He is quick to recognize unusual phenomena and patient in tracing out their source.

As befitting a man with these out-of-the-ordinary gifts he comes equipped with out-of-the-ordinary body mechanics. As an instance, his temperature threshold is like that of no one I've met before. To say the least, he is hardy, comfortable when you shiver, sweating when you are comfortable, and carries on in all weathers as though out for the afternoon on Long Island Sound. I have seen him on a nasty cold and blowy day. Everyone else is huddled in heavy sweaters and watch coats. *Figaro* is heaving in an erupting icy caldron. Monk is at the chart table below, wearing a sport shirt and light sweater, his bald crown glistening with a mist of perspiration. Suddenly he is overcome with *mal de mer* in this gyrating capsule. Clambering topside, he heaves his lunch up to the sea, scoops up a handful of seawater, rinses, and then with a pleasantry about the fine standard of cooking on board, which enables food to retain its flavor even when being disgorged, he goes back to his work.

His industry and patience are fabulous, his ship husbandry a miracle of order. But his insistence that his shipmates live by these same habits of neatness is the cross of the younger men who in bad weather stagger from bunk to table to deck and back to bunk, dropping stray bits as they pass through their vale of trials. At such times, they run head on into his peppery side.

Bobby Symonette (SIB—citizen of Nassau in the Bahamas)

Simple Island Boy, a sobriquet he chose for himself to disguise one of the wiliest minds since Benjamin Disraeli. When he uses "I'm just a Simple Island Boy but" for openers, you brace for the verbal karate chop. In 1960 he was a member of Bahamas' Parliament and its speaker to be. If any man ever graced that latter position in the various Parliaments of men, Bobby did. In his white wig, black silk gown, silver-buckled shoes, he was an impressive sight. So much so that Bucky, who had received all of his formal education in Jesuit, Benedictine, and Dominican Schools, and thereby acquired an early relish for costumes, ritual, and titles, would start every address to Simple with a ringing "Mr. Speaker" whether it concerned the speaker's turn to wash dishes or change a sail. But that was later.

He has always remained "Simple" to me, even as I am "Parsimonious Pete" to him. This latter name and its connotation is unfair. It is the attempt through silver-tongued forensics to disguise certain excessive behavioral characteristics in himself. The name has its origin in one single exchange

during the Fastnet Race of 1957, when, we, at Simple's insti-
gation, he being a boat pusher, had blown out two spinnakers
in a useless desire to look like a racing boat. It was blowing 40
miles an hour; we could have gone downwind in that stuff just
about as well if we had hung out a pair of his drawers; besides
no one was around to photograph us. But he, caught up in the
rapture of the sea, and never having paid a yard or sailmaker's
bill for *Figaro,* called for another spinnaker—our last. I was
horrified by the suggestion. I had already been fighting off
qualms attendant to taking a dicey boat (she was dicey then)
downwind under spinnaker in a howler with a big sea running;
the bill for new sails kept jumping up before me with a ding for
each like the white tabs in the display window of a cash
register.

The incident took place during a blowy morning after we
had rounded Fastnet Rock. The way up had been miserable.
Continuous gales and half gales, the wind never dropping
below 40 mph. We were on the wind the whole time. Meals had
been difficult to prepare and our appestats were turned low.
Now with our back to the wind and the boat modestly upright,
we all crowded below to have breakfast. French toast, maple
syrup, and coffee (Francis Chichester, our navigator, thought
this a strange concoction, *fried bread and treacle*). Only Ed
Raymond was left on deck. The seas behind us were enormous,
and when we sank into the trough behind one of the rolling
hills, the wind would be partially cut off and the spinnaker
collapse.

Ed would shout, "She's breaking," and we would say, "What
the hell, fill it."

Suddenly he called out more excitedly than ever, "She's
gone." We rushed up to help, but he had stated the facts
clearly. The whole center of the sail was gone. Only the tapes
stood out boldly in the breeze, sort of limning the shape of the
sail that was.

I asked Ed, our sailmaker, whether the dear departed was
one of his.

"Yep, I think so," said Ed, a laconic New Englander, who put his energy into his craft rather than into paragraphs.

"I haven't paid for it, have I?"

"Not yet."

"Well, I won't. That sail was made of inferior material."

Bobby interrupted these subtle negotiations with an impatient "Let's get another up." Ed Raymond, for natural reasons, supported him, but Francis Chichester, our quiet navigator, later to be knighted by the Queen as a famous lone voyager, came to my aid. I argued that it was our last chute and should be saved, for when the wind came light and behind and we would need it. Francis knew when to put out and when to lie low; besides he had a feather-edged stomach and had been heaving its contents at an alarming rate. But Simple kept making his obscene suggestion until I said, "You can put it up but not without a deposit."

All negotiations were stalemated until Francis, through a stroke of genius and by means of lightning calculation said, "Our course to the Scillys Islands requires that we sharpen up."

This made a spinnaker unnecessary and a confrontation was avoided. But the wind never did go light and we lost another relatively close one. I have remained "Parsimonious Pete" to Simple since that day, because I would not commit our final spinnaker.

In spite of his careless attitude toward my exchequer, Bobby is a refreshing member of our afterguard. He is a pragmatic boat pusher. He runs over with Caribbean folklore and sayings, a veritable Poor Richard of the subtropics. He is a great seaman, sail handler, and downwind helmsman in strong winds and big seas. (I've always thought this to be the real test of helmsmanship for the ocean sailor, rather than the ability to take a boat upwind.) He is an all-around sportsman and I, a designer, consider him the greatest designer I know. Who else could have designed such a life for himself? Racing, sailing, shooting, game fishing all around the world most of the year. He is able to take this time off because of his organizing ability and a gift for getting others to work. He is the perfect chairman of the committee. The ultimate proof of that is his house, which I designed.

Simple's idea of a home was an enlightened fishing camp. His beautiful wife, Diane, still remembers the stately homes of England. As the designer, equipped with his own ideas and caught between these extremes, I should have been doomed. Yet the result is a handsome and happy home brought to fruition through delicate concession by all hands. I see it often from the East Bay when sailing on my way to the Out Islands. I am proud and happy for all of us. I stay in it when in Nassau and like living in it, which is the ultimate test.

These three men and myself constitute the afterguard. Whether this be true or not, in my table of organization we, the chiefs, represent experience, sagacity, and are the obvious fountainheads of all wisdom. Our young members, the Indians, are the troops who although not unexperienced are not yet savvy enough to call the turns. They carry the burden of doing and supply most of the muscle in the event of sail changes, trim, etc. Our Table of Organization seems somewhat tipped in favor of the chiefs. This may be so, but, alas, my friends grow older with me. However, do not get the idea of a decrepit afterguard living off the strength of the young crew, of multiple counterparts of Tiresias sapping the vigor of our adventure. All of the afterguard are capable of performing every task on the boat with almost equal éclat. For that matter during the three to four days' passage of a cyclonic depression, followed by the first hard day of the overtaking high-pressure system, they may be carrying the better part of the burden. It is true that after a time you cut out such dashing feats as working your way to the end of a spinnaker pole in order to change spinnakers while keeping them both flying, or walking out to the end of the mainboom while it is squared and you are roaring along, alternating between one and nine feet above a roiling sea while the boat is in a spate of rhythmic rolling. You just figure out another way of passing the reefing pennant through the leech cringle. It is true that in this case you pull the boom in or go aloft in a bosun's chair rather than hand over hand, but these are minor shortcomings—the job somehow gets done. It takes a little more time and you may slow down briefly, and it certainly does not have the dash and verve that makes everyone swell up a little and say, "Man! That's racing!"

This last, beyond the reality of being the major workers in the vineyard, is the blessing of an experienced young crew. They bring with them another brand of racing. Nothing seems impossible; tasks are executed with a view to cutting seconds rather than just getting the job done—the last is taken for granted. Looking past this pragmatic aspect, they bring a brightness and different kind of laughter on board. No matter how optimistic and positive a man's nature, once he is past the blush of youth his brand of humor is bound to be shot through with irony, cynicism, and paradox. It is simply the illusion lost and a core toughened by exposure to events.

I look back at such instances when, as a young student, full of optimism and dreams I thought if only I could get to Paris and study, then the muses would descend and I would become a great artist-architect. Hadn't that happened to Jean Christophe and to every hero in every novel and biography I had read? Paris was the wizard alchemist, turning common clay into pure art. I strove mightily and finally got there on a scholarship. Before long I began to suspect the Parisian magic, but I waited patiently for the muses to wrap the mantle, a two-bit Don Quixote deluded by his romantic reading. The Paris of Stravinsky and Diaghilev, of Hemingway and Fitzgerald, was gone. The École des Beaux-Arts had been founded by Richelieu. They had changed professors several times but not the traditions. Only years later did I acknowledge the whole thing to be a frost. But then it was very late. Paris had other and more interesting lapses of virtue to hold me in thrall.

But our young companions have not yet had time to be truly

disillusioned. One should remember that this race took place in 1960—only a decade ago, but it was a wholly different world, before the war in Vietnam, drug culture, police, Panthers, and student confrontation. Nevertheless, the new young crews who race with me now are still as they were back then, although their hair is much longer. Their clothes are studiedly ragged, but with the headbands on, they do not look unlike Nelson's iron men. They are happy when sailing. It could have something to do with the enchanted world of *Figaro* or that their disillusionment is in great part that of intellect rather than experience, that of being a witness rather than a victim. I don't know and they can't tell me.

The laughter of our young crews, then and now, is based on sheer enjoyment, on the fact that they are pitting their young bodies against an ancient adversary, that they are locked into a competition for which there is no reward other than saying, "I was there," and in learning a skill not worth a nickel in trade unless they wish to become a professional yacht hand, which, in some quarters, is thought more a useful escape than a trade. Their fun is full of wisecracks and pranks, which give an air of youth and bounce to the whole undertaking.

Bruce Burgess

It is difficult to think of Bruce gone. He was killed in an airplane accident during the writing of this book. He left behind a loving wife and two small children and a host of loving memories. For that matter, I saw him briefly during this writing, much of it done on board my boat. We were at anchor in Padanaram just below New Bedford where he sailed in from a long voyage on a sprightly small green schooner. She was a character boat designed along traditional northeast coast lines. Seeing the *Figaro,* he popped into the dinghy, once the anchor was down, and came over. We had a long gam, and when I told him what I was writing, we talked long and lovingly over the race memories.

I will not write about him in the body of the book as being

gone. To the degree that I can I will keep his memory fresh as when he sailed with us. His young children, perhaps too young to accurately remember their father, can have some idea of how he was loved and admired by his friends and shipmates.

I met Bruce through another old friend and shipmate, the redoubtable, ever-young Mr. Chips of St. George School, Norris Hoyt, PhD, pedagogue, yachtsman, and *raconteur extraordinaire*. Bruce was one of Norris' students. Anyone coming to you from Norry possesses three characteristics. He is decent, open, and forthright, loves sailing, and is bound to be a photographer. Bruce had all these qualities and more. He was a little less prankish than our other young'uns, projecting an air of earnest responsibility. As a matter of fact, while very young, he became headmaster of a new small boys' school. It was while photographing that school from the air for a brochure that he met his fatal accident. He was a strong, even-tempered young man who possessed the marvelous quality of following an order given. There was no necessity to point out first, causes, reasons, historical variations of a particular job. He did it first and asked questions about it when done. A valuable man on board who never hung back at an all-hands' call, he could be counted on for coolness in a tight moment, doing his job with his pipe clenched in his teeth.

Bruce was almost an academic-born, having learned the Socratic method well. He could ask a very penetrating and annoying question, annoying because you could not answer it easily, and pursue it relentlessly until he was satisfied. But he was a gentleman and did not pin you like a butterfly if you could not answer his question satisfactorily. You knew, however, he would go on somewhere else until he found out. Unlike Steve and Cleody, Bruce knew exactly where he was going—he would be a teacher. Perhaps that accounted for his being a bit more settled.

If he had any quirks at all worth mentioning, it was his appetite. He was a steady, all-weather eater. Among the picky, bad-weather feeders, he would sometimes be called the ship's gull. This may have been jealousy. In idle moments various scientific reasons were adduced for this appetite, but no imagination was equal to his rate of consumption. He could warm the heart of any amateur Brillat-Savarin of the galley, greeting every gastronomical delight with enthusiasm, cleaning his plate and going back for seconds as long as they were offered.

But nature has a way of applying the old equalizer. Yin and Yang crop up everywhere. He was victimized by irregularity at sea. I could not see why he should be bothered by his infrequent visits to the head; it happened every time he went offshore—he should have become accustomed to this problem, one which he shared with many other reasonable men. A goodly number consider the world and themselves run by a split-second biological clock. If the balance wheel is upset in any way, their world is threatened. Since I am captain and ship's doctor, my advice and counsel is sought. I generally tell them to keep eating; it has to go somewhere. If this is not enough, I give them a mild laxative, and if it works, the ship resounds with their public joy.

At no time did Bruce's affliction interfere with his duties or appetite. He looked harassed only when he remembered his problem. The public discussion of his travail was the source of much invention.

Steve Matson

All of the young men had made long voyages with us before, all but nineteen-year-old Steve Matson, a young fellow from the Pacific Coast. Steve was recommended by "Simple." The summer before, Bobby and I had raced the Trans-Pac from LA to Hawaii, but on different boats. Steve sailed on the same boat as Bobby and had impressed the latter with his ability, agility, and eagerness. I signed him on, sight unseen, for the races to Bermuda and Sweden. During the bad spell of weather in the Bermuda Race, Steve and Cleody, both in the same watch, enjoyed a spell of seasickness. Neither missed a watch, and both saved their upchucking for the time between tasks. Their watch captain spared neither of them; we were racing—that is why we came. It is a wonder they still remained friends. Steve is a good all-around hand and a good companion aboard.

Both Steve and Cleody were at a very early crossroad of choice. Neither knew what he wanted to do, but with a kind of pride peculiar to young men, perhaps most men, they were reluctant to appear so undirected. They skirted subjects which would reveal such a state. Each worked on the other as a catalyst, however, and as our voyage settled in, their hesitation faded and they seemed eager for information, even guidance. It took the form of questioning me about my career. Afternoon and evening watches became great times to talk about art and architecture, with liberal doses of personal philosophy interlarded. The focus soon came down to architecture, a career which I supported strongly. It is a treat to have both occasion and time to talk to young men at the outset of their mature careers, especially about things reaching beyond stale pragmatism. Steve was a wonderful listener. As a man who relishes delivering himself of an opinion, I could ask for nothing more.

Since this race to Sweden Steve suffered a most unfortunate accident. Daring and glorying in his young strength and exuberance as always, he had joined a game—jumping off the wind-eroded cliff-edge of huge Pacific sand dunes. Like ski-jumpers, they fling themselves out into the air, impacting somewhere in the middle, and sliding down in the piled sand.

Steve in one traumatically mighty leap cleared the slope entirely and hit the hard compacted sand at the bottom, snapping his spine. At first he was given up as totally immobile, but he went on fighting for the privilege of living. He regained mobility in everything from his hips up. He went on fighting, studied architecture (perhaps I helped him decide), and now practices his profession and is a cup-winning yachtsman. He sails a small boat in regular regattas. Strong stuff, our Steve, with his bright blue eyes and big grin in his then-closecropped blond head. I have not seen him since but hear about him from time to time. "Give 'em hell, Steve."

James Reardon

Jim, "Bucky," is something special, a fourth son by emotional adoption to Betty and me. Fred Lawton, one of the great professional yacht captains, introduced us. Fred had spent the first year of *Figaro III*'s life with me and was leaving yachting to go to work for an electronics company. Fred must have felt as kindly to me as I did to him in bringing Bucky to me. Jim had worked as "Ship's Tiger" when Fred skippered *Bolero* for John Nicholas Brown, himself a fine gentleman who ran *Bolero* in the great tradition of yachting. I was forced to make some accommodations to that tradition just to keep up with Jimmy's training. Flags whipped up and down the starboard yardarm when I left or boarded the boat. When I boarded, the first thing I heard was, "Hup! The captain is coming aboard." It was all I could do to keep from turning and saluting the quarter-deck. He insisted on flying the Union Jack on Sundays, and on one Sunday, when we were lying alongside the flagship of a club, the commodore's lady told me politely that this was the privilege of the commodore alone. Bucky ran below, hunted for, and dug out a book of flag etiquette for yachts, which indicated it was a privilege the United States, in all its thundering majesty, extends to all its sailing citizens. I took it down anyway. She was a charming lady.

Bucky was due to start college when he came with us and stayed on for the next six sailing seasons. He and his lovely wife, Janet, now have four blond, blue-eyed children. He assures me that while it does not show on their baptismal certificates they each have Fastnet as a middle name. He has gone from being a buyer at Macy's to running his own import business, but he still sails with me, now as a gentleman Corinthian. My life, while interspersed and tempered with some disappointments, has, by the agency of such as Bucky, been provided with an unbroken continuity of good things.

Bucky is a tireless worker, a fine and daring seaman and a fountainhead of good feeling. He is my masthead man and alternates with Cleody as hookup man in the bow during sail changes. There is a tough competitor in his short, compact body which comes tearing out of the bunk and dashing topside like a firehorse at the first call of, "All hands."

William MacLeod "Cleody" Snaith

If I found it impossible to be objective about the others, how can I possibly be so about Cleody, my eldest son? All of my sons, Cleody, Skipper and Jock, have crossed the ocean with me, but of the three the one who has taken to sailing most is Cleody. He captained his college team, met his adorable wife, Sandy, during a small boat race (he picked her up one afternoon at a college club meeting and said, "How about racing with me?). It was her first time in a boat, but he must have liked the way she looked and behaved on the Charles River. And she did not mind getting her seat wet scrunching down in a small boat because she became his crew and a few years later they married. He is my mate, but I am having increasing trouble getting him out of small boats into mine. In a troubled lifetime this is one thing I never anticipated. Early in their lives, I told Betty, "We must guard against letting the boys become enamored of horses. They must be raised sailors." As long as I could keep them under my parental thumb we never let a horse on our property, and sailors they were. But the world is full of traps and enticements. There are girls, camping, and cameras. In Cleody's case it turned out to be girls, motorcycle racing, gliding, and small boat racing. This last is a blessing in disguise, for it gives him useful tangential skills. I am able to appeal to the latent loyalty of son to father, throw myself on his mercy and he comes with me. I unblushingly do this to all of my sons and enjoy their company on board from time to time. In addition to pulling the Bible on Cleody, I must promise the same kind of precision, tactics, and approach to our racing as he finds in his own variant.

At the time of the race he was not yet nineteen and was just beginning to blossom. He had a modest frame, but was strong, light, and agile, an ideal size for a bowman where you need these qualities in addition to quick hands. On the stemhead you want the lightest man able to do the job to avoid increasing the hammerhead action of the bow as it pitches in an unruly sea. Such pitching slows the boat. He was beginning to show an aptitude for this as well as in his steering. I put him with Bobby as watch captain. Bobby is a hard taskmaster and good teacher.

My own relationship with Cleody was close, rather father and sonish. I am not normally delicate in speech, and at sea my language turns even more colorful. Scatology and libertinism in conversation run rife even with Cleody within earshot but, for some reason, never directly to him. Perhaps it was because of his mother who only after these long years lets my verbal improprieties fly past her without a visible reaction. The boat has always been an extension of the family circle.

But during the race to Sweden we passed a meridian in our relationship, so slight as to almost pass unnoticed. It was then, however, that I accepted Cleody as a man not a boy. The event itself was ridiculous.

I had come on deck to find Cleody at the wheel. It was a dreary morning. In the clinging fog Cleody's oilskins looked like the aerial view of a flooded plain. Lakes of condensed moisture formed, swelled, and burst their restraining boundaries to make rampant streams which cut wriggly paths across the glistening orange surface. He showed me his hands which had been wet for days. The fingertips were puckered like pale raisins, the skin peeling in soft-edged flakes. In such conditions little cuts and scratches will not heal; they stay on, just this side of suppurating.

"Sailors call these wounds sea cunts," I said.

The designation is inevitable. The vagina-shaped gashes are surrounded by puffy edges like the lips of that sacrosanct orifice. The color of the wound is pink-red and the gash pearls with serum.

It is a decade since that morning, but I remember having qualms as soon as I said the word "cunt," even though it had the edifying prefix "sea" attached to it. In his nineteen years I had never exchanged such a word with Cleody before. Strange when one thinks of encountering this word and other four-letter beauties like it now in theaters, books, and thoroughfares, instead of being wholly restrained to lavatory walls. In all my life, my father never said any such word in my hearing, and I remember at a tender age hiding a piece of paper containing a quatrain from my mother because I thought it dirty and salacious. The word that made it dirty was "harem."

Since then we have heard and seen all the extant words and a few newly minted ones and yet the Republic has not fallen.

Cleody's answer was a noncommittal, "What will they think of next?"

"When there isn't any around, you can trust Cleody to make his own," Steve threw in to prove he knew the score.

I recognized that I was talking to hip young men and not innocent boys. That day a speech barrier disappeared between the generations. It's a screwy sample to show a coming of age between father and son.

6

BRUCE is putting a lunch of soup and sandwiches together at his own pace. It is a deliberate speed, slowed in part by snacking, but the slow pace of preparation owes more to the weather. I can damn it least by calling it uncooperative. A heavy swell is running. Utensils slide from side to side, threatening a leap into space from the galley counter without benefit of countdown. Bruce is strapped into the cook's belt, a junior iron maiden. However, it does help him stand erect, giving him the use of both hands, saving him from a constant clutching at the grab rails. Despite this, he regularly slams into the crash bar built in front of the stove. Contact is harsh and unyielding, but it does restrain him from being toasted over an open flame which is bared from time to time as the soup pot slides off. He goes doggedly on.

The oncoming watch, having been officially called, struggle out of their nests with appropriate complaints. Instead of glorying in praise of the sumptuous couches I provided, they sounded more as if they were returning from a spell with Procrustes. After listening to their collective complaints, all adding up to a most agonizing stretch in the sack, one wonders why the approaching period in the open air is not greeted with more enthusiasm. The offshore syndrome strikes again. One day a watch will roll out of their bunks full of hosannas for a refreshing sleep in a dry berth and in a room atmosphere tempered to their most exacting needs. On that day I will regain my faith in the essential fairness in men. Until that time I comfort myself in the knowledge that this is the way of sailing men and that I am treated no better or worse than any other yacht owner whose every thought is to the comfort and well-being of his crew.

Lunch is eaten and duly commented upon. Bruce is praised for his fortitude and gymnastic abilities. Small mention if any attaches to his culinary skills. He replies politely and adds an account of the horrors to be encountered in the head in this condition at sea, but no one chooses to pick up his opening. There is a noticeable lack of ravenous hunger which is not quite covered by loud talk. The rolling about has awakened and stirred unfriendly juices sufficient to turn down the appestat. We are a company of picky eaters today, frequenters of ladylike tearooms, all but Bruce who, while not up to his usual style, munches steadily on. And Monk who eats reasonably and steadily and treats this day like all other days. It could be that he has kept himself too busy to notice the rolling about.

Reading the signs, I can visualize a downward dip in morale. It is clear as the chart of air-conditioning sales for the month of February. We may be overwhelmed with an endemic apathy. Nothing slows a boat more; something must be done. Hiding my feelings behind a lot of irrelevant chatter and disguising them by a demeaning laugh, I remind them of the spirited dedication we made just before the start. It was almost a ritual beginning, battle orders, dedicated words from the captain and consecration to our cause. I believe! Words and images move mountains and men.

Most men are romantics and generally cherish the simple acts and stirring words that attend a victory, after and before the fact. A simple phrase or action becomes the companion symbol to a moment in history, like a trademark. It has the happy faculty of arousing the stalwart of the Imperial Guard asleep in some of us. The *beau geste* in action or phrase, the one final fist shaken at the heavens, fixes an event irrevocably in mind and makes us proud to be of the same flesh as the heroes. The Crimean War is a splash in the great river of history but fixed in memory because "Into the valley of death rode the six hundred." Bastogne will be remembered in a welter of individual actions because General McAuliffe on being asked to surrender said, "Nuts!" By an act of transference, we become capable of the same nobility. It is not the great historical importance but the memorability of the attendant words or incidents that counts. A transferable image or idea fixes memory.

We have forgotten the reason and outcome of the war between the Philistines and the Jews, but we remember and accept the story of Samson whose weakness came on him after Delilah cut his hair. We do not even consider the more likely probability that Delilah, reputedly beautiful beyond comparison and an expert in womanly arts beyond hairdressing, held in her quiver of enchantments a more certain method of scissoring the strength from a man. But what is the point of such a version? Since men have been telling stories, weakness in bed only diminishes the scale of heroes. Except for his acknowledged brief spell as a weaver's assistant, the Greeks who knew a lot about heroes always held Heracles to be a splendid performer in Hellenic beds. It rounded out the list and added scale to his other feats. It is true that ancient bards gave Kings David and Solomon a rough time in the business of love's arrows, but this could have been politics; besides, as Kings, they had a lot of other things going for them.

In the matter of courage and daring many men have died bravely and unsung. But Thermopylae is forever fixed in our minds by the calm and noble behavior of Leonidas' 300. We don't know their names but remember that they spent their prebattle hours cleansing themselves, each Spartan soldier combing the long hair of his friend and scraping the anointing oil from his body with a stirgil. We accept these as purification rites before battle. Why not! The event would lose nobility in a

61

heterosexual society by the reminder that Spartan relationships were dedicatedly homosexual.

Phrases have the power to make an event stick in the mind. As long as Englishmen write history we will remember Lord Nelson's signal to the fleet before Trafalgar, that "England expects every man will do his duty." We turn aside as inconsequential the thought that the battle message was composed with his one good eye on the London *Gazette,* Nelson being one of the early geniuses at his own PR, and the fact that a flag lieutenant offered a change in wording for easier transmission, "England" for "I" and "expects" for "confide."

But what does any of it matter? It is all the stuff of legend and history.

What does matter is that I am willing to learn from history. Before a big race one should have a message for the troops. It works. It's like having "In God we trust" stamped on soldiers' buttons or slitting a goat's throat before setting out for Scythia.

Yet it is not as simple as one thinks, this dredging up of an infectious glory phrase. My problem is that it is difficult to devise a prerace strategy for a long race, other than saying, "I will personally kill the son of a bitch who tears up my .75-ounce spinnaker." I have difficulty thinking of anything directly pertaining to the race. But the moment for the utterance finally came. Unprepared and haunted by the need to say something worthy of the event and of the Perrys, Farraguts, and Nelsons who set the style before me, I pushed myself into an autointoxicated excess of zeal and heard myself say, "We will sail her to the point of discomfort—a 3,500-mile sail around the buoys." It sounded great—noble and inspiring. The crew were pleased, and for that reason and for others perhaps more shoddy, so was I. Little did I know how a phrase, spontaneously uttered in an instant of momentary rapture, could come back to haunt me.

This cold day on the Grand Banks, I went through the cabin like Washington at Valley Forge, like Henry V at Agincourt, seeking to hearten my troops. But there was no touch of Harry in this night; perhaps my smile was not as reassuring as that of George with his wooden bridge.

When I reminded them that we were dedicated to sail the boat to the point of discomfort, I was greeted with blank, even sullen stares. Someone uttered that "Discomfort is one thing; trying to sleep on a boat steered by bus drivers is something else." Of course I took no obvious notice of this almost hostile atmosphere, for the tiger can always read fear in the handler's eye. It was better to give ground fearlessly, so I retreated to the company of Knud who finds any phrase in English a remarkable experience, to be reheard, reinterpreted, savored, and tasted.

All things come full circle at sea. Soon the relieved watch struggled hard, in their fashion, to woo the sandman in the same oscillating snuggeries, and the watch on deck gave their own inimitable versions of bus drivers lost at sea.

The swell continued, if anything growing larger.

As the afternoon wore on conversation gradually died. Soon the dominating sound was the creak of the mainsheet in rhythm with the roll and the sound of the bow wave. When one is on deck, in the fog, hearing the bow wave is a little like listening to a taped recording of the sea. But below, here in my bunk where vision is clear, the sound is normal and the boat seems to be going well, even though the hand rocking it is stronger than needed for our cradle of the deep. I have created my own set of wedges and buffers and doze off from time to time only to be awakened by some new intruding sound, heard over the normal susurrus and creak.

Another waking sound. It is Monk, restless; either he cannot sleep or he is getting edgy because of the lack of fix for some time. We want to sail the shortest possible course to Point Able, an invisible but mandatory turning mark, a given latitude and longitude set by the committee to avoid the reported southern limit of drift ice. We cannot climb to any higher latitudes in search of strong winds until this mark is passed. We can sail any course with this wind, but where are we?

Disappointed before, he is going to try for a sight again. He turns on the radio in search of the Canadian time signal. We prefer the Canadian to the American time station. The Canadian station comes in every minute calling the time in a plain language signal. The American calls it every five with code signals interspersed. Wrapped in this eerie fog, the taped, calm, and passionless voice of the announcer calling out the minutes gives every promise of normalcy. The rate and difference with our chronometer being duly noted, Monk prepares to go on deck. Monk's idea of dressing for the deck for a short period is to put on as few clothes as he can so that he will not get them wet. It always seems to me inverse reasoning, holding up to mockery the whole business of invention of clothing, but he is happy in his logic and Monk's logic is backed by a whim of iron. We stopped discussing small matters long ago; I think it best to save the dialectics for subjects like politics, Zen, archery, and girls.

He covers the sextant with a Pliofilm bag to keep off the spray, puts his hack watch in a pocket, and, clad in a light sweater, shorts, and an oilskin jacket, is ready for the deck.

I decide "What the hell" and go up on deck with him, but dressed a little closer to the style of Roald Amundsen than to Mr. Henry Stanley. I will take the time at his call of mark, but we are a long way from any such call. The sky above is overcast, the horizon hidden in the gray blanket, but at times we sail into brighter patches. That's what makes us hopeful. We both settle in, waiting for a clearing. It is a long wait. The sea in its present mood is not only unfriendly but demands a great deal of patience. Since it has no memory or feeling, there is no court of appeal except to the overall regulators, and no one would consider using up one of Aladdin's wishes on one of those "You grant this Oh Powerful Earth Shaker and I will say ten Hail Poseidons" just to get a sight.

Unhappily, neither of us is blessed with Joshua's gifts in matters of heavenly control. The sun will not peek through, much less stand still. The sky will not open. The sun cannot be seen through the overcast and the horizon, even in the brighter patches, will not move more than a few hundred yards away from the boat. All through this, *Figaro* keeps rolling along, perhaps wondering at the fuss and the vocal disappointment. She at least knows where she is. Monk goes back to his charts and a study of the deck log.

Navigators have an unwholesome suspicion of deck logs, viewing them as an exercise in fiction. It is the duty of a watch captain to see that an entry is made in the deck log every time the wheel is relieved. In it, the course and speed made good, along with wind speed and direction, sail changes, and any notable event during the period are entered. Unfortunately, the duty is not strictly maintained, especially while on long unchanging courses. When finally the entry is made, there is a reconstruction to be done. It is at this time that the deck log becomes more heavily devoted to fiction, for the relieved helmsman sees the entry before the one he is to make as a challenge, knows that his own course was a little faster and straighter, and helpfully informs the navigator of that fact.

Taking up their hash of truth, subjective judgment, and downright ego trips, the navigator adds his own factors of probability derived from the pilot chart (drift of Gulf Stream or Labrador Current) and his experience (leeway under given sea conditions) and comes up with a distance and direction of advance in the recorded period. He ticks this off on the scale at the proper latitude with his dividers and, measuring from the last recorded position, places a pencil dot surrounded by a small circle. He labels it EP, for Estimated Position, along with the date and time for the period of record. Until such time as a celestial fix proves the contrary, this dot is taken for the position.

This kind of navigation, or pilotage, is known as *dead reckoning*—a chilling thought, which is only slightly tempered by the knowledge that "dead" in this case is derived from *DED*, an abbreviation for *deduced*.

Before the start of Happy Hour, we took another sounding of

the tanks. Happy Hour is an ancient and honorable custom on board all my *Figaros,* it being the hour before dinner when both watches fraternize and exchange pleasantries. It is a device that prevents interwatch rivalry and tensions and, along with battle slogans and other devices, is a morale builder. A rum punch is served to the nonteetotalers. It is also the moment when the two lower transom berths are empty, so the tanks beneath can be sounded. It is necessary to stay on top of this problem for very practical reasons. It also serves as a constant reminder to the crew that life is real, life is earnest and is not just an empty dream.

It is a breathtaking moment when the measuring stick goes down the filler hole of the port tank and is withdrawn, then "O Nobilissime Visione," she holds water! The enjoyment of Happy Hour is redoubled.

Shortly after dinner is eaten by both watches and the first night watch settled in during the long northern twilight, a freighter steaming SW passes us astern and close aboard. She is flying flag signals W.A.Y. and dips her ensign. After an undignified scramble through the U.S. Hydrographic Office publication, we discover her signal to mean, "I wish you a pleasant voyage." We fly no ensign to return her salute, and so we wave madly, using a damp shirt for our banner.

The conjunction of two such pleasant events are taken to hold good auguries, and so they prove to be, for at 2000 hours the skies clear as though they had been cleared by a magic wand, and we are able to get a three-star fix. This is the best kind, for with a triangle small and tight (in Monk's peerless phrase, "like a heavenly snatch") made by the intersecting lines taken from different azimuths, you have a fix equal to reading a street intersection sign hung directly under a mercury vapor lamp and painted in black Helvetica lettering on a silver day-glo background. We used Arcturus, Jupiter, and Vega, the biggest planet and two bright stars of the first magnitude. Only the best is good enough for us. In a while Monk was able to transfer the longitude and latitude from his plotting sheet to our course chart. He firmly inked in the position marking it STAR FIX. Now we, as well as *Figaro*, know where we are. All things considered our EP was well within our reckoning.

The lines we use to find our place at sea are physically non-existent, yet we have become so accustomed to them that it is as though the earth had been born with them. They are a set of mathematical divisions of the earth which were invented, refined, and revised as men increasingly sailed out of sight of land and as their knowledge of the earth grew. By now they are as precise as though they had been etched into the face of the Earth itself, into the land, sea, and sky—the lot. All this because of international agreement (for those who despair of achieving anything through international amity, be ye heartened). In matters pertaining to the sea at least, by common consent, seafaring countries have agreed upon such things as the location of the Greenwich Meridian, the length of a sea mile, the convention that maps will be printed with north on top, a common set of rules of the sea, a common set of signals, etc.

Soon after midnight, the wind blew back in, still aft. The starboard watch set the 1.5-ounce chute in place of the .75, changed to heavier sheets, set and trimmed the mizzen staysail without calling for help from the other watch. They duly noted and emphasized this fact in the deck log. On its face this note looked like an unnecessary bit of preening, but the suspicion is afloat that this is advice toward building up an IOU collectable from the other watch some future day. (Poor single-handers, they can collect from nobody, nohow.)

This accomplished—the water now rushing by the hull at a livelier speed—the ship settled down, *Figaro* to cutting through wave tops and the crew to sawing wood. Nothing of consequence happened or at least was noted until 0330 hours. Then a comet, a spaceship, superman, or visitors from outer space passed over our heads. In Knud's fine script in the deck log, the event is noted with this comment: "From den Saturnen yet." I have come to believe he is putting us on with a comic Swede accent to amuse us. He is a very kind man. The comet or vehicle went off into the ENE trailing a halo of light roughly the size and shape of the full moon with a brilliant point source of light at its top or head like this:

A light fog returned during the early morning hours, but the wind holds firm. The swell is still with us, and the 1.5-ounce red-topped spinnaker is doing the same sort of dance as indulged in by the blue-top. But now in the heavier wind the movement is more ponderous, the less than enchanting backside of the go-go girl is gone; in her place a firm-haunched matron is doing her stuff. We are accustomed to the rolling of the boat. While it is not one of our favorite motions, we have learned how to live and sleep with it. Our guard is gradually letting down. We are dulling the fine edge of awareness.

But you dare not take the sea for granted—it brings you up short. In order that we not be lulled into complacence, the fitting at the head of the spinnaker let go. Something or someone is determined to let us know there is a boss out here and we transit his realm by sufferance. The two halyards are fixed into the fitting as well. The cloth came down, the halyards remained aloft—double trouble. There was no advance warning. One moment all was well, the next the spinnaker, intact, still full of the breeze, floated out ahead of the boat and slowly sank, like a soufflé top subjected to a rude inspection while still baking. If its descent was an accurate mirror image of our sinking spirits, the very length and duration of the fall turned out to be a stroke of luck. As a rule, one is so horror-struck when suddenly confronted by a developing disaster that the mind has room only for a catalogue of calamities growing from this first happening. The normal stimulating buttons are not punched; action is frozen. Our helmsman happily was not thinking. He had time, brief as it was, to see a strange, ghostly apparition loom ahead of him and instinctively jammed the boat upwind to get out of its way. This put us with our beam to the wind. The spinnaker going downwind drifted out to leeward and fell free of the path of the boat although it was still securely held by the sheet and spinnaker pole.

But for the helmsman's reaction, we would have overrun acres of fine nylon which by the forward movement of the boat would have been drawn around every shape and protuberance of the underwater body and would have clung to these shapes with the ardor and persistence of an amorous octopus or of Cerberus as a puppy at feeding time. Freeing ourselves would have been a long unhappy process. We would have had to cut ourselves free losing time and a spinnaker.

First the acres of cloth, now acting as a sea anchor, had to be retrieved and, while this went on, another spinnaker had to be set. It was an all-hands' deal. Soon the deck was swarming with clothed and unclothed yachtsmen, some in oilskins and boots and others in sopping long johns and wet socks. One group rove a halyard through the spare center block aloft through which we had a thin messenger line for just such an emergency. They hoisted the 2.5 bulletproof spinnaker which was set and drawing while the other gang brought the sopping red-top aboard. We were sailing again in a shorter time than I thought possible after my first sight of the shambles. We had time to examine the head of the spinnaker. The trouble proved to be a lousy fitting. Manufacturers ought to be made to go to sea with their own fittings before putting their stuff on the market. As diagramed, a section through the fitting looked like this:

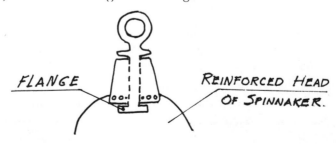

FLANGE

REINFORCED HEAD
OF SPINNAKER.

The trouble and its cause were simple enough. The fitting was made of bronze when it should have been stainless steel. In the almost two days' wear of go-go swiveling, added to earlier erosion, the soft flange at the bottom of the spindle had gradually worn down until the spindle slipped through the barrel of the cylinder like bath soap through a wet hand. Fortunately, we had spare swivels aboard (unfortunately, of bronze) and the spinnaker could be easily repaired. By careful handling and great good luck, no tears or holes were inflicted on the cloth during retrieval.

We were saved a major disaster but not squared away yet. We had two, not one, halyards at the masthead with no way of getting them down except by going up after them. The reason for the two halyards was due to my sailing the Trans-Pac to Hawaii last year. That race is downwind in the trades, and as in all ocean races, chafe is the great enemy. In the case of the Trans-Pac it is even more so because of duration, lively speed, and almost constant direction of the wind. I noticed many Pacific racers carried the spinnaker on two halyards simultaneously, the load always carried in the leeward block, the other halyard eased. In this way no spinnaker halyard could chafe against the head or outer jib stay. After a gybe one took up on the new leeward halyard and eased the old one from the deck. So that this can be done, the crane atop the mast is built like a three-tined fork. The two outer tines carry the port and starboard halyards. The center tine holds a block in which we carry a messenger line and is a utility block to be used for jib or spinnaker at will. It is now carrying the 2.5 bulletproof spinnaker. We must bring the other two down to be prepared for anything to come.

Our man at the masthead—Bucky—is ready to go aloft. The boat is rolling and the arc of swing at the masthead is many times that at the deck as is the case at the end of any pendulum. Now the swing will be more pronounced because as his weight goes aloft the righting movement of the boat is reduced, its stability is lessened.

70

He ties himself securely into the bosun chair which in turn is clipped into the wire jib halyard. He is set. He holds onto the shrouds to keep from swinging too wildly and to keep from banging into the mast. He goes up, taking an occasional slam against the shrouds, but as he nears the point where the shrouds and mast converge, he takes a two-way buffeting. He tries as best he can to hold himself off by legs and arms. In addition, we have a guideline tied to the bottom of the chair and take a strain to quiet the action. It is a help but not much. Once at the masthead, in between times of holding himself off from battering to bits, he removes the temporary center-line halyard and transfers the two halyards into the head of the sail now flying, then ties a haul-down line into the pair of halyards in case we have a recurrence of accident. In that event, we can bring the halyards to the deck without sending up a man. What is the use of putting yourself in the way of trouble if you can't learn something from it? We make all the necessary adjustments at the halyard winches; he fastens the center halyard to the chair and is ready to come down.

He reaches the deck a little the worse for wear. Slipping hurriedly out of the bosun chair, he moves to the shrouds and relieves himsel of the roil he has stirred up while taking the shellacking at the masthead. He had become seasick up there but managed to hold everything back until he finished his job and reached the deck. The masthead in a seaway is a rough place to be even for the toughest iron guts. In a while his spasms quiet. He comes back to the cockpit to rest and take the air in a semicheerful state, and soon his normal ebullience returns. Bucky is a hard man to keep down.

We, in reaction, reflecting on the suddenness of the event, ponder on the quick pouncing sea, always searching for, if not in fact creating, little cracks in our defenses. If it finds one, how it comes piling through, exploiting any weakness into trouble, sometimes even up to the point of a major tragedy. Suddenly you recognize that you no longer operate in a world of hard and fast rules.

On land we have organized the sea's geography by latitudes and longitudes; we have charted its edges and plumbed its depths. From that vantage point it is another frontier, tamed and within our governance. At sea, however, in a small boat we face an uncontrollable element; its restless power, its animosities and terrors rearrange our thoughts about order. On land when a vicious northeaster beats at us, we do not leave the house or we scurry for a taxi under an umbrella or work our way up the street dodging from canopy to canopy. At sea you must stand out in it, watching each oncoming wave, estimating how best to guide your boat through it while keeping an eye on the sails for the first indication of trouble. There is no hiding place.

It is as in the beginning. Little wonder that ancient man endowed the sea with so many beliefs and superstitions, which at the drop of a barometer come back to haunt us. Ordinarily the vacuum left by the loss of belief is partially filled by our new and sophisticated technology. But suddenly confronted by the sea's unyielding and capricious power, we find ourselves worrying the edges of old superstitions. We begin to wonder how much of our lives operate within immutable laws and how much is a result of chance and accident. The sea becomes an enormous arena of chance but with another meaning because within that framework it adds challenge, zest, and flavor to living. Yet it is the same sea that Columbus sailed. It is the same experience shared across time by ancient and modern man, an encounter stretching across the ages. In another perhaps sublimated way it enlarges our spirit. We no longer are reduced to integers, just so many genes doled out, measured, strained, and added up in some great volume of laboratory notes. Chance and our individual persistence must have played a great role in our existence, mutation, and survival.

In existential terms, sailing the sea broadens a facet of an idea set forward by Camus in the dedication of his book on Sisyphus. Sisyphus eternally pushed a rock toward a mountain top only to have it roll back short of the top. Using this idea in his dedication, Camus says, "The universe from now on without a master seems to him neither sterile nor futile. The struggle toward the summit itself is enough to fill the heart of man."

Each day the wind-sailor faces another set of problems. At intervals he fights for survival. In this daily effort to move forward, he wins and savors the desire to go on.

7

CLEARING skies, lifting spirits, and at first light a beautiful three-star fix. We use Fomalhaut, Vega, and Altair, brilliant first-magnitude bodies, as fixed and eternal as when the Arabian cosmographers first named them. Then, as the horizon brightens to set the stage for the rising sun, we see our competition.

Slightly ahead and to the starboard, we identify Sven Hansen's bright-hulled *Anitra*. "Bright," in this instance, means varnished as against painted and is not a conjunctive qualifier as in deep-browed Homer, ox-eyed Hera, or the wine-dark sea. She is almost a sister ship to *Figaro*, the same size and shape hull, but designed with keel instead of centerboard by Olin Stephens. She seems to run slightly better than we do—a fact which is slowly seeping into my consciousness, leaving with it a pain and unbelieving surprise.

I have always lived with the belief that centerboards are automatically superior downwind. The core of this belief centers in the idea that all I need do is pull up part of the board, thereby reducing the wetted surface, and wave good-bye over my stern. But my scenarios do not in reality come out to such a happy ending. I cannot get myself to accept the results as a proven case; rather I attribute the apparent superiority of a keelboat downwind, in certain conditions, to better steering control. A keelboat is more forgiving. Anticipatory steering is not as demanding. A centerboarder, as then current, with its shorter semibarn-door rudder goes out of control rapidly as the boat heels to a point where the rudder begins to act as a diving plane. Short of this calamity, the centerboard, having less directional ability, still needs more rudder action unless it is in smooth water where the lower wetted surface can assert itself. The newer designs with their newer rudders begin to level out this inequality, although the ever deeper ballast of the new keelboats turns them into stable lead mines. A centerboarder, such as this *Figaro,* requires better helmsmen. Conversely, I am happily surprised to find my boat a great on-the-wind boat and a superb reacher. This year *Figaro* is going much better. The fact that we are so close to *Anitra* after a few days running in a seaway shows the keel and rudder changes I made last winter are successful. The reasons for the change were not so much rooted in a desire for more speed, although this is a consummation devoutly to be wished, but as the result of a horrendous experience. But more of that story later.

Now back to the competition. Abeam and to starboard is Tom Watson's *Palawan,* also a bright hull, a centerboarder, and larger than us. She should be well ahead. Abeam to port in a white-painted aluminum hull is Hank Dupont's *Cyane,* a keelboat, counting among her souls on board our sometime shipmate and always dear friend, Norry Hoyt. I am sure if we all keep quiet, we can hear his voice, even here—enthusiastic, catchy, almost bubbly, at the point of laughter—telling an oft-told tale which his hearers welcome each time just as did listeners to ancient bards, skalds, and troubadors.

Behind us is *Constellation,* a 90-foot schooner! She belongs to, and is being sailed by, the only lady skipper in the fleet, Sally Ames Langmuir. Being too big, *Constellation* is not racing officially. The Cruising Club of America limit size is 73 feet. The committee gave her permission to sail with us. Even recognizing a certain lack of motivation she should not be behind—she is just too big to be back there. No matter how little the motivation, by sheer size, if not out of pride, she should have been out of sight ahead. Perhaps the early days of sailing hard on the wind, shifting to light running, is just not her bag, or maybe she's had some serious gear failures aboard.

Except for the big boats (other than *Constellation*), which must be off and away ahead, and for the small class behind, we had been seeing most of our class competition regularly until the fog set in. Now here they are again. It is not usual in an ocean race except in those with a very large entry list, such as the Bermuda, where the sheer weight of numbers and, at times, generally shared weather conditions make encounters likely. In the Fastnet the course bends around the southwest coast of England. The St. Petersburg–Fort Lauderdale goes around the Cape of Florida. Sailing the shortest course makes bunching likely. But this is rarely as true on a long race out on the open sea. The ocean is wide and each boat has its own best sailing angle. Until one learns differently, the tendency is to think of weather on the ocean as a single big pattern, meting out the same wind, speed, direction, and state of sea to each boat. This is true in a great overpowering storm system, but ordinarily there are significant differences within 50 to 100 miles separation of isobars. This difference, plus course adjustments to a boat's best sailing angle, and the skipper's idea of where to find the best wind, generally separates boats.

But now we hang together like the tattered section of a migrating flock, as though we are seeking the comfort of the group automata with unvarying behavioral responses. Yet this is really not so. Each boat is a universe of its own, peopled by its own inhabitants with their own eccentricities, likes, dislikes, their own idea of fun, and their own dreams. It is a culture center of its own. Ocean racing is a curious sport. The boats as a group have a common goal—they race to a common port and each wants to win. By and large skippers and crews do the same things, respond to challenges and stimuli in the same manner. Even techniques are carried from boat to boat by wandering crews and by observation. Yet taken together, a boat and its crew constitute an individual community. It is a tribe existing by itself and isolated from any knowledge of what may be happening elsewhere. It is a state of mind and being such as I have come to love, this being shut off with your own friends, unified with a single although many-faceted concentration. How to win and what you must do next in order to do so.

Not everyone cherishes the same attitude. As a matter of fact, this is the first Atlantic race in which the proposition was put forward by some contestants that regular radio communication be set up at a regular time each morning. They were to exchange positions exactly as it is done on the Trans-Pac. Both Dick Nye and I objected and said we would not join. *Figaro* and *Carina* are two of the yachts not participating in the exchange. First, on the grounds that if anyone gave a position far ahead it might spur the crew to greater efforts, but, conversely, it could have an equally demoralizing effect, might in fact generate a "what-the-hell" attitude. I like the idea of hope burning bright up to the end. If your spirit is to be crushed, let it happen at the end rather than at the midpoint. The second reason is that we like the splendid isolation. That's why we go to sea. If we wanted a kaffeeklatsch or cocktail party, we would have stayed ashore.

I may be overly romantic or else a misogynist, but I feel that in some way the singular experience of sailing across the ocean in a small boat is lessened, the sense of exhilaration, of winning over adversity, is flattened and made ordinary by chattering away with people, even if they are in another nearby part of the ocean. It may have been comforting for the settlers who braved the wilderness gateway of Cumberland Gap to clear the forest land beyond, to know they had a neighbor somewhere over the next ridge. But we are not here to settle or tame a wilderness; rather we want to try ourselves in this hostile environment, win if possible, and leave the roaring wilderness of water exactly as we found it. The idea of a daily electronic kaffeeklatsch not only reduces the undertaking but affronts my sense of style. If I may look ahead, the next thing to expect is a small boat from one of our competitors coming alongside on a calm day to exchange copies of skin magazines (a stout part of any ship's library) in the hope that you have grown as wearied as they with your first selection of the unreal if roseate and pneumatic creatures. (The eye and mind is soon clotted with so many antierotic still lifes of commercial beauty contorted out of all reason in order to give you a simultaneous view of a plump arse and fulsome tit, that you look forward to the next revelation for some minute indication of reality, in the hope of a clearing vision.) But to go with the gam, the exchange effected, the finer points of the surrendered icons pointed out, a little over-the-rail gossip exchanged, an attempt to borrow a bottle of rum successfully evaded, they leave for their mother ship.

The picture is overdrawn. It is hyperbole. The situation sounds ridiculous, but, remember Jersey City was once a menacing wilderness of forest and savage. Nevertheless, the idea of electronic chatter across the fence sounds so snug and cozy, positively reeking so much of suburban domesticity, that to a degree, once permitted, it will invade another unspoiled frontier of the spirit. What then happens to our splendid isolation, the chance to cut oneself off even for a moment from that frantic pileup of bodies, machines, and stupefying repetition? What happens to the opportunity to reflect and revitalize? Now, viewed with a decade of perspective since the time of that race, what with living in the presence of urban decay inadequately disguised by a pother of new architectural decorations, and at the same time being exposed to the pressures of social breakdown and disruption, we are witness to the loss of human dignity in that miracle of evolution—man. We see that magnificent balance of musculature and brain now reduced to scrambling and scrounging in an ignoble environment and social structure. I know now I was right to resist any intrusion (real or symbolic) into that precious isolation and peace that I had found. However slight or comforting, such intrusions should be kept out of certain holy places.

Point Able is our reason for being so close together, and until we pass the southeast corner of the path of the drift of ice coming down from Greenland, we will probably stay in a bunch. This is being done to equalize the chances of the faint and the lion-hearted and to avoid foolhardy accidents. From that point, with only one more *verboten* area ahead, we are on our own. We will all sail a great circle course, that is to say, a course which will follow the path of a string stretched over a globe from St. David's Head Light in Bermuda to St. Kilda in Scotland, our landfall in the Outer Hebrides. The forbidden area is Pentland Firth, an estuary between the off-lying land at the northeast coast of Scotland and the main body of the land of gillies, gullies, and usquebaugh. Pentland Firth has tidal currents which reach up to 8 knots. This is not only dangerous, exceeding the sailing speed of smaller yachts, but, more to the point, it is unfair as a racing mark. Any yacht reaching the entrance at the proper moment has an enormous advantage. The reverse is as unhappily true. Since yachts, through their differing size, cannot sail at the same speeds, it is arithmetically impossible for them to reach a given point at the same time. That's why we sail with handicaps.

We must, therefore, sail north of Ronaldsay in the Orkneys, and the course from there becomes once again optional. The race committee has done the best it can with trying to adjust the inequalities of boat speeds within the limits of that work of mystification and science fiction called the rating rule. Handicapping seems to be the yachtsman's problem in this era, equal to squaring the circle in bygone days. Yet with all their great distances, ocean currents, storms, and calms, out of sight (though rarely out of mind), it is surprising to find boats arriving at the finish line within minutes of one another. Two hours from the finish you saw no one. Then suddenly they converge from all points of the compass.

Our competition, seen and unseen, are dear friends and boon companions ashore. But at sea they metamorphose, growing horns and claws, and are steeped in the odor of sulfur. They probably grow webbed feet as well. In the case of Dick Nye, one could easily mistake the blue puffs of smoke he exhales when chomping on a cigar for tobacco smoke, but I know the shape and texture that comes from burning brimstone when I see it. For reasons unknown, most of our important competitors hold special relationships to the fates and the weather gods. In short, we race against a number of seafaring Fausts who care no more for winning than for their right arms, to say nothing of their souls; as far as I am concerned, when at sea they are totally devoid of souls. They are not like us, these monster-men of the fraternity; we are the little men, the workers in the vineyard, who fight for a small place in the sun and a quiet nook in the winner's enclosure.

We sail with a fair-sized ocean racing fleet, considering the length of the race and the port of departure (the logistics of starting one race after completing a first one and making the new start from a port with inadequate facilities is very complicated).

The fleet numbers eighteen with seventeen racing. In an approximate order of size, I list the yachts and their owners:

Germania	Baron Krupp Von Essen und Halbach
Escapade	Baldwin T. Baldwin
Barlovento	Pierre Dupont
Drumbeat	The Honorable Max Aitken—now Sir Max
Ondine	S. Huey Long
Hamburg IV	Hamburg Sailing Club
Dyna	Clayton Ewing
Palawan	Thomas Watson
Carina	Richard S. Nye
Anitra	Sven Hansen
Figaro	William Snaith
Cyane	Henry Du Pont
Windrose	Jakob Isbrandtsen
Delight	Wright Britten
Belmore	Sailed by Errol Bruce

Danegeld	Robert Lowein
Cassella II	Yngve Cassel

All of these boats, with the exception of *Germania, Drumbeat,* and *Belmore,* are being sailed by their owners. With the exception of the Baron Krupp, I am well acquainted with everyone in and connected with the race. I know the Baron Krupp, but my acquaintance is limited to politely warm exchanges over cold champagne.

I have special friendships with two men whose boats are entered, one sailing and one not. Let each man count himself lucky who has Max Aitken for a friend. Generous, adventurous, and bursting with the fun of living, he has the quality of transferring much of his own pleasure to his friends. The other, Dick Nye, is a nonpareil. He is a constant winner of races, which he performs with a mixed air that, on one hand, says, "After all, what did you expect?" and, on the other, claims, with a masquerading modesty, that he is but a lucky handmaiden to the fates. No less a student of life than Joseph Conrad said, "You can judge a man by his foes as well as his friends." Dick is my "dear enemy." If a man needs great competition to sharpen himself against, then Dick is my man. Vercingetorix to Caesar, Napoleon to Wellington, Lee to Grant, Rommel to Montgomery. I am not sure which is who. One could fill pages with tales of Max and Dick, but there are always court injunctions, suits for libel, and one must get on with one's own story, which for the moment has very little in the way of sprightly information to report, other than that by twelve noon we can count up the day's run as 180 miles and that as result of a running fix of our position the clock was moved ahead one hour to $+3$ Zone Time.

One could also mention a comment entered in the log by a malicious eavesdropper, who reports that while the Simple Island Boy and the captain were in the middle of one of their endless gasing sessions below (during Simple's watch on deck), an exchange between Steve and Cleody was reported:

STEVE: "What do you think of our watch captain?"

CLEODY: "I don't know, I never see him."

So endeth Saturday, July 2. We have been at sea two and a half days and have come 355 miles. Our 2000 hour fix had us at 35° 54' N–58° 55' W and the base course to Point Able is 80°.

8

ANOTHER clear morning and a star fix to fill the dreams of the most finicky navigator, the kind that works only with 6H pencils. There is a fat edge of satisfaction to Monk's voice as he calls "Mark" for the last time, followed by "That's it, thank you." I look at my watch. The glowing hands show it to be 0410 hours. I crane my head out of the covers and out of the bunk to look up through the companionway. A large square of electric blue-violet is framed by the darkness below, very beautiful, a backdrop for an old mystery or a bright beginning—the color of the world before God invented light and found it good. I try to lock the color into my memory, perhaps to be used in a painting, but the cold morning air leaks into my blanket cocoon. It pours in at the edges where I have broken the carefully engineered seal against the night air. With that, I snuggle back into the covers, goose-pimpled but aglow with the inner warmth that comes from a sense of well-being. There is time for one last nap before waking and dressing for the morning watch.

Monk clambers down the companionway ladder and starts to stow the sextant. The morning air has a bite. I hear him pause to rub his hands and arms as though to stimulate circulation. I whisper, "Did you shoot a good set, Monk?"

"The best, Captain," he whispers in return, "Altair, Vega, Mars, and Alpheratz, all hanging up there—big, bright, and steady as lanterns, like spearing fish in a barrel."

"That's great, Monk," I reply in the same happy hush and just for something to say.

He goes back to his stowing. I hear the soft, short clatter of the hack watch deposited on the table, the snap of the chronometer lid, and the slap of the notebook. Then he starts to undress. An intelligent man who knows a good thing when it stares back in his face, he is returning to his bunk to sleep and will work out the sights later this morning.

My body heat once again held in by the covers begins to spread a cozy warmth, the last of the goose pimples disappear, I start to drowse. The boat is quiet except for the gurgle and rush of water going by immediately outside the hull, a murmur which makes me feel even warmer and safer, like hearing rain on the roof during a summer afternoon shower. The last thing I remember thinking is that we are sailing in a plethora of goodies.

I wake once, briefly, to the clang of a pot, then doze off again only to come up from the deep, struggling hard to remain asleep against the compelling perfume of ambrosia. The smell of frying bacon and percolating coffee fills the cabin. It enters through my nostrils, settles on my taste buds, and invades my whole consciousness. (I wonder at the vagaries of men. I love Max Aitken dearly, but he cannot abide the smell of frying bacon in his cabin.)

Later, after breakfast and the change of watch, the morning drones on. Minor adjustments are made on the sails. Small tasks of ship's husbandry are undertaken and disposed of. Parceling and other chafe preventives are applied, and we are always peering at the horizon to see our friends. They are still with us but in alternating relationships to us. With two fixes and a wind direction that lets you change course at will, we have decided we would do better by sharpening up, that is, heading slightly north to bring the wind more on the quarter. We will get more drive from the breeze at hand. This course change brings *Palawan* slightly ahead, *Cyane* on the starboard hand drops back, and *Windrose* suddenly pops over the horizon to port.

Once the new positions are established, there they stay. We have a bit more angle of heel and *Figaro* is moving faster.

We settle back into the mechanics of passage making. The wheel is relieved every half hour and entries made in the log. The more knowing helmsmen, on taking the wheel, call for an alteration of trim and harry the crew until the boat handles to their satisfaction. This is a peculiar idiosyncrasy and privilege of the helmsman unless vetoed by his watch captain. Each boat driver likes a certain kind of response from the boat and a certain feel to the wheel. Sometimes the change is minuscule. I remember serving as a watch captain on Huey Long's 58-foot yawl, the second *Ondine.* We were in the Southern Ocean Racing Conference (SORC) and in this race, the Miami–Nassau, we were sailing hard on the wind across the Gulf Stream toward Great Isaac Light. Jack MacManus, a skillful helmsman from Boston, was attached to my watch. We were standing watch and just the two of us steering for the whole period, relieving each other at half-hour intervals in order to stay sharp and maintain concentration. We had a beautiful evening, easy sea, a true and steady wind. Jack liked a slack helm; he was a dinghy racer. I liked one with a slight weather component so that the boat aways had a slight tendency to windward. On taking the wheel, he would slack the mizzen three inches. When I took over, I would get the three inches back. Those were our major changes for our watch period, and as I remember, we did very creditably.

Noon, hot soup and sandwiches, a change of watch, and after a noon fix a report of the day's run and our position. We have run 180 miles since yesterday noon—not bad, not exceptional. The watch settle back once again to the long business of grinding out the miles. Our competition is fixed on the horizon like stamps, and we take only occasional looks to see if anything noteworthy is happening. But everyone crowds the rail to see a steamer going west. She has nothing to say to us or we to her. We settle for waving, hoping that her radio operator will mention us in a message ashore and that in some way our families will know we are getting on and taking nourishment.

It is slow, unexciting work, perhaps because it is July 3. We are saving our energies for tomorrow—*the glorious Fourth of July.* At sea, aboard *Figaro,* the Fourth of July has taken on special meanings. Perhaps it is because we are so far from home and sailing toward a foreign port. We treat it as an extension of the celebration for our household gods, if, in fact, there's room out here for the lares and penates as well as the finny varieties. It is all accompanied by an underlying though not overly persistent sentiment of patriotism. As captain and master of entertainments, I am largely responsible for stirring up the scale of the celebration. Making a to-do over the July 4 celebration is not within my inherited family traditions. I owe these feelings largely to my wife Betty. It was she who created and nailed down a tradition for our own family.

I was slow in arriving at any special sort of attitude toward Independence Day, having been born in Brooklyn, in a section inhabited by a wide spectrum of nationalities who were at most two generations away from immigration. They had moved here from a one-generation stop in crowded Manhattan, into modest brick and wooden houses arranged in rows on tree-lined streets. They had brought with them various old-country celebrations and traditions. Close communities of ethnic groups were formed, living no more than one street apart, sometimes even sharing a single street, dividing it east and west. At one time or another, St. Rocco, St. Patrick, or Rosh Hashanah were being memorialized, but the impact seemed to be swallowed and subdued by the overhanging trees. Trees were important because our street did not have as many trees as some of the others. My maternal grandfather planted a Norway maple in our pocket-sized front yard. It has always been difficult for me to reconcile this tree with my grandfather, who was an intensely urban man.

If ideas about my grandfather are difficult to reconcile, then thoughts about inherited customs and traditions are utterly irreconcilable when I think of my grandmother. That magnificent woman who raised me after my mother died had come to this country as a very young bride. She crossed in a ship which, from her description, was either a sailing ship with auxiliary power or a steamer with auxiliary sails or just a sailing ship. I could never get her to be more accurate because the trip was seemingly endless and traumatic. She was seasick all the way and scared of boats ever after, so much so that she would become seasick when boarding a Hudson River side-wheeler excursion boat while still tied to its dock.

She was a simple and modest woman. Our pleasures were humble; the grand life, a distant view of things enjoyed by inhabitants of another world. Yet here I am, her grandson, on my own yacht, reveling in an Atlantic crossing and about to celebrate the Fourth of July. The first she would have thought consistent with punishment meted out by the Grand Inquisitor, and the second, some sort of pagan holiday endured to the accompaniment of exploding firecrackers. There was little reason for her to be better informed or more with it. She was a very private woman, not fully integrated into American life.

My grandfather knew a bit more. He was mildly political, a sort of block captain for the then-powerful Tammany Hall—his job, to see that his constituency voted early and often. It could not have been a very rich duchy, for we lived in very modest circumstances, in a very close and familial circle with private joys and celebrations, covered over by the trees. I knew about great national holidays through going to public school. The Fourth of July was mainly distinguished by being associated with firecrackers which we would set off under tin cans in the street and endless rolls of paper caps for the cap pistols which we would shoot off in honor of George Washington, whom I vaguely associated with Independence Day. The cap guns also served the greater glory of Tom Mix and William S. Hart, the then-reigning cowboy movie stars. At night we would burn sparklers and see and hear distant fireworks over the high horizon made by the trees. Sometimes we would climb to the flat roof of a house in the warm dark of the summer's night in order to see more of the faraway display.

As I grew older my ideas of the Fourth clarified, but I had neither the occasion nor the desire to celebrate it in any particular way. Betty changed all that. She comes from Minnesota, and while she was that exotic thing called a ballet dancer when we met and married, she comes from and has never forgotten a very American land and people. Instinctively, her hand is joined to the hand that held the plow that broke the plains. For her, July 4 had always been a day of family picnics, games, and refreshments stretching into the evening when you stayed on to see the fireworks. For her father, she remembered it as a gentle boozing with friends or a baseball game before dinner in which he was catcher. After we began a family of our own we moved to suburban Connecticut, with one intermediate stage from an artist's loft in New York City, our last gasp of the bohemian life, but we did not know that at the time.

Now all of my reading of a younger America came to the fore—about a time when Independence and the American Dream was more keenly and kindly felt, patriotism livelier, picnics rowdier, and generally capped with a two-hour peroration by Daniel Webster or a pale aldermanic imitation. The proles would relieve these rigorous exercises by gargantuan meals and watermelon-eating contests, and the pages of fiction swarm with lovers who, wandering away from the ruder mob, stole kisses and virginities in the dappled sunlight of a hidden and unspoiled grove. All of this, the real and the fantasized, were rolled into a collage which had come to mean the Fourth of July for us, a familial celebration with semipatriotic overtones, an amalgam of past and present. This remembered aura is never so much cherished as when I am at sea, for often the memory and anticipation are sweeter than the fact.

Whether the crew share my particular feelings about the Fourth or have a few of their own or none at all, seems to make little difference. In our situation, a break in the regimen, centered around a formalized celebration, sends waves of anticipating pleasure out ahead like outriders or like a swell before a storm.

As master of revels I direct the formalities, but its skeleton and flesh are provided by Betty. As planner of our food and supplies, the accouterments of a party are also in line with her job as ship's provisioner.

Evening and another star fix. We are steadily running down the miles. The line of inked positions on the chart are beginning to reach out along the Great Circle course. At this very moment I could be sailing the reverse course of the one that brought my grandmother to America, but I can't tell. The sea carries no marks and covers over all trails.

9

THE dawn of July 4 raced toward us at the precise rate of 15° longitude every hour. Each morning is a special miracle of rebirth and an invitation to adventure, yet withal a clockwork phenomenon which has been observed, timed, and calculated to the flicker of a computer. We may not have penetrated the ultimate secret of the cosmos in its first cause and dimension, but we have its schedule down cold. To the upwelling of spirit which comes with the return of light after the unseen threats of a night for us at sea, one can add the sense of wonder voiced by the marveling scholar who said, "What a wonderful thing is mathematics."

A few hours ago this dawn passed over England, searching out quiet mossy graves, touching them with a blush of pink light. It had filtered through the stained glass of venerable windows, speckling gray stone with tints of blue and crimson. Of all things abroad this English dawning, only the sun seemed to memorialize the day as it picked out the final retreats of George Grenville, Charles Townshend, Lord North, George III, and the other bewigged statesmen or pantaloons who played roles leading to the events of 1776. On this morning gentlemen in England now abed did not think themselves accursed nor hold their manhood cheap because of this day. Very few of the dormant or quick, those turning over to nuzzle in the warmth of the soft familiar shape alongside; those yawning, stretching, trying to stir the laggard life juices under rumpled pajamas, recognized this as the anniversary of a day one hundred and eighty-four years ago when so much of their history and ours changed.

But then why would they—so much had happened to them before and since. Hastings, Agincourt, Trafalgar, Gunga Din, the Light Brigade, Mafeking. (Once an American student at Oxford electing to read in American history was asked by a puzzled don whether he thought there had been enough of it to constitute a course of studies.) Indeed, why should they remember it? Enough that it was celebrated in London by the Pilgrim Society, the American Chamber of Commerce, and by an Open House at the Embassy in Grosvenor Square and that these aforesaid events will be duly noted in the inside pages of newspapers alongside the pictures of the latest Miss Malt Ale of Cardiff wearing a smile and a bikini.

The same pink-violet light which would later touch Benjamin Franklin's grave in Boston's old Granary Burying Ground, lying in comfortable distance from the large window in the member's bar of the Union Club, the same light which will spread its glow over the great stone shaft of the Washington Monument and the columned beauty of the latter-day version of Hadrian's Tomb that holds Jefferson's effigy, found us on an uneasily rolling sea under gray skies.

For those of us who had served the last night watch, it was not a very prepossessing morning—cold, damp, holding out little virtue and less promise. Its only grace lay in that, with its coming, our watch was over. We'd had it and were in no more temper to greet the day with hurrahs than could be found among the early risers or night owls of London. I wanted nothing so much as sleep. Other than that there seemed to be nothing that one could offer to raise my interest level one millimeter. Sometimes the beauty of a dawn hits a hidden atavistic button and you feel refreshed and reinvigorated, truly going through a reborning. No wonder so many rituals take place at sunrise. But this rosy-fingered dawn did not jazz up the system or inspire gobs of poetics. There was nothing for a muse-ridden bard worth reporting. The brightness did not extend for more than three handbreadths above the edge of the world. From there, beginning with a harsh and definite line, a heavy impenetrable overcast overlaid the ocean making a lowering ceiling whose bottom limits consisted of low-flying scud, handfuls of gray matting torn from Poseidon's beard. We were certainly under a big system going rapidly east, but since the wind was still aft it did not fit any of our accustomed patterns. The depression causing this must be far to the northeast and very large. But this is only supposition. We receive no weather information.

I had little appetite for breakfast. Perhaps if someone had offered me a large, very cold glass of fresh orange juice to cut the phlug of a long night of smoking and swilling coffee, I would have taken a fresh view of the world. But no one offered because it was not available, which, all things being equal, seems a solid reason. Bucky slipped below early to start the breakfast. It takes longer than one imagines to prepare. I notice, however, on very cold or wet mornings that he starts much earlier than usual. There is always the hope you can rouse the other watch a little earlier, but I would rate that likelihood about equal to the psychokinetic transportation of the body and form of Raquel Welch by the will of an off-watch dreamer. Also one cannot escape the fact that the galley is a pleasant place to be on a cold, wet morning. Shaving ten minutes of deck time at the expense of the other watch is a coup to enjoy in silent straight-faced glee. However, the other gang is just as agile. The attempts go on and the desire to pull a fast one always brings about silly situations.

I remember one late watch when, the weather being particularly miserable and our first turn in the bunk being sleepless, I was overwhelmed by the desire to be anywhere else but at the wheel. I suddenly had it—up to the very armpits. I spoke as though under deep autohypnosis. My voice became an unconscious servant of a wish. I turned to Bucky at 0400 with two and a half hours more to go and, without really meaning it, said, "Feed those pricks and get them on deck." (It must be recognized that I hold no hidden animosities toward my shipmates. They are dear fellows. But at 0400, anyone sleeping below, while we yawn, nod, and shiver on deck, is automatically a prick, doubled-dyed and in spades.)

Bucky, nothing loath, always the faithful hand, slipped below and had a splendid breakfast going before I could retract the order. And I never did. Rather, I sat there transfixed, awestruck at the audacity of the idea, even if it was mine. I never said a word to him, and he did not talk to me for fear perhaps that I would halt the operation. Soon breakfast, no matter how extended the niceties, was cooked and ready to serve. Then our nerve failed. We called no one, and no one stirred. Not even the fragrance of coffee and bacon moved a soul. That compelling perfume lost its magic in the presence of the sound of rain on the overhead. So we wound up eating it ourselves and spent the time until they awakened picking our teeth and getting sleepier. Naturally, when the time for their breakfast came due no one held any tender thoughts about cooking. Their meal was a ragged affair.

This Fourth of July morning I went to bed without eating, and as for any idea of celebration, they could take it and stuff it in the least likeliest of places. The idea of patriotism, commemoration and the lot were the last items on my list of things to do.

I wakened sometime late in the morning before time to change the watch. It had not been an easy and refreshing sleep. The sleep of babes has been eluding me these many years.

Whoever or whatever it was this morning, I wakened out of sorts, out of the wrong side of the bed. Since there is only one side by which you can enter or leave a bunk, the difference must be which hip or leg you thrust outside the limits of the bedclothes first on rising. In any case, it must have been the wrong side this morning. Not having eaten breakfast before retiring, I felt a bit peckish and, thinking to prepare some fluffy delight, went to the galley, only to find a mound of uncleaned pots, pans, dishes, and utensils cluttering the counter, sink, and stove. I had to burrow down and clean a few in order to provide a starting place. That tore it. By the time I finished I wanted no breakfast, only revenge and the skins of the beasts who had perpetrated this indecency on me. I wanted their hides to nail to the head door.

Up until now there had been little conversation. I had been greeted with a cheery "Good morning, Captain" to which I replied with an undecipherable grunt and so I was let be. Now the need to speak welled from my every pore.

"What the hell kind of ship are we running here? This watch is supposed to clean up," I said to the man at the wheel who just happened to be the Simple Island Boy.

"Are you displeased, my captain?" he asked blandly, his tone not at all in keeping with a black beard beginning to sprout and already making him look as piratical as the men his country claims to have expelled at the time of its forming.

"Displeased, hell! Do I have to clean up for this watch in order to get something to eat?"

"You were sleeping so soundly we hesitated to wake you with any clatter. Besides we are only following orders, helping you sail to the point of discomfort."

"Discomfort, my eye! I don't see any of you layabouts on deck suffering any discomfort."

"We are always thinking about you, my captain."

One of the most unfruitful lines of pursuit is a single angry idea in the face of unfailing good humor. Besides, none of the things I said carried sufficient barb and acid, so I sliced off on another tack.

"In spite of the loyalty to your own bloody rag, you know this is an American boat and this is an American holiday, why aren't we displaying our colors?"

"You heard the captain, lay aft to raise the ensign," he said to some mysterious being forward, over the heads of his mates lolling in the cockpit. As far as I could see, the whole watch had congregated there at the first rude sounds from down below.

Cleody rose from a sheltered place under the dodger, reached behind him and, taking the folded ensign aft, hung it from the mizzen boom and made a ponderous salute. Matson was sent below to finish the washing up, greeting me with a "Hi, Captain" as though no heat or criticism had been exchanged. There was nothing I could do or say in the face of such unflurried and pleasant manners, and since there was no longer room for me in the galley, I headed back to the main cabin and my bunk, perhaps to plan the proper use of the rest of the day or perhaps just to sulk in privacy. But the silver-tongued one could not let it rest with that.

"Is there anything else we can do to please you, Captain—a cigar perhaps?" It is enough to make a man plot mayhem.

"No, just keep your attention on the boat; we're still racing—this is not a cruise whatever else you and your watch are thinking about." Not very good for a curtain speech, but the best I could muster at the moment. I didn't even listen to his, "Aye, aye, sir."

Monk, lifting his head for a brief moment, said, "A clear case of insubordination, Capting."

"You can say that again. I'll hold a captain's mast before the free drinks are served this evening." I climbed back into my bunk and, marvel of marvels, had a wondrously refreshing nap, sleeping the babe's sleep at last, until I was called for lunch and the change of the watch. All the world looked beautiful and friendly. But Bobby's watch had lost some of their good humor. Their sallies carried an edge.

At first the other watch fielded the shafts in the spirit of fun but soon caught a whiff of acid and the repartee took on a degree of heat. This was the moment to dissipate the possibility of flare-ups. I used up part of my stock of authority in the attempt.

I thought to remind both watches that, in spite of this being a holiday and although entertainments would be in order later on, we were still and always racing, and I suspected that the pure white flame of dedication had become somewhat polluted. I made out a sample list of complaints. For one thing, there was far too much casual conversation in the cockpit. Did they really find the racing so dull and the sound of their own voices so enthralling? If they insisted on talking, let them take it out of earshot of the helmsman. For one reason or another the nonsense being exchanged was immensely interesting to helmsmen and therefore distracting. Good steering requires concentration.

Furthermore, the cabin looked like a Chinese junk. I, for one, did not propose to live in a pigsty or good-will storeroom. Any stray socks, T-shirts, etc., not claimed and stowed would be shoved into the ship's rag bag. I reminded the crew that just a few decades ago if anyone had tried to *make* them live this way, they would have mutinied and rebelled before this. Well! I was rebelling now.

Lastly, *now hear this,* I do not approve of the game invented by Bobby's watch, and all players are hereby called on to cease and desist. I must describe this insidious game, which came into being quite innocently. Because of our lack of water, all wash-up is done in seawater and, unless it is stormy, on deck. Normally, the water is dipped from the sea in a canvas bucket. Unhappily, it was discovered that the lee waterway could be flooded by dipping *Figaro*'s rail. It is a very simple trick while the boat is running or broad reaching to sharpen up slightly, thereby causing her to increase her angle of heel. Since *Figaro* has a low freeboard and a pronounced dip in the spring of her sheer (very lovely), the water wells aboard and goes swelling aft in a torrent down the waterway. It makes a veritable washing machine, furnished with endless supplies of clean, if salty water. The men washing up in the corner of the cockpit can rinse clear of detergent and fouled water by simply asking the helmsman for a dip.

It may have been the chemistry of youth in Steve and Cleody working on the generally more sober Bobby, but it was not long before it became apparent that this same rush of water could be used to fill a shipmate's boots while he relieved himself at the ship's alfresco pissoir, the lee shrouds of the mizzen. The reliever stands there, vulnerable, his feet grasping prehensilely at the deck through his boots, a lamb ready for sacrifice. Oilskin pants have no buttons or zippers to help gain access to pockets and the more pressing openings in the trousers worn beneath. The primitive design requires that oilskin pants be lowered, the act to perform. A man in the situation of active dehydration is in a relatively helpless state because of the encumbrance of the oilskins draped around his legs. His agility in getting out of the way of a sudden onrush of water is severely hampered. The game is not very old but already shows up as a nonrespecter of age or office; several shots have been aimed at me. Because the game is so young, rules and scoring systems are still evolving. These scale upward depending upon the degree of difficulty of the shot and the anatomical location of the territory flooded. Filling a man's boots ranks somewhere near the bottom of the scale, but if one can splash water over the temporarily opened high apron of the oilskin pants, thereby filling the pantlegs and worse, then the jackpot bell rings. The points are generally agreed upon by the player and his witnesses; this is the only democratic aspect of the game. However, there are no points awarded for successful evasion, nor does the victim get a chance to vote. To date no award has been agreed upon for the accumulation of the highest score for the day. The roots of any pleasure derived from this game can be found in a basic competitive urge, the lingering heartlessness of primitive man, or the simple fact that it is there, a dispassionate experiment, a test of technical skill, emotionless and without contrition. In this last respect it reflects much of the behavior characteristic of the anomie of our lives.

The game is getting out of hand. Scores are being claimed for wetting by inadvertence, such as the accidental dousing of the man working on the bow. This could get dangerous. I told the crew that they were behaving like so many lemmings;

whatever they did could be paid back with interest. Remember! Dry things and places to dry out wet clothes are in short supply on the boat. Besides, *goddamn it,* the shortest route to a given objective is a straight line and all this swerving from the course, minute as it might seem, adds up to considerable distance when multiplied by the number of times a day and the number of days, etc. Races are lost by seconds. I know, it has happened to me.

They looked properly hangdog, but I have the distinct feeling that we have not seen the end of the game. There is no earthly use in inviting problems by subtle imaginings, so I went over to a happier subject—our dinner party. With a party in sight we were once again a single crew and not two separate clans ready to do battle.

We discussed the afternoon program. We would decorate the cabin with the things Betty had put aboard. Happy Hour would be extended. Anyone moved to sing or make a speech could move above the salt, and we would have a big dinner. Everyone but Bobby and Cleody joined. These two said they were sleepy but would join us after a bit of sacktime. Knud and Bucky were detailed to hold the deck, but each took turns hovering at the companionway when not steering—giving advice and even darting below to demonstrate a suggestion. Betty's Fourth of July supplies were in a sack in the forepeak. This was exhumed from a pyramid of wet sail bags and, when opened, proved to be filled with cabin and table decorations, place favors, and paper hats. The artifacts of the party are those meant for the pleasure of ages four through seven. Wine and food should bring the party up to our age level. We found Betty's paper goods in fair shape despite the wet sail bags. Betty understands ocean crossings. Everything had been placed in Pliofilm bags.

The work of converting *Figaro's* cozy if sometimes sloppy cabin into a festival hall went forward. Streamers were hung diagonally across the cabin in a graceful catenary from grab rail to grab rail. It reduced the headroom to a height better adapted to midgets. Garlands were festooned around port lights and hung from any likely protuberance. We followed no plan or theme; improvisation ruled. Everything was red, white, and blue. In a short time we looked like a Munich *Bierstube* at *Fasching* time, reduced and encapsulated in a children's playhouse. The ocean outside remained unmoved by the spirit within.

Cleody found the excitement too much. Sleep became impossible in such an atmosphere. He joined the decorators. Bobby, on the other hand, earplugs inserted, his eyes shaded by a black mask, remained impervious. He either slept or made one hell of a pass at faking it. Everyone involved seemed as happy as a clam at full tide. The exuberance was contagious; even Bobby, if asleep, could be enjoying a happy dream.

I left the decorators to their own pleasure and repaired to the galley. I intended to cook a dinner worthy of remembrance in the annals of ocean racing. The culinary tradition of this holiday requires certain dishes. Turkey or ham as the basic viand surrounded by regional side dishes—boiled white onions, candied yams, etc., all in keeping with the preferences of the thirteen original revolting states. All of our ingredients came from cans. To give it a more festive air, a modest Bordeaux would be served (a good one would have been stirred up like a milkshake by now). I gave a fleeting thought to asking someone to *chambre* the wine but finally reckoned this as being too showy; besides I do not trust *Figaro's* movement to that extent. The stained front of my Jaeger long johns can attest to that. When a bottle jumps from the table at sea, it has an unerring habit of choosing me for the target, making me look for all the world like a sodden Silenus. During Happy Hour, plates of hors d'oeuvres would be at hand —pâté, cheese and crackers, sardines and herring for those who want the zest of a bit more salt in their lives. For the red, white, and blue finish—hot apple pie and cheese and coffee and a thimble of brandy (we are still racing). The grand dentertainment would finish with low-flying, loud-banging firecrackers and song.

I first set about making the pie in order to get that out of the way and leave room and time to make a sauce for the turkey. We need an extraordinary sauce in order to disguise the fact that our turkey is tinned.

From my perch in the galley I shared the fraternal enjoyments. No doubt part of our pleasures come from being transported by imagination to other times and places when we were preparing for a party. Perhaps it is a recall of simple childish fun. Perhaps there is a deeper longing to reestablish contact with endearing memories and institutions. Perhaps in an excess of desire to recapture these past reverences we are like so many St. Johns of the Cross, being carried in spirit across whole oceans (although the only other thing we share with that intense *religieux* at the moment is celibacy).

If one looks at this party from a cold-blooded functional point of view, it is a waste of time and energy which could be better used to push the boat harder. It is childish, an excessive display of chauvinism, a diversion from the business at hand. But the last is exactly what we need, an important interval, a break in an extended period of pressure and tension, a tension that promises to continue. We need a change, a fresh start, something to mark an ending and a beginning. We had slipped from one situation to another without making the change. For several days we had raced under the momentary threat of abandonment. Now we have committed ourselves to the spare mercy of the ocean. No sacrifices have been made, no propitiation offered to signal the decision, and we invoked no power for benign influence. Even though the precise moment of decision has passed, the tension is working its way out to the surface. You could sense that in the way the two watches had at one another during the lunch break. We needed a change.

High morale ranks with good sails as an ingredient for winning races. The extra effort, the willingness to suffer discomfort, even pain, in order to push the boat to her optimum potential is a powerful factor. High morale is epidemic in effect; it passes from crew member to crew member. If a crew responds willingly, the watch officer does not hesitate in making difficult changes. We have no bosun mates using starters to whip the men out to the end of the yardarm. The circumstances still militate against us. The fresh-water situation will stay with us, always on the narrow edge of sufficiency. The weather has been consistently unpleasant. Not unusually so, but the stuff dished out to us these last several days is not guaranteed to add to the gaiety. There is little excess joy to be milked out of our racing performance. It's not bad but nothing to put into the log and signify by exclamation marks!! We can hold station with our competition, not much better. Of course, on board the larger *Palawan* they may feel differently, and her company can be feeling considerably worse. We sure as hell can use a lift. An arbitrary occasion might do, one such as a captain's dinner or declaring a national bilge-boys day. But there's nothing like a good, solid, honest reason, like this holiday, for instance, replete with associated traditions and pleasant personal memories for each soul on board.

Because it is a holiday, a suggestion is made and enthusiastically seconded that we listen to the radio telephone to hear the chatter passing over the waves. We have been maintaining radio silence since we did not agree to the proposal that the yachts exchange a report of their positions daily.

We feel honor-bound not to listen to the position broadcasts, but I had agreed to monitor 2182 and 2738 kilocycles for distress signals at another specified hour. We had not been doing that regularly. That hour was not now, but finding ourselves overflowing with the milk of human kindness, eager to help anyone in distress even in off-hours, and recognizing this as being a gregarious type of holiday, I gave in to the importuning of the younger members of the crew. I turned on 2738, struggling all the time with my principles and trying to convince myself that this is no less than would be expected from any good Samaritan.

Immediately we hear Pete (Pierre) Dupont on *Barlovento*, one of the bigger boats, calling his cousin Hank on *Cyane*. They cannot make direct contact but use Tom Watson on *Palawan* as an intermediary. Hank, it seems, is having trouble with the glow-plugs on his diesel engine and is seeking advice. The doubling up of all questions and answers and the garbling of words has a little bit of the feel of a comic working with a straight man. The situation itself is in the highest tradition of the sea. Hank is about to take out an appendix with a jackknife and is following the instructions of a distant surgeon. That drama over, *Palawan* calls *Constellation*. Is *Connie* about to call the States, they want to know. Yes, she is. *Connie,* having a very powerful set, is willingly or unwillingly becoming the communication center for the race. *Palawan* asks her to pass along a message, so does *Cyane*. What the hell, these fellows must be riding along with their sets on constantly, just like fishermen. This sounds exactly like the electronic kaffeeklatsch that Dick Nye and I had stood out against. "O Poseidon, Odysseus, Magellan, James Cook, and all you magnificent ones whose shades haunt the deep, *the rot has set in!*"

Our splendid isolation invaded, the drama of our private travail cheapened, the entertainment palls. We knock off the set. In order to bring us back to a sense of our own basic realities, I order the port water tank to be sounded. The level is holding. We have 10⅜ inches of H_2O—"*O Jubilato.*" Now we have something for which to be truly happy.

The boat is charging along at a crisp pace, reeling off a steady 8.5 knots, hour after hour. We are carrying everything we can from front to back. We are wearing the spinnaker, spinnaker staysail, main, mizzen staysail, and mizzen. If anyone had an oversize ballooning shirt we would have hung it on the stern pulpit to dry. Everything is pulling like hell—all's well with the world.

The pie is baking. I turn to the sauce.

10

THE practice of gastronomy on the home kitchen stove is the last of the do-it-yourself enthusiasms to be taken up as the frontiers fade further into the past. On *Figaro* the culinary arts are pursued for their pleasures, for style, and, not the least, considering the means available, for their challenge. Today, July 4, however, this served less as a reminder of *la dolce vita* than as an invitation to a near-disaster. It is ever thus, any surrender to the sensuous delights dulls our guard and opens the gate to the never-sleeping enemy outside.

There is a tradition that says the sea and hard living go hand in hand, but these are changing times. We live in a high-calorie society spurred ever higher by lavish illustrations of gourmet delights in magazines and on package faces. The yachtsman is no stranger to these enticements. Imagine, if you will, today's sailor living on the diet fed Nelson's tars. Even if they could somehow manage to hold the slumgullion down, half of them would give up the sea with their lunch. I cannot imagine a yachtsman, ardent though he be, putting up with the sight and smell of weevily hard tack and bully beef aswim in a gummy cask of brine, much less eating it. Our man may basically be a simplistic biological concept such as Pascal's thinking reed (seagoing version), but one cannot expect him to quiver with delight at the simple passing of nourishment through his tube. After all, he has pursued the bubble taste from Hamburger

Heaven to Gino's Pizza Parlor or, in his three-star categories, has been guided by Michelin to the Grand Vefour in Paris or Le Pyramide in Vienne.

The approach to the Cordon Bleu is basically traditional but happily or unhappily has not been left untouched by an evolving technology. Ingredients come from cans, frozen food packs, and freeze-dried containers. Stoves come in a variety of models up to a high-frequency radar range. But, in spite of all this Tom-Swift-and-his-electric-chef routine, men's basic food attitudes have been unchanged through the millennia. Their appetites for certain comestibles may have shifted—peacocks stuffed with jellied eels may have slipped on the charts—but the underlying delights and fears are almost the same as when a man scratched up a few obols and blew himself to a feed at the corner cookery on the Agora. The organic-food nut, nature's very own test tube, eating wheat germ, brewers' yeast, parched rice, and downing a steady hail of vitamin pills, is brother at the table to ancient Egyptians. If we are to believe Herodotus, the figures profiling and hieroglyphicking on the red sandstone believed that most human illnesses had their roots in the kind and manner of food digested. And as for Mr. Forty-six-inch-waist-size gourmand at the cocktail party, who dips up gobs of caviar and cheese with both hands every time the tray goes past, whose mouth is so full of potato chips that he can scarcely free his tongue long enough to give vent to his views on blue movies, the red or yellow menace or the greening of America—this same heavy eater could have been seen at the Trimalchio dinner quaffing and stuffing himself to distension as observed by Petronius.

On land and sea we try to carry on the traditions of a great gastronomy with the help or in spite of a juggernaut technology. We keep the names of the innovators and tradition makers green and lively in spite of monosodium glutamate, lysine, calcium silicate, and other nonorganic ingredients grown and festered in laboratories.

We watch oranges become more orange, chicken in frankfurters take on the color of beef, as we munch our way through strange earthly delights. From time to time we halt our chewing long enough to praise the name of great chefs.

The tradition of food is important to me. I have never thought of eating on board my *Figaro* as being merely a biological necessity to allay hunger pangs which might interfere with concentration on more important things, such as sail trim and ship's husbandry, although at times and in some weather we have eaten less than praiseworthy meals. But eating is also a matter of style and pride. All my *Figaros* have been known as great feeders. A foolish pride, perhaps, but one of my lesser sins. Galley setup and equipment rank with nautical supplies. Along with navigational books and hydrographic office publications are cookbooks: James Beard, Julia Child, and Escoffier can be found alongside Fanny Farmer's all-American entry. These, our guides to heavenly tastes, stand in their shelf over the galley stove, breathing the ascending perfumes (sautéing onions). Norry Hoyt claims, "On *Figaro* you first slice an onion, then think about what you will cook."

I would even consider carrying a book written by Marie Antoine Carême (1783–1833). He must have been a master indeed. Called the King of Chefs and Chef to Kings, he variously served Prince Talleyrand, the Prince Regent of England, Alexander, the Czar of All the Russias, and he finished his stint with the great uncrowned head of Europe the Baron Rothschild. I am uncertain whether my interest in Carême's book is for cookery or for a quotation handed on by Anatole France: "The fine arts are five in number, painting, sculpture, poetry, music and architecture *whose main branch is confectionery.*" The italics are mine.

Out of the mouths of cooks! This is a seriously intended avowal of his pride as pastry cook equaling the skills of a master architect. Taken in my context, it is an antic if prophetic comment. I hold the horrifying notion that architects are moving slowly and implacably toward the skills of confectioners. With borrowed engineering, the rush of stylistic changes reflect less the need to adapt to the occupancy of structures by ordinary mortals than the harsh demands of communications media. It is photography and the jargon of professional estheticians (whose own livelihood depends on the liveliness and originality of their views) that play such a role in establishing goals. Behind the media is an easily bored public who endlessly riffle through the categories of *now things*, be they posings of naked girls or a picture of the largest concrete erection in the land. Such an aggravated need for originality is hurrying the sense of discontinuity in our lives. Standing out as movements to stability in this restless culture are a few such scatterings as the Western Movie, the Recipe for Coq au Vin, and Small Boat Sailing.

But on to other digressions in and about cooking on *Figaro*. I must be sure you understand its importance in view of events in store. If not, then all this talk is a lot of balls, the stringing out of a minor passion.

I have said that not the least of pleasures lies in the challenge. Cooking at sea bristles with challenges. The one thing a sea-cook has going for him is the healthy appetite of his crew. But ambition is a spur. Masterpieces have been created out of necessity.

Where would Chicken Marengo be without the battle of the same name? Napoleon, we are told, ate nothing that day until the battle seemed won. Then, famished but at a great distance from his baggage train and supplies, he asked Dunand, his chef, an important member of the H.Q. staff, for dinner. Foragers were sent out who returned with six crayfish, four tomatoes, three eggs, and one small hen (with difficulty I suppress ending this catalogue with a partridge in a pear tree). With oil and garlic always at hand (Bonaparte being a true Corsican) and borrowing brandy from Napoleon's own flask, he created the now famous Chicken Marengo on this battlefield, using the crayfish for garniture. Napoleon, immensely pleased, patted his developing paunch and said, "You must feed me like this at each battle."

The story continues that Dunand, sensitive to the correctness of things, felt the crayfish to be an improper garniture. It is mostly in Spain with rain on the plain where mixtures of fowl and shellfish are universally accepted. Dunand made the dish using mushrooms instead. Napoleon, who once said he didn't want good generals but lucky ones, now, in the midst of battle and missing the crayfish, refused to eat, claiming it would change his luck. Crayfish has remained the official garniture, although nearly everyone uses mushrooms. I suppose we can flaunt Lady Luck when our battles take place at the table.

For that matter, Pomme Soufflé came into being because a train was late. I have been on many late trains but never remember anything good coming out of it. Nevertheless, during a short demonstration run at a railway inauguration in 1837, the train could not make the last stretch. The locomotive, huffing and puffing for all it was worth, could not make a hill. It is not clear whether the guests got out and pushed; in any case they arrived at the hotel where lunch was to be served, late, out of sorts, and impatient for their meal. Worse, they were off timing for the chef. The deep-fried potatoes had been prepared to be served on tick; now they had grown cold. Even before Mussolini they expected trains to run on time. (Dr. Ronan, are you listening?) The chef, in an agony of indecision, in desperation, plunged the cooled spuds back into the hot oil. Lo and behold, they puffed up beautifully into the delight we now know as Pomme Soufflé.

My modest ambition to seek a delight within the great tradition of cooking, using unlikely ingredients, led to our undoing. There is a rapture on the surface as well as in the deep. It started with the fact of the turkey breasts (tinned), a normally dry meat unless served with a sauce. Of all things, I, being in an advanced state of arrogance, had set my mind to improvising a version of a Sauce Suprême which is a compound sauce requiring a start with a velouté. The first step is composed of chicken stock and a blond roux, made of butter, flour, plus the trimmings of mushrooms. In keeping with the

111

nature of our stores, the chicken stock was powdered, the butter tinned, and the mushrooms dehydrated. First, these had to be advanced to a usable form. The idea sounds ghastly, and with time and reflection I have come to consider it so. But at the moment I reasoned my ingredients were no worse than those which go into any supermarket packet or bottle or that which issues from the average run-of-the-mill restaurant kitchen. Besides, we were at sea; this was a challenge, and to the base ingredients I would add a great deal of creative stirring and zealous watching. In short, I thought it a splendid, reasonable idea.

After almost three-quarters of an hour spent on the preliminaries and the velouté itself, I was ready to start the second mixture and then blend the two; the latter consisted of more chicken stock, butter, and thick cream. Here was the stinger! My thick cream would have to be a heavy infusion of powdered milk, hopefully adjusted and blended to approximate a pleasant texture and taste and avoid any suggestions of chalkiness. The world belongs to the brave, so I went on beating, reducing, mixing, and blending, engrossed in my task as I hovered over the stove, oblivious of the occasion, place, or other needs. Like a middle-aged, if not Middle Ages, alchemist I hunched over the steaming vessels, trying to make pure gold out of dross. It is hard now to imagine that all of this blood, sweat, and tears was intended to enliven the tinned breasts of turkey.

The gods of cuisine seemed to be with me. The sauce remained smooth, thickened, and its taste, after frequent samplings and infusions, seemed to improve with each taste. I was nearing a success, the triumph of willpower over the impossible, when Bucky Reardon stuck a sober face down the companionway and, in his best unconscious rendition of an undertaker's voice—in which the casualness of address cannot disguise the sepulchral undertone—said, "You better take a look at this, Cap."

I felt the quick, hot swipe of the hara-kiri knife once again, a slash of pain griping horizontally across the gut, as swift and sure as the afterglow of a bad oyster. My mind flashed signals in the subconscious network, "He never talks to you like this unless we are in real trouble. Christ! we are sinking! Moby Dick is back!" Variants of tragedies flashed through the contingency planning file as I ceased cooking. Disguising my longing to stay with the comfort and safety of the sauce behind my commander's voice, which everyone familiar with authority knows to be a blend of assuredness, calm interest, and cool, I asked, "What is it, kid? What's up?" He pointed aft, saying, "You better come up and take a look at what's behind us." Instant relief set in. The band of hot iron around my middle let out a few notches. At least *IT,* whatever *IT* was, had not caught us yet! We had time! With regret I pushed the saucepan to the back of the stove; I felt exactly as when called to the telephone while in the middle of a creative surge when painting. The sauce might curdle and clot beyond recapture—Goddamn all these things which come up behind.

With rumblings about the indecencies in the timing and tyranny of inanimate things, I went up on deck. Knud stood at the wheel, turning to look astern every few minutes. He, as well as Bucky, tried to approximate a view of unconcern over the sight of the phenomenon behind us.

To tell the truth it was not a reassuring sight. To say the sky was black is putting it gently. It was suddenly and abruptly black as the terminator line of sunlight on the moon, like the tenebrous shadings which hide fiends or avenging angels in a Gustave Doré engraving. We had been sailing in a mildly gray day on a gray sea flecked with a scattering of broken wave tops. But now the horizon in the west was black, the only proper qualifier is Dylan Thomas' "Bible black." It was certainly the hiding place for a vengeful god. It arched up into the sky where it abruptly joined the gray in almost a knife-edge resolution; no badger-hair brush had been used to blend and meld the two areas of color. This was hard-edge realism. Underneath this dark dark sky the gray sea took on a pale ophidian flecking, without shine. The flat highlighting of the breaking wave tops was dull and lusterless, giving the whole sector under the dark sky a pale, dead, and menacing look. Yet the intense reversal of the normal contrasts made it beautifully menacing, like a Winslow Homer storm scene.

I looked to see if this turgid mass in the sky held any flashes of lightning. None was there. Perhaps the breaking waves in the foreground hid the churning white line of froth under the leading edge of this black. Perhaps it was my experience last year in the Trans-Pacific. In that race you come to a point just before entering the Molokai Channel where you encounter a region of trade-wind squalls. Each is about one-to-two miles wide and wanders as an isolated patch of woe over the sea. Their whole shape, dimension, and the rain falling out of them can be seen plainly. Your boat in this race is burdened with so much go-fast that it would take ten minutes to disengage and drop the spinnaker; besides, the squalls come on with enough persistence and short spacing of time between that you would spend most of your time raising and lowering the sail. So you put your back to the squalls and run off. You have fifteen minutes of hairy going. The wind bangs in at about 30 knots. The boat rocks from side to side, sometimes dipping pole and boom, but in fifteen to twenty minutes you are out of it, having been pushed generally along your course and sailing smartly again.

Perhaps it was this or the fact that I could not read the weather properly. Normally when an overtaking menace of such proportion heaves into view, the wind will have started blowing into it long since. But our wind still came from the direction of the blackness. It was larger than a local squall; I could see no definition of limits. Now, thinking back to it and reconstructing the situation, I realize that this must have been the lower leg of a very long front arching out of a very deep and violent depression whose center lay far to the northeast. The wind had been blowing obviously along the face of that front for days. But I did not reason it that way then. Perhaps I wanted to believe that it was a squall, black-hearted it is true, but one which would not spoil our party, and perhaps it was my longing to get back to my sauce which, even then, I imagined, was drying into a curdled, lukewarm pot cheese.

By this time the decorators had joined the weather watchers. Talking to Watch Captain Knud, I said, "Take down the spinnaker staysail, square the pole and boom; take down the mizzen and run right off when it hits."

"What do you think it is, Captain?" Bruce wanted to know.

"I am not sure," I replied, "it looks like a big squall. It may look blacker than it really is because it is in front of the sun and the wind is coming out of it toward us so the change you get will be local, under the cloud itself. Ride it out with your backs to it and you ought to come out golden. Just get on your rain gear and stand by. I am going below to finish my sauce before it spoils."

"Captain, how about the spinnaker?" Knud asked once again, a gentle reminder of his own opinion. "I think it's okay, Knud. It's 1.5-ounce cloth, the same weight we used in the Pacific during the squalls. Just post a man each at the sheets, guys and vangs and be ready to let go if it's worse than I think." With that I went below, a bothersome decision over with, eager to see if the sauce had spoiled. It had not. Happily I put it back on the heat and started stirring again. A man devoted to culinary arts is not easily diverted by black skies.

11

THE front comes over us, not creeping on little cat's feet, but clawing and rearing like a tiger. One need no longer guess what to expect. Zeus loosed his thunderbolt, Poseidon's guts rumbled, and, with that, *Figaro,* below decks, passably neat until now, wearing her beer-hall decorations with decorum, suddenly looks like the morning after New Year's Eve. A great wind, overtaking, flipped her on her side with the unruly ease of a boxing glove sweeping across a toy shelf. A moment before her crew had been expectant, though at ease, like occupants of a California household filled with false cheer and lulled into a bogus serenity, trying to forget that the foundation of their cottage sat astride the San Andreas Fault and that the next instant the Fault might decide to move another few yards or even into the Pacific. One moment *Figaro* was going nicely, sailing relatively straight up with just enough roll to keep us honest, enough to remind us we were at sea, at least for those of us below who could not see or hear the bow wave or the hiss and smother of broken water alongside. Then in a flash, to the accompanying clamor of a great wind screeching in the rigging, to the pounding roil of water breaking down the waterway, she is sent reeling, knocked down and pressed, held by a great cruel knee between her shoulders, for a period slightly less than forever. Then, after this eternity in time, comes a heart-rending sound of tearing cloth and she

117

staggers to a more upright position, like a groggy champion struggling to his feet, dazed and semiconscious after a knockdown, knowing only that one must be on one's feet fighting back. Like a champion, she is urged to her feet by the shouts and yells of the men who serve and believe in her. She still moves forward, but irresolutely. On deck, the yells persist and grow louder.

Meanwhile, in that period of peace before the sky fell in, I had been standing loose, unworried, intent only in stirring my brew (the eye of newt and toe of frog, with cream, of course), when I was sent ass over kettle along with a plethora of objects—most of the loose inventory in fact. (After days of downwind sailing in an upright stance, little carelessnesses become major omissions. Objects are left unlashed. Once freed from a strict order, stowage becomes a system of first-to-hand rather than adhering to a rule.) As a result, all of the loose objects, party hats and favors, books and navigational tools, landed in a heap. We are first sent flying and then during the difficult reentry, my sauce, my lovely white sauce, already in its first tastings filled with so much promise, takes flight from the stove and hits the cabin sole. Alas, all of its promise is now reduced to that of a puppy's puddle. But the scene below reflects the barest lineaments of the disaster shaping up on deck.

I scramble to my feet with difficulty during a spate of wild careening, more shaken than bruised, my *amour-propre* indecently abraded, overwhelmed in part by fear of what may have happened and wholly ashamed and abashed at the thought of the figure I cut as commander of a gallant company and as meteorologist and weather caller. I look out on deck. Someone has cried us havoc. At the sight, a great weariness comes over me, an ebbing of the adrenalines. They may be rallying at some secret corner to mass up for our counterattack. In that moment of standing in the face of calamity my feelings run through a back file to a day in 1957 during the race to Spain. We had been running off for about one and one-half days in hard going, carrying the spinnaker, and reached the

Left to Right:

Moulton "Monk" Farnham, William Snaith, Knud Reimers, Bobby
Symonette, James "Bucky" Reardon, Steve Matson, Bruce Burges,
MacLeod "Cleody" Snaith

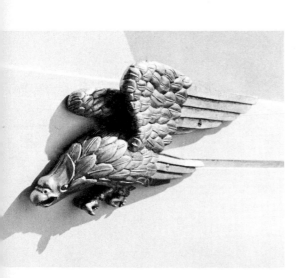

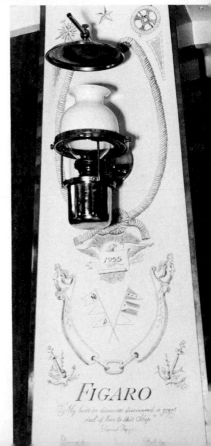

FIGARO

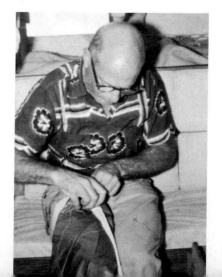

point where we thought we had it made. Everyone's taut nerves began to relax when suddenly we were knocked down. The spinnaker filled with water and, like a sea anchor, held us down. Then, as now, I picked myself up from the cabin sole, dazed and unbelieving, having been tossed from my berth. I staggered to the companionway and stared in horror at the cockpit awash, the water licking at the corner of the opening, ready to pour below and fill us. The lee rail had disappeared under three feet of water. We could not find the cleated sheet much less release it, and these were the days when the spinnaker guy was hooked into the pole instead of the sail, so it could not be let go by the run. The pole itself was hard up against the headstay. (When I reach this part of the story, I generally stop and, when asked, "What happened then?" I say, "We drowned.") But the story is even less glorious. I stood by the companionway as though hypnotized until I felt a strong shove at my back and heard the terse though not unkindly voice of Charlie Sheldon say, "For Christ's sake, Skipper, get up on deck or get the hell out of the way." Then, as now, I felt the cruel burden of years.

Now, unlike that time, we are in no imminent danger. We are sailing the same boat, but she has been altered in that the keel and rudder had been increased in depth, the center of gravity is lower, and consequently she has more stability and the deeper rudder makes for better steering control. But as I look out now, things are bad enough; our spinnaker and mizzen staysail are gone and we are thrashing about.

These losses have come about because of my arrogant underestimate of the blackness behind us, by my foolish comparison of a North Atlantic frontal system with a Pacific tradewind squall, by my hubris in thinking I could play at Captain Courageous and be a new-day Carême, all in one afternoon, while Old Devil Sea remain docile. Because of my attitude, we had hopelessly torn two sails which we might need later in another kind of going. I cannot fault the crew. They tried to warn me and, when I turned a blind eye, had done exactly as ordered; the main eased, the mizzen down, and men placed at ready by vangs and guys. But the wind, in hitting, swept these arrogantly few preparations aside. In its first strike it wiped out the spinnaker and the mizzen staysail. When I say wiped out, I am not overdramatizing the situation. There did not seem to be enough undamaged cloth between the tears to serve as a base for stitching. Even if we can succeed in sewing it up by hand, as one must do in these circumstances, the sail will be a bumpy sieve, a patchwork of blisters and boils, like a plague visited on the Pharoah's barque. Even the sails patched with flour bags, which one occasionally sees in the im-poverished reaches of the Caribbean, would look fresh out of the sailmaker's in comparison to our repaired spinnaker. Under normal circumstances the thought of repairing it would fall in the category of "It looked impossible, so we didn't even try."

On reaching the deck, I recover my voice, if not my aplomb, and issue a stream of commands. If commands alone can restore order, we are well on our way. First, we need to strike the shredding tatters of the spinnaker and mizzen staysail. Pieces are disappearing before our eyes. The crackle of the loose ends flagging in the wind set up a steady roar like a giant shredding mill or like the finger-snapping of a hundred Flamenco dancers, or if one has a bent in that direction, he can imagine the gleeful hand clapping of the imps of the sea on looking at what they have wrought.

No sooner do we start sail clearing than a deluge of rain hits. I choose to think that the lower orders of demigods in the sky, on seeing what their unruly cousins below had done, opened their heavens and wept for us—a mighty rain; nothing of or-dinary size happens to us. But there is no time for such speculation. Seeing all this precious drinking water go to waste, falling on our very own parched plain and running off unused, I am torn between setting a sail to carry on racing or catching water and going on three-fourths rations instead of one-half. The only way to solve a dichotomous problem is to deal with

120

both facets of it; so I tell Monk and Bruce to delay their own sail operations and get to water catching. They stretch and hang the water collector (which turns the deck into a giant slalom course) and then fix a canvas bucket on the inboard end of the main boom to collect a jet of water falling from it in a useless cascade. It is as thick as from a garden hose. The main is a dandy little rain catcher all on its own. The other crew members keep on with the sail change.

The first rush of wind goes through and its ferocity lessens; that much of my forecasting has been upheld, although I certainly misjudged the frontal force. The sea, however, is stirred up and *Figaro,* down to her main alone, rolls madly. Monk discovers how much when he goes below to open a filler hole in the tank. A spout erupts from the open hole that goes halfway up to the overhead. In his surprise and excitement, he drops the screw-plate closure somewhere behind the tank and, in his hurry to shut off more loss of water, grabs the first thing he can lay hands on to stop the hole. I was told later (and to this day hope this was not so since I gag at the idea) that he grabbed someone's old sock which just happened to be there and jammed the hole. By this time the water catcher has collected a respectable amount of water ready for transfer. When it is tasted, alas, it is found to be heavily flavored with creosote, a pervasive chemical not exactly suited to the preparation of soup or coffee; even its tonic powers as an aftershave are still untested, although the aroma speaks for itself. Creosote, by the very nature of its offensiveness, should be useful for something other than telephone poles, railway ties, and dock pilings. Monk is on the verge of tossing the lot overboard when I suggest that we pour some of it off in any containers available. "One day," I muse aloud, "we may even like the taste of creosote." This is done and the rain catcher struck, a most ingenious if unfortunate device.

The water falling off the boom develops a taste of its own—in this case, salt. The main sail and boom are coated with a patina of salt which requires considerable rinsing before we consider the rainwater coming off it potable. But by that time the rain slackens so that, on the whole, our gain of usable water collected as against loss by sprouting through the tank's blow hole amounts to about four gallons. But these are precious gallons even if they raise the salt content of the entire lot. Come to think of it our present mixture is no worse than the lot that had been loaded and lost in Bermuda. Of course we have a small backlog supply from the Great Creosote Spring. It is difficult to imagine oneself drinking any of it, but its taste might improve if we are floating, dismasted, and helpless on the face of the sea. It may require a rare bit of judgment in choosing this against slaking our thirst with a spot of crankcase oil.

The operations in water collecting are peripheral tribulations; the main concern still involves the sail change. The rags are taken down, ruefully examined, stuffed in bags, and stowed in the deep reaches of the forepeak. We are now without a new 1.5-ounce spinnaker, the most useful weight aboard, filling most of the needs of middle-range winds. In its place we raise the famous borrowed bulletproof spinnaker. It belonged to Blunt White of *White Mist,* and after his death, I managed to borrow it from Mel Grosvenor who bought *White Mist* from Blunt's estate. (I could never get a sailmaker to duplicate it; the cloth was no longer available, and they always wanted to sell me an invention of their own.) Once up, the sail begins to pull with joyous abandon, oblivious of the broken body of its 1.5 cousin now interred. After all, what fine racing sail pays any attention to past failures?

How marvelous to see it standing steady to the wind, no nonsense such as oscillating or collapsing. It is a most forgiving sail even for a relatively inept helmsman or bad sea. She had been built for this kind of going, and by, or without, the grace of the gods she is doing it. I have felt an attachment to that borrowed sail almost near that of love for a boat. Sails are generally a sometime thing, but if I ever evinced any feeling for a shapely bit of cloth, this sail was it. (Could it be because she belongs to someone else?)

Figaro, given the tools, goes to work once more, showing us how to surge down seas. The speedometer never goes below 8.75 knots and hits 10½ to 11 in the surges. *Man, this is why we came!* Our troubles fade away; we've had that kind before. The experimenters and jury riggers hidden in every racing man find a way to hang our spinnaker staysail aft as a mizzen staysail. It is smaller than the ruptured sail designed for this position, but it stands solid and draws well. We cannot detect any increase on the speedometer, but this instrument is pumping up and down with the surges like a slide trombone, so a great deal of the speed estimate is by guess and by god. The way the speedoneedle is moving up and down the scale reminds me of a time when we tested a new hull in model at the Stevens Institute Tank and watched its small projected light jiggle up and down the telemetry scale as the model indicated its resistances. I was handed the results worked out to three decimal points. When I exclaimed, "How the hell do you get three decimal points from a bouncing light?" I was told, "It takes a trained eye." The same is true in this instance with the speedo, the needle bouncing around so that it takes a trained eye to measure the increase. But the sail stands so firm and proud we know it must be adding its might to our performance.

The deck now cleared of all signs of trouble, new sails up and drawing well, I turn the helm over to the duty watch and the rest of us go below to get on with our preparations for the party. "The show must go on." First we rid the cabin sole of the strewn clumps of sugar, hard-boiled eggs, screwdrivers, pliers, blankets, and pillows. My once-glorious sauce has clotted into a repugnant mess. It gets the same inglorious treatment as the ordure it resembles. Our decorations remain intact and look incongruous until the surrounding havoc is cleared. I did little about the cleaning up but went back to the galley to get on with dinner. The gods be praised, the pies are intact. I stowed these against any possible accident. In all other respects my ambitions are humbled, thoughts of Carême, Brillat-Savarin,

Louis Diat fade to join frustrated dreams of yesteryear. I prepare a simple workmanlike sauce which will fulfill the purpose of a tasteful lubricant for getting the turkey breast down (a very dry meat no matter how ardently basted).

Soon our party is ready to start. By now a halfhearted clarion, as master of the revels, I call the guests to table. Bucky and Bruce volunteer to hold the deck. We set to, halfheartedly, our paper caps not worn quite as jauntily as would have been the case an hour ago. We make passes at merriment, but hanging over us like a pall is the thought that this was a $1,250 blowout, expensive even with me as chef. Since we all feel that we are eating funeral-baked meats, and that it will be unseemly as well as unwise to turn it into an unrestrained wake, only one glass of wine is served to each. After all, when one feels the need to have one's soul and body purged and shriven, some sacrifice must be made. In spite of the suppressed lamentations, we enjoy our penance.

There seems to be a pattern to my Fourth of July at sea. On another Fourth during a race to England we broke our main boom. Someone out there is trying to tell us something.

Figaro surges on. She is uninvolved with holiday parties, guilt feelings, and shamefacedness. All she needs are the proper sails, properly set and trimmed, and a reasonable intelligence in command, making a decent average of good decisions, and she is off and running, tireless and brave.

Bucky and Bruce come down for the second sitting, elated and exhilarated with the charging surges and sight of the soaring speedoneedle. They sound so happy I join them, taking a second cup of wine. After all, my spirit had been most brutally abraded; I need the most cheering, and a captain does retain certain prerogatives.

For all intents and purposes, so ends the glorious Fourth, another midyear behind us, another crucible passed.

12

USUALLY after the leading edge of a frontal system passes we suffer a few hours of squally weather followed by indeterminate winds and generally miserable conditions. Then a clearing wind gallops in from the northwest and we are off to the races—usually, but not now. This must be an enormously deep system with its center somewhere way off to the north—it just keeps pouring over us. It is as though we and the weather were traveling at the same speed, but that is impossible if we consider the rate at which it caught and passed us. Perhaps its path is diagonal, making sure we get every last drop of the locked-in goodness in its hypotenuse. Whatever the reason, we sail under constantly unhappy skies. The winds inside this zone are uneven and disturbed, taking turns, blowing us up and down from every direction but in no regular order. One moment we are bowling along, riding down crests, all sails and lines stretched and thrumming; the next we are in heavy rain, the wind killed, the sea flattened except for an uneasy heave—*Figaro* rolls in frustration, all aboard are miserable, those in their bunks only a little less so.

We work through a senseless procession of sail changes for little net gain. But each new direction and velocity must be met with the proper sail and trim. It might make just as much sense to say "screw it," but would that be racing? It is tiring work with no shiny crackerjack prize as payoff. One impetuous entry in the log speaks for all of our frustrations. In caps and underlined in red, standing in blazingly angry isolation, in the center of a line, is the word "BALLS!" Under it a plaintive comment in the best of terse nautical styles: "Rain squall, no wind in it."

The early morning hours before the dawn of the fifth are the worst. The wind blows its softest, and our speed drops below the magic number of 7 knots. Our lightweight spinnaker is up for the greatest percentage of time during this period (in the squally bits, the wind sometimes blows from ahead until the local cell passes through). The sail is taking cruel and unnatural punishment. With the coming of daylight things pick up. If I were a true believer, I could imagine that Zephyr, god of the west wind, wakened from a quick forty, has decided to blow a lively tune in our rigging. We have visibility but no sunlight. But visibility is all our identification squad needs. Who's around? What happened during the squall and afterward? One sloop is visible ahead. After much palaver it is thought to be *Palawan*. We turn on the radio telephone—it is not the hour for position exchange, by narrow margins we remain innocent of the charge of sneaking a position plot, but the kaffeeklatschers may be telling one another about squall damage—nothing much. *Constellation* and *Palawan* are talking; these two are talking over the back fence all the way across, but then Tom is a factor in the communicating business. *Palawan* reports *Figaro* and *Anitra* behind her, with *Cyane* farther back. *Palawan* ahead is confirmed; we must have opened on the others during the night. No damage reports; could I have been the only one making a sauce?

Another semidisaster. At eight forty the blue-top, our lightweight spinnaker, lets go at top and floats out ahead of us. Again, alert helmsmanship averts total disaster—we do not overrun the sail. It is recovered and examined. The stitching of the cloth to the metal swivel has given way. The swivel, aloft in lonely and useless splendor, is hauled down and repairs begin immediately.

Goddamn it! I had suggested taking the sail down and replacing it only ten minutes earlier but was persuaded by the debating champions in the crew who know of sailmakers only as resources and not as accounts payable, to hold on to it, "The sail is doing us a lot of good in this stop-and-start going." I had pointed out that now at 8 knots through the water, almost anything would do, but they countered by pointing out the fluctuations in the wind meant it had not yet settled in. Curse and damn all democratic institutions. There is still something to be said for the Bully Waterman, man-driving type of captain who would fix his sheets in place with chain and locks to which only he had the key, *and be damned to you.* It is true in this case I would be a Bully Waterman in reverse, but the end purpose would be the same. At least, I would never engage in debating with the Indians. With the greatest restraint I refrained from saying, "I told you so." It is a small kick to one's ego and affords only momentary victory. On the other hand, it feeds an "I'll show the smart bastard" attitude in the affronted crew member. Besides, if I really wanted it down, I could have ordered it done instead of inviting opinions. You can say, "Let's get it down," instead of "I think that ought to come down."

We put up a spare old Raymond chute. It is battle-worn and scarred with sailmaker's patches, stretched out of shape and bulbous. It is unlovely, like one of Toulouse-Lautrec's lumpish brothel creatures, the once silky smooth surfaces now dappled and sagging. There must be something about spinnakers, me and the ladies. Where spinnakers are concerned, my mind is in a rut or maybe just in rut. I notice that I have at one time or another likened them to hula girls, go-go dancers, and even a firm-haunched matron. Now, of all things, I am moved to compare this misshapen bulge to one of Toulouse-Lautrec's girls. The persistent female imagery must be a product of being at sea and away from women. ("That's what I think about all the time, Dr. Rorschach. Doesn't everybody?")

Women or no, there is every reason to frame images in terms

of art. Art has been my vocation and avocation. At one point of time it invaded all of my consciousness. Now I seem to be undergoing a final sea-change toward an aspiration once accepted with the regularity and naturalness of breathing. The months prior to this have witnessed a growing crisis of belief in the virtues and verities of the art around me. Loss of belief is the unhappiest state of man, desperately so when it is for a thing which had come to replace most of the inherited and formalized credulities. All of this interior ferment burst out in a *cri de coeur* published in the *Saturday Evening Post* series, "Adventures of the Mind," as the "Anguish of Modern Art." (I swear this was not the killing blow that finished the magazine.) Later, I extended the ideas of this essay into a book which fell on barren ground. Its time was not yet; I was a swine before the pearls.

Sitting at the wheel of a boat during a long passage is a phenomenon like no other I know. It is a time that invites flights of fantasy concerning things which worry the corners of the mind. Under ordinary circumstances these will not be spared enough time for recognition, much less thought. These flights follow or take on certain patterns. They react to one another. I had equated a spinnaker with a hula girl, now this distended cloth, bulging in its unnatural restraints like flesh squeezed out at waist and thigh by an ungiving girdle, became in my mind's eye one of Toulouse-Lautrec's lumps of flesh, an unlovely woman in reality. But on his canvas it is a work of art. I give up thinking of women for the moment to contemplate the idea of beauty. This spinnaker is unlovely-looking, too, not at all the symmetrical soaring wing seen in sailmaker's ads, although it is taking us along at a good clip; yet I am offended by its looks. The idea persists that a better-formed sail would take us faster. But there is every likelihood that in this weight of wind and sea we are moving as fast as we can. If we are moving as fast as we can, why then the desire for a beautiful sail? Looking at this question in another way, what if an ugly boat could sail one knot faster than any other, would I, as one who loves pretty boats, take pleasure in her? The answer must be I would make one hell of a try at loving her.

For that matter, most of our value judgments for beauty are disappearing or at least changing radically. The Apollo Belvedere in the Vatican, a thing of acknowledged beauty for millennia and, until a short time ago, considered by popular consensus to be the most beautiful art object in the world, has fallen out of fashion. Once art lovers from all over the world came to see it. Now it is neglected and stands almost forgotten, as it had done for centuries before its renaissance.

For a while we were given a poetic aphorism to help our judgment—Truth is Beauty and Beauty is Truth. It listens good but the idea rankles. Who is to tell us which is truth? Lautrec painted unlovely harlots. Is that the single truth about harlots? Jules Pascin and George Grosz also used whores for subject matter. I almost included Dominique Ingres, but his odalisques are harem creatures and, for that matter, creatures of the flesh in name only, coming from his brush as unscrewed and unviolated as porcelain figurines. Not one of his pneumatic inventions seems to have known the hot thrust of a sultan's loins or the coldly administered lash of a eunuch.

But the other three worked with the real thing. Toulouse-Lautrec and Pascin lived in whorehouses; Grosz haunted the cabarets of a troubled Germany in its pre-Hitler and gathering-storm period. The latter saw impoverished hollow-eyed women selling themselves to the successful scavengers of a broken society. Pascin's women erotically sprawling in arse-high shifts come through with all their curvaceous and sensual femininity, but their persons are overwhelmed by the musky perfume of the whorehouse. Toulouse-Lautrec saw great sullen clods of female flesh, degraded and misshapen perhaps but in some mysterious way retaining the eternal monumentality of women. Grosz projected all the horrifying overlay of artificiality in a dissolute society. All the women of these painters are members of the same sorority. Each tells his own truth, yet none of these is beautiful.

The unhappy truth is that we really have given up the search for either truth or beauty. Originality is now the only name of the game, and how can any upstanding art critic knock that? But it is a game played in an arena which has dropped any hint of standards. It is as though the world having been destroyed, we are starting all over again. In the end it must prove to be a pointless game, for history has a way of telescoping time. The man who first got attention by assembling the rotting parts of old Buicks will be lost in the assessment of a time as will the importance of his work. And, conversely, who now recognizes or cares that Bach was once considered behind his times, an old-fashioned fuddy-duddy when all around him the world was bright with its exploration of the new sonata form. The trouble is that whoever devised the biological timespan of our lives paid little attention to the telescoping effect of time on ideas. G. B. Shaw had the right idea in *Back to Methuselah,* but then he was a notorious carper, the lover of paradox for the sake of paradox.

Something is decidedly wrong with the pace of change when a culture can give rise to two such diverse polarities of genius as Picasso and Klee, enshrine them in some unreachable heaven, then sweep aside all that hard-fought-for knowing and discipline and greet with equal glee the minimal work of a man or the maximum try by an ape in the Cincinnati Zoo, all in the sweet name of art.

So much for the sea-change of a long voyage. I can chart my reactions and offer it as a bit of home laboratory proof. Whereas I once felt vigorously about the onrushing dehumanization of art, I am now being rapidly overcome by a vast indifference. Boredom is one thing art cannot long survive.

As long as one is going to carp about fashion, why not cut through to something nearer and dearer to all our hearts? The vagaries of fashion on flat canvas, molded sculpture, or a page of music are bad enough, but starting in the twenties in aftermath of the First World War, a new standard of beauty in women has been lurking in the mirrors of the world. It is

enough to make a drinking man give up the grape. *Vogue,
Harper's Bazaar,* and other organs of chic are offering bags of
bones as the supreme models of the new-day woman. Older
standards and measurements, the endearing phrases of older
literature, like "the honey and wine of her sweet round belly, a
plump calf, thighs as round and white as marble pillars, well-
turned ankles, and pear-shaped bottoms," have fallen into
obloquy. The newer judgment turns the Venus de Milo, with
or without arms, into a fat broad.

True there is a predilection for big mammaries and jiggling
haunches in certain quarters. Marilyn Monroe, Jane Mans-
field, and Ann-Margret have had their champions. But even
as the praises resound, starting with the formal entry into any
Hosannah, "Man, did you see her—?" the pejorative word
"cow" is heard through the land and the various champions
are accused of having been weaned too early. In fact, this may
be the first time in the history of man since the mysterious
Easter Islanders made their carvings of starved figures, the first
time in the history of sexual appetite, when the gaunt and
haggard have been placed in the running for exaltation to the
role of love goddess. On the other hand, this may only be the
subconscious expression of guilt by an overfed society while in
the presence of starvation in so many other places. Or it can be
a manifestation of the ever-intensifying war between the
sexes, the hungry reach by women to regain the lost ma-
triarchy. After all, there is nothing so warranted to release
women from the bondage of being sexual objects as the reduction of their overt sexual enticements. If there is a larger truth
in any of this, please make the most of it.

I am steering and, as just witnessed, indulging a wandering
mind while work goes forward on the repair of the blue-top. At
0915 hours we observe *Palawan* ahead (we have been cutting
into the distance separating us); she is having spinnaker
problems. The nature of the trouble is not discernible from
here, but any action generally betokens a changing wind. She

131

replaces the one she is carrying with a new broad-striped affair. In spite of the change she is not doing well. Still carrying our misshapen old Raymond chute we are walking up on her.

By 1000 hours the wind comes in again. Too much for the old Raymond. We set the *White Mist* bulletproof and the speedo hovers at 8.8 knots in between the downhill rushes. We are on the old ski slopes once again. Joyful sailing, *O Jubilato*—all's well with the world.

Downhill schussing in 14 tons of ocean racer is a thrill not precisely matched by any other sport. It is not as imminently threatening as the large curling top about to break over the big wave surf rider; not as breathless as guiding a snorting, throbbing, skidding machine at 170 miles an hour over a race course. But in the ocean racer one is hundreds of miles offshore, away from help or witnesses, and the helmsman holds the fate of his companions within his competence, as well as his own well-being. But, unlike most other sports, in this one time stretches out; there is no immediate cessation in sight. One has yards of time to recognize and estimate the growth of the oncoming threat and he has not the option to withdraw and try again some other day. He also has time to see and register the immensity of the adversary and soak in its peculiar beauty and exhilaration.

His fervor is encapsulated by the broad sky overhead, a single unifying agent which holds all this diverse immensity together. In the trough between waves his view of the sky and the surrounding sea is restricted by the containment of the moving green walls, but in another moment one moves on to the crest. Then the sky is endless and unchanging to where it meets the horizon. You are in an immense inverted bowl of churning water, the waves moving implacably in a main direction, hurrying to a distant rendezvous. When the wind force mounts, the tops of these waves blow off, eager to get on, impatient at the ponderous movement below them. They are giant horsetail whisks, each flicking annoying intruders from the brow of its own monstrous champion. The falling scud leaves long trails of broken gray pockings, stretching downhill on the slate face of the sea. There is no relief or ease anywhere in sight. But that is not the search. Here one at last recognizes the great secret of ocean racing—you do not think of ease; rather you are concerned with how best to harness this wasting energy, how to go faster. You can sleep when you get to shore.

The helmsman stands or sits behind the wheel, never quite relaxed; he is on the *qui vive* for any break in pattern. There is a pattern. After a time he develops a response in cadence with the rhythm of the sea. Out of the corner of his eye he sees the forerunners of the oncoming wave. This is its steep side. The wave and wind are not in direct relation to each other owing to the Coriolis force. He adjusts to get the maximum energy out of both. Like the surf rider, he places the boat in a slightly diagonal position across the face in order to get the longest, strongest ride. He steers carefully; if he oversteers he will miss the wave altogether. The boat begins to climb, starting in the trough as the sea comes under her. He makes a correction as the building force of the wave pushing under her windward quarter attempts to heel her down and make her change up to windward. In a severe sea the boat is placed squarely stern-to, else the great combers can roll her over. But now all of his preliminary moves have been right and the boat is caught by the wave and, gathering speed, begins to rush forward. The speedometer needle starts its climb—9, 10, 11 knots. Once in a while, a big one, a real graybeard comes along and we hit 12 and 13 knots. The helmsman, the wheel vibrating in his hands as the rudder is locked in a fore and aft position by the force of the water rushing by its sides, lets out a howl of triumph. It is almost an animal cry, a natural outlet, welling up in a geyser of exhilaration. He has the feeling of having harnessed the angry forces of nature to beat it at its own game. He has pulled Poseidon's beard. The crest is coming closer. Water begins to break over the transom and goes tumbling down the waterways. The whole boat is humming with vibration as she exceeds the speed for which she has been designed. Ahead of him the helmsman sees a dark abyss. The boat no longer appears to be totally afloat in the sea but is borne on broken water which starts at a place alongside the mast and aft. All the rest ahead of this section is a steep slope, invisible from the steering position. When standing on the bow at such a time you feel hung out over a great falls, a great rushing trough in the sea. The run is near its end. The helmsman uses it to the last of its usefulness, while the boat settles in the leftover smother, he is maneuvering to catch the next one. That's important. It is better to ride each one rather than milk an individual run. That's what eats up the distance, riding every wave that comes your way. It is an endless surf ride, no land to break this wave—only the weight and speed of the boat stops him from riding all the way to the distant shore where it will break.

It is a pattern which repeats hour after hour. Helmsmen come and go, watches change, night falls; perhaps in the dark you miss a few, but *Figaro* charges on in daylight and in dark. If the helmsman is sloppy, she does her best in spite of him. If he is good, her response is thrilling, chasing down the hills, climbing to the next one and rushing off again.

This year she is superb. She handles beautifully, is responsive and obedient to the wheel. There is no fight, no fuss. She was not like this during the race to Spain. She was a dicey boat then, although very fast downwind. But last winter I made changes. They are paying off now. All I need do is keep us in spinnakers.

We are in the downwind routine. The exhilaration of running downhill on the seas is a constant; it has become a state of being. With that our watchfulness has increased. This is the time when we have the greatest problems with chafe. The light staysail, now used as a mizzen staysail, is lowered from time to time and examined, parceling and hoses as chafing gear on spinnaker sheets are readjusted, and all sorts of downhaul jury rigs are tried to keep the sheet from rubbing against the boom.

The sky has cleared; we have a beautiful moonlit night, a swift running vessel in a steady wind and sea. In the moonlight, with exaggerated shadows, the seas look monstrous.

Just before midnight a tanker crosses our bow close aboard. She came from nowhere—nervous moments.

13

SOME days take on shape only when you look back at them, not unlike a large mosaic wall which cannot be comprehended until you are far enough away to see the whole thing. In either case, there is no singularly dramatic incident to serve as an organizing center. Rather, the day, like the wall, is made up of separate glittering happenings, spread out in separate sequences. Yet these are held together by a dominating background of color and texture and have a consistent line and rhythm. They are not extraordinary days, yet more than commonplace. This day did not match in splendor anything to be found in a Byzantine basilica nor was any part of it as intense as an icon screen. Rather, it was a day bound together by a single glorious mood, a happy day made up of small pleasures.

It did not begin that way. Shortly after midnight fog settled over us, the wind softened, the speedometer dropped to a disheartening 7 knots with intervals of even lower speeds. Just as despair began to invade the heart, the wind would return and the needle jump to a sprightly 8.3 knots, only to sink again. The bitter end of night was hardly a herald of the day to come. Nature's refrigerator door had been left ajar, and the vast store of air held in Greenland's icy mountains rolled down over us. Knud, Bucky, and Bruce, the stalwarts of the last night watch, normally so bubbling and voluble were stilled by the cold and damp. They said very little beyond a brief report when Monk and I appeared topside at 0430 hours. There would be no morning stars for navigation this A.M., a fact which seemed to disturb our near-frozen mates not at all.

Only Bruce of the off-going gang applied himself seriously to breakfast. Since this watch ate after the other group had taken to the deck, Monk and I joined him in another cup of coffee in order that he not eat alone, although Bruce did not visibly mind his lonely task. Knud decided, after weighing matters carefully, that even a moment spent outside the comforting folds of his blanket would be ridiculous disposition of time. Bucky had been warmed by the kitchen fires so that his body fluxes should have been nearing a normal level, but he had lost his appetite for breakfast during its preparation; a phenomenon known to most sea-cooks. I teased Knud for his apparent surrender to Mediterranean languor. As the only old, reliable Viking aboard, we expect more hardy pacesetting from him. We have northern rigors still to face. This is not the behavior we anticipated from the race that homesteaded Greenland.

He too was surprised by this, he said, snuggling deeper, his voice furry and soft as comfort crept through him. He did not understand how this rejection of cold and longing for a warm bed had come about and could only put it down to the season in the sun spent with me, racing in Florida and the Bahamas one winter. It all stemmed from that Southern Ocean Racing Series, he thought. In some way, and in a manner best understood by Dr. Jekyll, his blood chemistry had altered. The tendency must have developed by exposure to all that unrelenting balmy air. It evinced itself from time-to-time on cold days by a soft, subtle yearning, in no way resembling an aching joint before the onset of rain, yet to the same effect. But withal he was not aware of being made unhappy with this phenomenon until I brought the matter to his notice.

At 0600 hours the fog began to lift and the sun came out. There were no boats in sight. Suddenly we were the lonely occupants of an empty and sunlit sea. By 0830 magnificence overwhelmed us. The sky was clear bright, crushed lapis lazuli suspended in the most transparent medium, applied in pure level washes on a hard, white gesso ground by a Renaissance master's hand. We sailed under an azure vault, on a green sea flecked with brilliant diamond points. The breeze, booming at 17 knots apparent (which meant we had a 25-knot breeze since we were sailing away from it) pushed *Figaro* along at a roaring clip. Our spirits soared with her, top royal high. There were still no boats in sight.

The Simple Island Boy—his cigar somewhere at midcareer —apparently in need of an excuse to stay out of the wind and away from Cleody's growing ironies about upper-class prerogatives, went below to compose a few deathless phrases for the log and perhaps solve the mystery of the absence of boats on the horizon. After days of waking each morning to the sight of one's friendly enemies nearby their abrupt disappearance leads to all manner of uneasy or braggart conjecture. He gingerly turned on the radio receiver to the talk-between-ships channel. Bobby treats all such instruments as visitors from Mars. He turns the knob with a delicacy implying fear that with rude treatment the instrument, filled with all these charged particles, might blow up in his face or at the very least sting back, something like the renowned oranges of Southern California which, when being sucked, suck back. It is not that Simple is unsophisticated in the matter of technological advance; after all, he is a graduate of MIT. His attitude reflects a conditioned state of mind. It may be accounted for by the fact that while the Bahamas are a maritime nation, its people sail mostly in small boats equipped with the most rudimentary aids. Bobby, a true son of the Bahamas, was introduced to sailing when mainsheets were manhandled with tackles, and halyards went up by the run. Since this race Bobby has been bitten by one-design racing. He is an Olympic contestant. Cleody has sailed with him in a 5.5 in a gold cup series in Finland. Now, new and very technical equipment runs through Bobby's fingers like gold past Croesus.

But to return to the radio—naturally the Reuters of the fleet, *Constellation*, is on the air. She reports *Palawan* abeam. By some fine rationale of his own, Bobby reasons that they are both slightly ahead of our beam. An additional bit of gossip reports *Cyane* as having suffered a serious spinnaker wrap, no extent of damage, if any, reported. We are probably the only fools to sustain a lasting injury. This bit of news leads Bobby to note in the log that "Sally Snaith's Sewing Sorority" is still busy repairing the Hood light chute. (Once repairs got under way we found more extensive damage.) My uneasy sense of exactitude on quotations is jostled by the use of the Christian name Sally. It should be Betsy—Betsy and sewing go together like Madame Defarge and knitting—Penelope and weaving—and Omphale and spinning, etc. I am sure that Bobby would have used the correct name had he not loved alliteration more.

Whatever his taste in prosody, the relevant matter, nevertheless, is proper grist for a log. But what comes next is a gratuitous slander of myself as commander. It goes as follows: "This sail was ripped up in a very careless fashion by the starboard watch, personally observed by Penurious Pete, correction, Parsimonious Pete, alias Bill the Ripper." Without doubt, this entry, challenged in any maritime court, would be considered an inflammatory remark tending to reduce the crew's faith in its commander and leading to mutiny. For the sake of a happy ship I treat the matter lightly.

By advancing the sun line and a local noon position we get two notable fixes, the first L42° 38.6′N—LAT. 46° 17.0′W gives us a day's run of 204 miles! Not bad for a forty-six foot boat! In the second position later that afternoon we turn Point Able at last. Leaving it to port we square away for the next mark, North Ronaldsay in the Orkneys, at the northeast corner of Scotland. We are on a course of 068° on a great circle route with Ronaldsay 1,820 miles away. Our landfall, St. Kilda, in the Outer Herbrides, will come before that.

Shortly after noon we receive a visit from the behemoths of

our earth; a great pod of whales came by a "spoutin' " and a "bellerin.' " We count at least seven in the herd. Monk strikes a heroic stance in the windward rigging, screws an imaginary peg leg into an imaginary hole in the deck and bellows, "Lower and away all boats." We the men of the *Pequod* out of Nantucket feel an atavistic tingle. We join the hardbitten souls of another century.

The sight of these leviathans disporting themselves in the sparkling sea leads Bobby to reminisce. He tells of a fantastic spectacle once observed in the Caribbean; a pod of whales engaged in amorous dalliance, a stupendous gang-bang. A bull whale in rut must be an awesome sight. All the souls on *Figaro* rush topside to see the leviathans, and Bobby's announcement aroused everyone's bump of biological curiosity. He is showered with questions. How is it done? Who's on top? What length, circumference, and angle of dangle is the bull's instrument? Bobby is either overwhelmed by this rush of inquiry into heretofore-unrevealed aspects of leviathan physiology (never covered by Melville) or else lost in bemused reverie at a sight not to be forgotten. In any case, he cannot supply enough satisfactory answers. As is their wont in such cases the young fill in the gaps of knowledge with certain raucous images of their own. Cleody and Steve outdo themselves in creative reconstruction. The seminar breaks up with the subject thoroughly exhausted and the whales clear out of sight.

Something about the sight of these great innocent mammals cruising at play in their sparkling environment, away from the cruel wounding irons of the hunters, makes us feel unclean. There is every real justification for the feeling beyond that stimulated by this vision of innocence. We are not very clean. We have been encased in layers of the same clothing for days, making sure to retain all body exhalations by keeping the whole lot firmly jacketed inside oilskins. This latter casing has the magic property of permitting water in but none out. The degree of strength which body ammonias attain through proper nurturing and fermentation is astounding. The olfactory nerves have a built-in self-preservation system by becoming dulled and quiescent when overexposed to unpleasant experiences. Nevertheless, after a period topside, when cleansed by the fresh, salty tang of the sea breeze, these nerves momentarily revive. Then suggestions of horses, goats, and zoo cages intrude on one's consciousness as the nose works hard to sort out and classify each new attack until it is once again subdued and sinks back into quiescence. One considers one's shipmates from a wholly new point of view until the realization hits that, even though they are gone, the offense seems to follow you about. An offense in one's own nostrils becomes more than a line of Scripture.

Cleanliness and godliness have suffered changing relationships through the decades. They were together in the Greco-Roman societies; bathing and cultuure were hand in hand in the bathhouse. But when the Dark Ages fell on Europe, bathing as a way of life blackened out as well. Piety and male heroics both became associated with nonbathing. This path to heaven was not open only to early Christian eremites who attained sainthood through scrofula and prayer, but to certain religious orders within the Hindu culture as well, indicating a degree of universality to the paradox of the cleanest soul inside the dirtiest cover. As to the Middle Ages' male heroics, we have only to consider the insides of a crusader's tin suit. No wonder Saladin, fresh from the perfumed fountains of his seraglio, was so quick and cunning in ambush of the armies of Louis the Good and Richard the Lion-Hearted. The invading armies must have been seen for miles by the malodorous fog riding over their heads in the desert air. The taste for randiness and strong odor persisted even into the time when the Renaissance enlightened the Dark Ages. Meat that was well hung and ready to fall from the hook by its own weight met every fancy, and François Premier of France, no mean connoisseur of Life-Style, Art, and Women, would lose his cool and perhaps his ardency, we are told, when the lovelies called to his bedchamber had been permitted to wash at any time within the week of the royal summons.

We are not so distant from our own hardy recent past when it was customary to sew one's self into long johns at the first blast of winter and not remove the stitching until spring was well established. And as for our own hero symbols, one has only to think of the bold men of the West. The cowboy spent weeks on the trail but never seemed to carry anything behind him on his saddle but a blanket roll, coffee pot and frying pan.

But nowadays, with the availability of water and the constant TV reminders that most of our failures in business and the pursuit of love come from giving olfactory offense, we have been conditioned to a daily shower and the use of numerous chemicals packed in aerosol dispensers. As our machismo slowly succumbs to the mores of an androgynous society, we have come to consider nonbathing as the mark of the beast.

It is hardly likely that all these conditions surged through our minds after the departure of the whales. Instead, like lemmings, we suddenly feel an urge to bathe and so we do. But unlike lemmings there is no abrupt plunge into the sea. That would be an invitation to suicide either by stopping the heart with shock or being left behind at 8 + knots. Instead, we pour the liquid ice over us in bits.

Since the boat is rolling along, there is room for, at the most, two at a time on the bathing platform, the deck area just aft of the mast. You, and at times a mate, pour buckets of Greeenland's melt-out over your head. There is no singing under the shower; whatever sounds emerge are bellows and shouts. You are led to this near-death by freezing in stages. The first shock comes when, stripped, you step out on deck. Then the body, swathed in layers until now, suddenly spread to the brisk air, recoils in a manner not unlike that of a slug exposed from under a rock. When the water hits, you writhe, dance, and shout in an attempt to restart the flow of blood which has been seemingly shocked to a halt. The water is so numbing when it hits, the first sounds are involuntary gasps. Vocal chords constrict; it takes an eternity to regain the ability to shout. If before you were dancing to the wind and running its tune up and down your newly exposed frame, now you are a dervish or else caught up in the last dying burst of the tarantella. Your skin gets hard and bumpy as that of the goose about to be slipped into the pan. The impact of the water is so cold the sensation is almost that of burning. You scrub as though your very entry into heaven depended on such shriving. But by the time the rinsing buckets come over you it is not so bad, rather fine as a matter of fact. Now your shouts are tinged with crowing, the gooseflesh disguises the uncried cock-a-doodle-do. The friction of the towel is your passport into Valhalla; you have joined the heroes. You are gloriously alive and feeling clean. It is as though Joan of Arc had been lifted from the stake, all earthly stains burned away, and taken to the cool verandas of paradise.

By this time you are aware that your precious private parts (I too am fond of alliteration) have shriveled alarmingly. It is the Brass Monkey Syndrome. But since this is a common phenomenon to which you have grown accustomed by repetition in like circumstances, you are left only with profound admiration for Eskimos. What enormous obstacles they must overcome to survive as a species. Do you suppose there is a Darwinian development to meet this circumstance? Is the male Eskimo most deserving of our admiration or does the female possess secrets never known under the philosophy of her presumably hotter sisters to the south? What goes on under all those furs?

Not the last of the pleasures following a bath at sea is getting into fresh clothes, the most innocent of all sensuous delights. You can, that is, if you have been able to keep your replacement wardrobe from becoming wet in its locker or drawer. (We insure this today by packing all groups—socks, underwear, T-shirts, shirts, and sweaters in separate Pliofilm bags inside the locker.) You almost need an occasion on which to make a change of wardrobe. It is so easy to roll into the bunk without removing anything but the outer layer. I remember a gross character telling me his own test for a decision to change.

144

"You throw your socks against the bulkhead," he said. "If they stick, it's time to change."

Our sudden devotion to personal hygiene and sanitation gives way to a general frenzy. We no longer can stand the cabin in its present state. Bedding is stripped and thrown into the laundry bag. Mattresses and blankets are taken topside and spread to the sun and air but out of the spray. We use some of our creosoted freshwater to wash down the walls and bulkheads and overhead. The invisible encrustations of salt and grime are scrubbed away. There is no creosote when the walls are wiped clean. The cabin sole is swept and scrubbed, leftovers of dinners, crumbs, lint, and unnamable detritus are gathered and given the deep six, the bedding brought down, new sheets spread and we are born again. The cabin sparkles. We are off to a new start. *Figaro* during her high colonic has not missed a beat.

A proud entry in the log: "The blue-top, GODDAMN IT, is finished!" The sewing crew, fingers aching from plying the sail needles, eyes strained and red from incessant peering in bad light, drink a beer in weary satisfaction and then flake out. They have been noble, relieving one another as watches changed and fingers played out. They were racing against a probable time of need for a light spinnaker. It is that kind of devotion that wins races. I am humble in their presence.

Hamburgers (tinned) are on the menu. Canned hamburgers are just one step up from dog food. As a matter of fact, I shiver when I remember what happened to a neighbor of mine in Weston, Connecticut. His wife, an ardent horsewoman, went off to take part in a horse show and left my friend and his children to fend for themselves after setting up the household and doing the necessary marketing. Everyone looked hale and happy to see her on her return. One of her early tasks on returning was to feed the family dog who had suffered a bit of neglect in her absence. After a fruitless search for the cans of dog food, she wondered aloud to her loving family, "What happened to all the dog food?" They looked at one another in consternation! No one barked.

I found the only way to make canned hamburgers palatable is to throw away all of the built-in gravy, scraping the meat clean of that unnamable concoction hidden in the congealed fats. As a base for a new sauce, I sautéed onions (naturally) and thin slices of linguica, a Portuguese sausage, a favorite of the Portuguese fishermen who go out on the banks without refrigeration. The sausage is so rife with hot spices that no degenerating microbes dare invade it. I learned about these from Fred Lawton, a Newporter and therefore a person aware of the niceties of Portuguese culture, who was my captain for a short time. Anything good enough for Fred and the descendants of Henry the Navigator is good enough for me. Until a later *Figaro* came along with mechanical refrigeration, linguica was a standard item of stores aboard for long, cold passages.

I must have evinced some displeasure with the job of cooking for Knud appeared by my side and said, "Skipper, you have had a hard day, let me take over." And soon, starting from my planned pedestrian meal, he had put together a wondrous thing. To my basic onion and linguica he had added tomatoes, wine, and finally a lick of brandy. Both Carême and the manufacturer of the canned burgers would have been proud. It proves that a delicious meal can be made with the most ordinary central elements. Canned hamburger, in this case, simply becomes a textured vehicle to carry marvelous tastes.

During the dinner while discussing the phenomenon of taste, one splendid adventurer decides to try the salvaged rainwater. Almost as in a wine tasting, a cup is handed around. Universally we agree on a name, "Old Circus Tent."

After dinner we are treated to a magnificent sunset. Turner in all his glory let loose with an enormous brush. Flaming shafts of orange bursting out from behind purple clouds, the color lessening into pinks, violets, and blues as it climbs the vault of the sky. The sky to the east is a reflecting screen of violet and pink. It is too beautiful for anything but con-

146

templation. So Bobby and I sit there happily sucking on our cigars and letting the digestive juices seethe and settle. Nothing is said. It would be a gratuitous denigration of beauty to say that this beautiful sunset, this magnificent sky, with its roil of bright colors shooting from behind the majestic edifice of clouds, meant rain tomorrow. What the hell! There is nothing we can do about it. Tomorrow will take care of itself.

It is time to turn in. Tonight we have not only the events of a splendid day over which to ruminate, but the incredibly sensuous delight of slipping between fresh sheets.

14

FOR those of us on board who raced to Spain, this past winter's change to *Figaro*'s keel is a source of continuing wonder. It is paying off in pure gold. I feel like the experimenter who has brought off a successful mutation or separated a Siamese twin. Changing the rig, or underbody, of a boat is not a sport for the timid. It proceeds on shaky grounds. Beginning with conjecture, it slowly moves into heady belief, and then suddenly you must put your money where your ideas are. When you finally get her away from the persuasive extortion of Ali Baba and his forty thieves at the boatyard, you take her out for her first trials with the new changes. Ah! What a tremulous day! What hopes and dreams agitate your inner being as you stand coolly at the wheel, powering out of the harbor. Outwardly, no one betrays the interior quaking and shaking at this final testing of months of discussion and planning, to say nothing of all those payments. None of the crew says anything about it; they respect the fact of an idea being laid on the line. There are deep studies of her wake as she powers out through the calm harbor water. Is that the start of a quarter wave? Is there a ripple where no ripple should be? Does she steer well?

Later on, if she sailed well against a trial horse, then what a glory feel, like the effect of five martinis without being stoned—but if she didn't make it! I remember two occasions when, returning to the boatyard to the faraway accompaniment of dirges, I was asked by the yardmaster what I intended to do now. After an eternity of tight-lipped, rather blank staring at him, then with a long look at the boat I croaked, "Find Hymie the Torch—burn her!"

Those are two days that stand out in my memory, but I refuse to remember at what psychological and monetary costs. By some happy chemistry, the self-healing properties of the mind turn off the flow of such offensive memories, else experiment would be nipped in the cradle. But it is not ever thus; more often the changes have been successful. In one way or another, I have changed every boat I ever owned and I do not indulge in one-shot changes. Once begun, I am hooked—I continue a series. It takes but one success to become an addict.

Certainly the main thrust of change is toward winning races. But one should not put aside another motivation, the search for answers to a seemingly eternal question—"What makes a sailboat go faster?" It is a continuing wonderment and part of the magic for those madly in love with sailboats. Perhaps it is not as fine a madness as loving a woman, not as mind-robbing as that *grand malaise*. Yet, for those who have given their hearts, it is almost equally compelling, equally persistent. This does not mean that one should immediately form a picture of a stricken boatowner mooning around a boatyard like Mr. Swann haunting Odette's home. Yet there is more to the comparison of loves than rhetorical similarities.

To begin with, a boat, like a woman, is a mystery. However well you think you understand her, she still keeps her own secrets and mysteries, and creates her own slaves. Both are complex creatures with whom one is joined in ecstatic unity for given moments. (This is an analogy and not an order of rank in emotional magnitude—although you may have difficulty convincing a yachtsman's wife.) Nevertheless, for either of those lovers, the afterglow of either victory or fulfillment is short-lived. Even as repletion ebbs, a new kind of hunger sets in. The mere fact of possession or experience of momentary oneness is not enough. Appeasement is insufficient. The quality of love is to be strained. The lover of the woman now wants to know the depth of her love—"More than anyone else?" "Has it ever been like this before?" He wants eternal assurances. The boat lover, less emotional yet equally unappeased, sits among his silver cups and wonders, "How much more response lies unawakened in my inorganic mistress?" What gives these disparate and disproportionate desires commonality is that there is no absolute measurable assurance for either lover.

There is a growing, though still far from complete knowledge about sailboats. Until now, they were designed as an exotic concoction—to a dash of science you added a splash of intuition and mixed these together with the basic ingredient, experience. Before, discoveries advanced and even retreated at times, all because of the sweet uses of empirical reasoning and the impact of various rating rules (handicapping systems for racing). Now discovery has speeded up. Ideas can be more readily tried by test tank and computer. But even with these seemingly irrefutable scientific aids the right things are as likely to be attributed to the wrong reasons (although hopefully not with the prevalence of the trial and error days).

In a way it will be an unhappy day when the design of sailboats is reduced entirely to computer formulas. Perhaps because it is fossilized locomotion with no economic or political spur to move it out of the back room of technological study, it has retained lovely mysteries and remained just a very pleasing machine-creature which does not threaten man, his society, or his environment. This lovely creature-thing, man and nature each occupy a side of an isosceles triangle in a balanced duel of forces, a marvelous face-off in which man generally wins if he has the edge in skills. But as this lovely invention becomes more machine and less creature, more complex and sophisticated, men may lose their traditional roles. While nothing happens without man, yet his areas of mastery and involvement are being reduced. In some fields he becomes simply inventor and programmer.

We are making the full run as foretold, prophesied, and lamented by our priests, prophets, and exorcists. From Francis Bacon, who took time out from writing Shakespeare's plays (he was a busy fellow), to foster and foment the advancement of technology, even giving his life in pursuit of his ideal (he caught his death playing around with some screwy idea about food being preserved in cold), we can go to Samuel Butler, who in *Erewhon* advocated the destruction of all machines in order that man be saved. Now Roderick Seidenberg tells us in *Posthistoric Man: An Inquiry* that it is almost too late; we are already programmed and about to be digested by the machine and its inevitably constructed society. If one continues to mine this doomsday lode in terms of its prophets, we are headed toward our ultimate evolution as in G. B. Shaw's *Back to Methuselah*, ending up as whorls of thought occupying space; desire and urgency gone with the gonads, along with all our bad habits and sneaky pleasures. If we try to escape that much evolution we will wind up with Hermann Hesse's *Magister Ludi* playing the bead game. In short, my friends, we better get sailing; we are losing our glory as a human animal and the No. 1 slot on our own hit parade. Our natural world, under attack, is disintegrating. Sailors of the world, arise! Down with the machines! You have nothing to lose but your decay.

All this sounds farfetched—a philosophic abstraction too kooky for credence; nevertheless I had a fleeting glimpse of such a future the day I attended an Apollo moon-flight launching. It was an incredible experience which, until the moment of ignition, I confused with being a highly spectacular event, one already seen on television. It was also an extension of our business. I am president of a firm closely associated with the space program (we are habitability design consultants to NASA). In my role I have been kept abreast of many developments as they emerged. During briefings one is overwhelmed by the quality of the minds solving problems in every discipline touching on the program. The intricacies of the ideas and mission requirements, the brilliance of the solutions in planning and equipment never cease to amaze. Man is at his loftiest, completely in charge of a magnificent technical adventure. One's admiration is objective and clear, and yet, even when you are involved, the whole thing fails to touch you directly. It must be even less so for those who looked at it only as an event on TV. You hold that conviction until the moment of ignition.

Suddenly, the silent, graceful white giant, until a while ago a mildly animated abstraction enfolded by the gantry arms and tied to the earth with umbilical hoses, a feather of steam from her liquid oxygen life supply wisping off her side, takes on a terrible reality. For then, at the end of the countdown, in itself a drama challenging the fantasy of Orson Welles' radio show, comes the call, "We have ignition." Hope, fear, and the barely suppressed tinge of a victorious halloo, all intermix with the raucous tones of the public address system. The Saturn 5 belches out a great flame, then some seconds later you hear a roar like all the dragons of the world in anger. It is a sound that not only fills your ears but drubs your body. You are being prodded by invisible hands. The angry monster rises ponderously, then majestically a great tail of flame thrusts downward. Vicariously you thrill wth all those who worked on the program. You are one of that same race of men—puny little creatures who have taken the place once occupied by the behemoths of the earth and now by the pure exercise of your mind and skills have fashioned a devil that enables you to leave your planet and explore the once-distant and unreachable districts of Selene, goddess of the moon. It is an exhilarating and intoxicating thought. But almost simultaneously you are overwhelmed with another idea in the presence of all this roar and flame. My God! Up near the nose of this monster, roaring out over the Gulf Stream, lie three men, their heartbeats being counted in Houston, Texas. It is hoped that they are on their way to the moon, an impossible odyssey. What if something should go awry in these first microseconds? All that malarkey at the briefings about escape methods—you know in your heart that this fire-belching monster has taken over. For those incredible first moments the men inside can do little to help themselves should this monster run amok. It is a Frankenstein creation. Three men are sitting on 6,000,000 pounds of explosive fuel, developing 7.6 million pounds of thrust. Later, they may be able to guide and steer it, but for the moment the machine has taken over—it is in command. Tomorrow the world! *Heil* Adolf! Or is it HAL?

Happily that same flash of thought takes us to the man in a yacht. Buffeted and beaten though he may be, he is always in command. His world still is governable. It is fine that his small vessel is stubborn and gives ground slowly to technical mastery. If nothing else, it is a symbol of his own pertinacity in survival after having fallen out of that tree. The yacht is a lingering remnant of a more charming life.

Which leads one to ask: How come, if we are so technically proficient, there are so many mysteries after thousands of years of use and development? The pragmatic answer is that there would be no more mysteries if the navies of the world, war and commerce, relied on sail. But steam and the internal combustion engine coming suddenly into use switched sail into a gentle backwater. It became a sweet and lovely retarded child and remained so for many centuries until leisure itself had become a tyrannical pursuit.

That is one kind of explanation and very close to the whole truth. But there are myriad complexities hidden behind that graceful vision of delight, a white-winged sailboat, effortlessly gliding over a blue sea.

To begin with, while a boat is borne on a single body, the sea, it is subject to differing environments within that body. Part of the hull is immersed and responds to a relatively constant order of fluid dynamics. The other is on top and subject to the sport of the waves. Water is incompressible. As a body moves through it, an equal amount of water is displaced, which thrusts against the layers next to it and flows into the void just created. The resistance and drag of the hull to forward movement resulting from the patterns of flow past has a direct bearing on speed. The bulk of a hull has several distinct functions. Quite obviously it provides living space for men, their gear, and their supplies. The keel acts as a weighted pendulum keeping the boat erect against the heeling force of the wind. The immersed part of the hull and keel together provide lateral plane or resistance so that the boat will not slide sideways owing to the side force of the wind against the sails (the effect of lateral plane is like the resistance in trying to push a shingle sideways through the water).

Yacht designers are in a pother of exploration in regard to underwater shapes, trying rounder or sharper entrances, differing midship sections. For the moment at least most have agreed upon longer and finer trailing edges. The amount of wetted surface of these shapes contributes directly to the drag of the hull. As this is reduced, it takes less power to move the hull faster. (You have only to trail a rope behind to prove the drag of wetted surface. As the line is let out into the water, the weight of the drag on your arm, despite the fact that the rope floats, increases correspondingly.) However, the reduction of wetted surface is only one of the areas of witchcraft in design. Form is a factor in reduction of drag as in quantity. There is no yet precisely known point at which to stop adding or cutting. A number of factors working at cross-purposes are involved, leeway or side slipping being just one. Steering, righting moment, and draft of the boat in relation to your home body of water are all involved. The boat gains a quality and loses another with each addition and subtraction, and the areas involved can be done in a legion of shapes, enough to suit every designer's dream and whim. This is the point at which yacht design is still involved with witchcraft. The designer has all sorts of newfangled indicators to tell him if he is on a good thing or no. Strain gauges to measure drag, observation of direction and crossover of flow from the positive pressure to the negative side, the separation of layers, and the eddies formed are all part of his scientific sorcery in judging underwater shapes.

On top of the water, however, the boat is not only making waves but being affected by them. These waves can and do come from every compass direction while the boat struggles to move forward. A small list demonstrates some of the more ordinary perversities which show up in an ill-considered hull.

1. If because of fullness or imbalance in forward and after ends she pitches or bobbles in small waves, energy which otherwise would go into forward drive is dissipated.

2. If her shape between wind and water causes her to plunge and rear in steeper seas, the mast whips, shaking the wind from her sails.

3. If her bows are too blunt, she may be slowed by the impact of waves. If too fine, she plunges and buries and lacks the power to carry large driving headsails.

4. If she has an improper keel shape, or if it is wrongly centered in relation to the center of effort, she will carry a heavy weather helm on a close or broad reach, requiring constant rudder correction which in itself is acting as a braking force. Only a sphere is perfectly symmetrical as it turns. A boat's underbody is not; rather it is an elongated series of faired convex and concave shapes. As a boat heels to the wind, it buries the wider part of its beam while lifting out an ever-narrowing part of its underbody on the opposite side. As a result, she winds up sailing on a wedge shape (the deep part of the wedge down) which is forcing her up to weather and therefore requires rudder correction. However, in keeping with the subjective judgment still rife in yacht design, be it noted that there is disagreement among some British and American designers as to the effect of this dissymmetry.

In brief, like a whale or a nuclear submarine, what may make for a speedster underwater could be the slow boat to China above. These are only a few of the factors and paradoxes to be ameliorated in order to give us that vision of delight, the white-winged vessel on the deep blue sea.

So far we have been talking about the hull in water, but

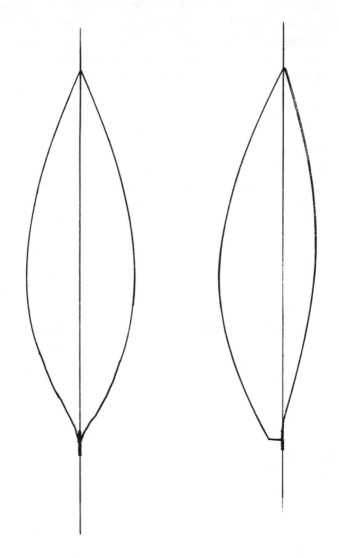

Figure 1 Upright shape -   Figure 2 Heeled

there is another element with which to contend—the wind. It, like the waves, can and does come from every quarter while the boat moves forward. Here a whole new order of mysteries comes into play—the design of sails. There is not a sailmaker alive who does not believe that only he and he alone knows the proper camber of a sail and how to get it—knows where the high point of the chord should be in relation to the total curve and how to control it in varying conditions. And he believes that he of all makers knows best how to create the shapes which interact between jibs and mains that give both the greatest driving force. "You pays your money and makes your cherce."

But in line with taking mysteries for granted, we accept with equanimity one remarkable phenomenon—*a boat sails forward against the wind.* In fact, her fastest sailing speeds other than surfing come when she is close reaching, that is, with the wind blowing from 45° to 70° on the bow. Incredible as it sounds this is a fairly recent ability. It was millennia long in coming and finally made possible by the adoption of the fore and aft rig and the improvement of sails. In fact, in that lovely tale by Conrad, *Youth,* Marlow tells of his first voyage as an officer on a square rigger out of Liverpool—how they beat their way fruitlessly from Ireland to Wales and back again, hung up in a muzzler, and grooving a track in the St. George Channel for one week, until worn and discouraged they went back to harbor to wait for a lifting wind. They wore ship through 170° on each change of course and, what with leeway and all, wound up in the same place each time. Today a smart sailor like a twelve meter will tack through 60°!

How is such a thing possible! How can a boat move forward against the wind when you see the wind drive everything else before it—dead leaves, girls' skirts, yesterday's newspapers.

In all humility, in the face of so much complexity, I offer a few simple diagrams on the phenomenon.

Figure 3 is the profile of a modern sailboat. The shaded area marked X is the immersed body of the boat. The cubic dimension of this area amounts to the displacement—the square footage of both sides of this surface in all its curves adds up to the wetted area—and the profile with all its curves and dips forms the lateral plane.

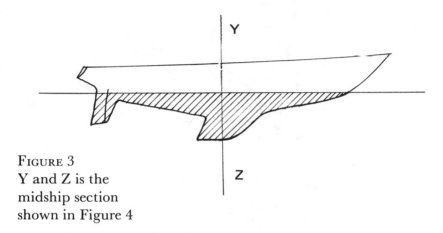

FIGURE 3
Y and Z is the
midship section
shown in Figure 4

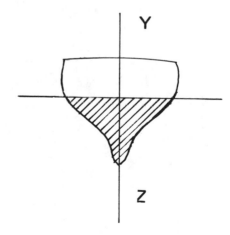

FIGURE 4
Midship section on Y–Z.
This complex form meets
at the center line at
the entry and trailing
edge. (There are as
many concepts for a proper
midship section as there
are designers.)

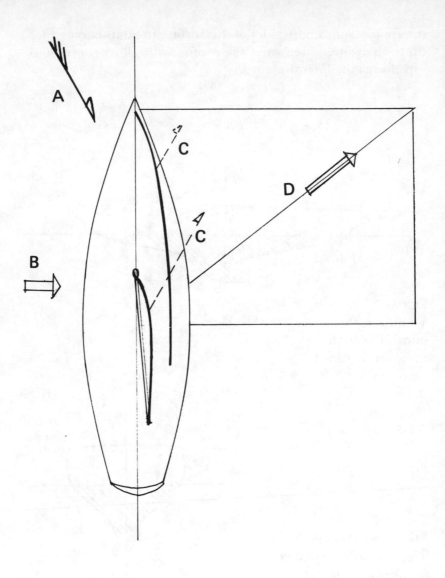

FIGURE 5 is a diagram of the dynamic forces of wind, sails, and lateral resistance that combine to move a boat forward.

A is the direction of the wind. Its energy is translated to *B*, a side force by *C*, the position, shape, and lift of the sails, which by their angle and shape convert the wind pressure to the side force with a forward component. *X*, the lateral plane in Figure 3, in being pushed against the incompressible water, offers resistance to this side force and the side force is converted to *D*, a forward vector. Caught between two pressures, the constant push of the wind and the resistance of the water, the boat acts like a seed pressed between thumb and forefinger and slides forward.

This is a gross explanation of one aspect of sailing. There are countless interactions of hull shapes, displacement, wetted surface, sail plan, and sail area which make a boat a good windward performer, a good runner or no performer at all. And lest we forget, all of these dimensions are factors in handicapping and therefore vulnerable to the hawk-eyes of the measurement-rules committees, for let it be known that one of the standard methods of winning races is to lower the handicap. (We have just come through a season of racing when Jerry Milgrim, the brilliant young professor at MIT, after a careful study of the new IOR Mark III handicap rule, in a radical experiment designed *Cascade* a *Cat Ketch* (!!) which was a winner that spread consternation in all measurement committee circles.)

This seems to have been a long overture to the telling of the changes to *Figaro*. But, just as the haunting, introductory single English horn prepares you for the coming woe of Tristan and Isolde at the start of Act III and the great chords of the full orchestra in the First Act Prelude announce the stately gathering of the mastersingers, so must you be prepared in order to give proper weight and understanding to the search, study, prayer, and travail that attends a momentous alteration to one's boat. Else it might very well be confused with the changing of spark plugs or the replacement of a windshield wiper.

15

THE idea of making changes on *Figaro III* grew slowly. One could put up with momentary knock-downs when racing past the mouth of Old Harbor on the eastern side of Block Island. After all, that's a wind tunnel during a smoky sou'wester, pointed right at you like a cannon, and other boats around are being treated with the same lack of ceremony—not all, that's true, but enough so you don't feel peculiar. But in the race to Spain we were knocked down and spent a time flattened on the face of the sea, 1,000 miles offshore. These were long minutes seemingly dragging into a lifetime while we were on our side looking at the cockpit abrim with ocean and sees the edge of that water lapping hungrily at the corner of the open companionway. Then one must cry, "Enough"—that is, unless he has suicidal tendencies or is just mule-stubborn. When the gods of the sea are trying to tell you something, you had better listen and obey.

I decided to make the changes—the questions were which changes and how. I wanted to accomplish three things: (1) to lower the center of gravity, (2) to add lead (both of these would increase her stability), and (3) to deepen the rudder. In a shallow centerboarder a rudder is of the moderate barn-door variety and which, in the case of *Figaro* when well down on her side, no longer acted as a steering vane. A diving plane perhaps, or even an aileron, but no damn good at all for

163

controlling the boat and helping it get out of its predicament. After long brooding, many sketches on paper, and a hint of directions from Gil Wyland, chief engineer of Sparkman & Stephens, her designers, she was taken to Bill Muzzio's yard in Stamford to be altered.

I turned over my boat and plans to the late Bill Muzzio, a self-taught mechanical wizard, he to figure out how best to go about the job. The problem—how to do this without altering the centerboard trunk and slot, and at an expense which would not take it out of consideration. We finally accomplished our objectives by taking out all the keel bolts and freeing the keel. Then, with the leading edge of the lead keel held in its original position to avoid a knuckle at the turn, a wedge was cut from the center top shown in Figure 6. The trailing end was bent up so that the draught increased by 6 inches and provided a space to insert a plug of lead of approximately 500 pounds between this new location and the wooden keel. New dead wood filled out and faired this trailing area, and it provided a leading skeg to a deepened rudder increased by 6 inches as well.

The old keel bolt holes in the lead keel were filled with molten lead. New ones were drilled in the lead to fit the existing bolt holes in the wooden mother keel. The centerboard slot remained untouched.

This is her first season out since the changes. The results of the earlier part of the season were inconclusive. I couldn't tell if she went better or worse because of the weather patterns. But here she is, in the kind of race and conditions for which the changes were made, a transatlantic race, and riding down the overtaking green hills as if to the manner born.

She is now a joy to steer, going straight as an arrow, responsive to a light hand on the wheel. The tendency to come upwind at the bottom of the toboggan run is lessened, and it does not require much strain or time to straighten her out and place her properly to take advantage of the next surfing run. The most significant fact is that now we miss very few rides down the waves but catch every one as it comes up on us. We

Figure 6

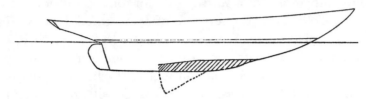

Original shape—shaded
area shows lead; dotted
line is centerboard lowered.

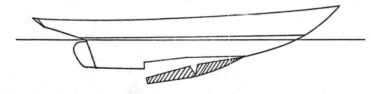

Keel tilted downward—
V-cut and back end bent up.
New plug inserted above it
at center of buoyancy and
rudder lengthened.

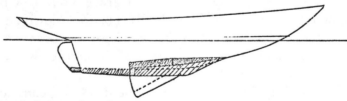

The shaded area showing new
shape, extended area of lead
and rudder and new lead plug
added.

now have the reliability of a commuter catching the morning eight fifteen (not to be confused with the reliability of the eight fifteen itself). When you are forced into excessive maneuvering at the bottom of a rush, you are apt to miss the next wave and lose the advantage of a surfing run. In some conditions of sea you are likely to miss one wave of every three. Now we can begin our placement maneuver near the end of the rush, and the misses will average one in seven, which is a fantastic percentage increase. When you consider that when the boat is on its toboggan slide the speedometer needle will go to 10 and 11 knots (we have two speedometers, port and starboard, labeled optimist and pessimist for obvious reasons), the increased percentage of higher speeds adds considerably to the miles run in twenty-four hours.

The crew love to steer her now. In average weather the watches are set up to give every man a shot at steering in regular turns, else life as a permanent foredeck Indian gets to be dispiriting during a long race. There is an unmatchable lift to the experience of sitting at the wheel in this kind of going, feeling the boat's life-energy pulse up your arms through the varying strains on the rudder, while the nerve-ends of your gluteus maximus feel the thrum of the hull, responding like a violin to the bow-arm of the water rushing past. Floating high on the crest of a gray-flecked wave you look out across the watery prairie of hills and furrows, each hill topped by a feathery crest, and then as the boat shoots down into the racing valley, you become conscious of a great mound of broken-topped water over your shoulder. It is bearing down on you. It is a bit scary despite the fact that you know the boat will rise on its forward slope and the broken top will simply hiss by as you are in the middle of the downhill schuss.

Underlying these visual excitements is the consciousness that the safety of the boat and of your mates is now in your keeping, while at the same time you are caught up in a challenge to get as much, if not more, out of her as the next man or the man before. I try to give each man a shot at steering in average weather, but when it blows up, steering is limited to the few in each watch who have the ability to handle a boat in a hard go. That ability has now been extended by *Figaro*'s new docility in this kind of going. By these changes, if nothing else, I have taken some of the bite out of Samuel Johnson's comment, "He who goes to sea for a pastime would go to hell for his pleasure."

While he was working on the keel, I asked Bill Muzzio to do something about the leaks. Without showing any signs of age this old girl kept making water at odd hours. Bill said the keel showed a lot of checks, which I presumed to be only natural since it began as a great balk of oak brought to the yard, adzed into shape by Joel, and then, having been set up in the building shed, it lay in the summer heat and winter cold for eighteen months while the boat above slowly took form. Building *Figaro* was a slow process. She was planked by one man, Louis Larsen, who went at his job like Mr. Hepplewhite laying in marquetry. Because it is a shallow centerboarder, even two buckets of water loose in the bilge create a discomfort level almost equal to a sprinkler system gone wild.

Bill Muzzio took an alemite gun, a plunger device for injecting high viscosity grease and oil, loaded it with white lead, screwed a few alemite fittings into places he thought likely, hooked up the gun, and squeezed mightily. The lead disappeared into the mysterious heart of the wood. None came immediately to the surface. I had visions of the boat bloating and growing her own version of goggle-eyed from this Draconian injection. Suddenly, about ten feet away, a thin curl of white lead came to the surface, a white gusher. Bill grunted his satisfaction and kept up the treatment, a cross, I felt, between intravenous feeding and a clyster. His treatment helped reduce the flow but never cured her. She is a wet boat. Water finds its way aboard through the driveshaft and rudder glands and, in bad weather, if we have not put on battening cloths, through the forward hatch and skylight. We accept these spirit and body chastening habits of *Figaro* as balancing negatives against all of her known delights. It conforms to

Emerson's laws of compensation, and in any case if she were all delight it would be a paradise, and we know that sailors must earn their way into that.

By the time I made these alterations to *Figaro III*, I had become a hardened veteran in planning and living through major changes.

Figaro I was an Alden, Malabar Jr., about 32 feet overall, 24 feet on the waterline, a nice boat with an average turn of speed. I am not sure how many owners she had before I bought her. Alas, as her new owner I had dreams of glory matched only by my own inexperience. One thing I felt sure of—if I added more sail, she would go faster. I also knew that to keep her standing erect I would need more ballast—end of theory and end of expertise. But who needed to know more? My courage was undaunted and my heart was pure and my mind unmuddled by facts. When I bought her, she had an 85-percent fore-triangle, which means that the jibstay was attached to the mast 85 percent of its height above the deck. That still left 15 percent of the forward side of the mast unused. I installed a 3-foot-long bowsprit, and from the end of this to the top of the mast I planned a new jibstay, which was parallel with the existing stay. In this way I added a considerable amount of sail. Her old jibstay now served as a forestay.

To keep the boat standing on her feet under this great press of sail, I added 1,000 pounds to the bottom of the keel (that being a good round number). I knew nothing about righting moments and cared less, and I carried the same carefree rapture over into any consideration of the strength of the mast or the rigging. There is a special providence that watches over those who take to the sea with a virgin heart.

The work was done at Joel Johnson's yard in Black Rock, Connecticut, the same yard which later built *Figaro III*. It was a small yard and ill-equipped to do these kinds of repairs—besides, Joel hated this kind of work, did not have the necessary equipment or supplies to fill out rigging needs, and had only a rudimentary machine shop. He had a great wood-craftsman's distaste for working with metal (I chose him to build *Figaro III* because of his superb wood craftsmanship). To cap all this, Joel was a fundamentalist in matters of his God, as well as of wood, and kept his yard closed, even to owners, on his Sabbath. Since Sunday is one day out of the two that most yachtsmen have to devote to their own passion, it required considerable patience and fortitude to endure it according to St. Joel. Joel, himself untouched by the aura of frustration which hung in clouds around his yard and home (some one hundred paces away), simply read his Bible.

The work moved very slowly. We were well into the racing season by the time she was ready for launching and trials. Unhappily when the mast went into the boat, the new headstay came up inches short, even with the turnbuckle let out beyond a reasonable safety limit. I needed a toggle to piece out its length. Joe didn't have the stock, the machinery, or the inclination to provide one. My internal pressure gauge shot up to the red line when I thought of not being able to get her away this Saturday—another week of sitting on one's hands! Don Jones, a close friend, a great shipmate, and a machinist of considerable skill, noting the steam coming from my ears, dashed off to his factory machine shop to see what could be done. He came back in a few hours, full of apologies. He could not find a proper piece of steel, and so he had fashioned a temporary fitting of heavy brass stock which would take us sailing today. By this time I would have been ready to accept a lash-up of string and wire. We put in the new extending toggle, took up on the screw fitting, worked our way out of the tortuous channel, and went sailing.

She was a dandy. Until one has sailed in an overcanvased boat one has not lived. She took off like a bomb and just kept going. I am sure the adage about Providence and fools is right. Had I known anything about the handicap measurement rules I probably would never have taken on the changes. My handicap shot up like a fever, but in reality it made little difference.

At that time, most of my sailing was constrained to the new

169

Dead Sea—Long Island Sound. In a 17-to-24-mile race around the buoys, speed is of the essence. The minutes of handicap between boats disappear. Time takes on a new meaning for the yachtsman whose boat has fallen into a hole in the breeze, as it must for the man with a noose around his neck waiting for the trap to be sprung. Rules, schmules, I wanted to go fast and so I did.

In her first series, the American Yacht Club Cruise, we sailed in Class C, or Division III, as you will, starting ten minutes after B. On board were Don Jones, his wife Jay, Betty, and myself, tyros all. The gods were kind and gave us a nice easy day for sailing. We took advantage of it by sailing through our class and most of Class B, finishing with the leaders of that class. We were so far ahead of our class that the race officials first decided that we had not sailed the course, or some other such idea, and discounted our finish. We disabused them of such thinking and won our first silver cup. I had had my first heady taste of Lotus leaves. I was hooked.

Being overcanvased and undercrewed has its drawbacks as well. In this very same series, the Sound inexplicably produced a decent breeze. We were booming along under a mountain of spinnaker cloth (or so it seemed to us then), going through boats with a scarcely concealed curl on our lips, when the wind drew gradually ahead to the beam. Before long we were sailing on our ear, pushing great gobs of water aside, entirely at the mercy of this formidable pile of nylon, each of us secretly hoping that it would decently blow out and relieve us of the decision to take it down. But it held on, just as advertised, until I finally surrendered. The takedown was an ungainly mess, the air filled with the crackling sound of sailcloth and the loud, ungallant shouts of contradictory orders issuing from me. We got it down somehow—how, is a blank to this day. I have a dim memory of Jay falling backwards down the companionway with a monstrous armful of nylon clasped to her bosom with the passion of Barbara Frietchie clutching the flag. That ensuing winter, as we sat by the fire, regaling ourselves with memories of the season just past, Jay told us that when she got home from that cruise and saw the blue bruises stamped over her fair body, collected in the various days of racing, and remembered my honeyed description of the luxuries, ease, and fun to be expected on the cruise (I was practicing the skipper's eternal task of recruiting crews), she broke down and laughed and laughed and laughed. Don said it was more like hysteria. Jay is a great girl; despite that first great denouement she still sailed with us.

We faced a small Armageddon that fall in the Off-Sounding Series. Our Plain of Esdraelon was Block Island Sound, a snappy bit of water, really an arm of the open Atlantic with Block Island set in the middle between Gay Head on Martha's Vineyard and Montauk Point on Long Island. The boat had been going so well I was loath to touch anything in fear of tampering with the magic. My hesitancy extended to Don's brass toggle. By this time I had added a few men to the crew; a good ship deserves to be well served. In the second day of the series, we were sailing a windward leg in a piping breeze. "Banny" Sprague, a fine racing man, acting as sail trimmer while I steered, called for one red hair more of trim on the No. 1 Genoa. That was the hair that broke this particular camel's back. Everything happened in a flash. First, a report like a cherry bomb exploding, the brass toggle finally tore like a piece of cardboard—the hole for the pin had been slowly elongating. The explosive sound came as a result of the sudden release of tension on the head stay. Following hard on the heels of that sharp report, we heard a slow, tearing sound, like a tree being felled, the long-extended crackle one associates with a forest giant crashing down. Indeed it was our own forest giant. The hollow wooden mast held in alignment by the shrouds had broken off about five feet above the deck. It fell straight back into the cockpit and over the transom landing between Betty and myself. After the realization of what had happened took firm hold, and not to be outdone by certain sea-fighters in history, I felt it incumbent that I mark this occasion with a suitably "deathless phrase." Never believing that I could match "England expects. . ." since I was a novice at the whole game, I settled for "I guess this puts us out of the race." Such was the pithiness of my remark that I found not one single dissenting voice—a remarkable thing in itself.

My surface imperturbability, pushed to the limit by the escape from the falling mast, so far offshore, was further to be tested. A submarine which had been watching the race, we must presume at periscope depth, surfaced alongside in order to be helpful. Her big black hulk set up a backwash like the sea bouncing off a cliff. Have you ever been inside a Mickey Mouse pendulum toy, going tick-tock rapidly from side to side? Neither have I—but that is what I imagine is the nearest thing to being inside a sailboat in a jump of sea without her mast. The lead pendulum of the keel without the mast at the other end of the fulcrum to slow her swing, snaps the hull back like a slingshot after each time it is heeled by a wave. Not only is it difficult to keep your feet, but it is a rapid invitation to *mal de mer*. The submarine was complicating the pattern of the sea with the rebound ricochet. They kept asking us what they could do to help and kept pressing coffee on us—the sovereign remedy. We, in turn, kept offering them beer as an inducement to go away. (In this matter of sovereign remedies, my childhood movie-going taught me that the moment the doctor entered a scene of sickness or childbirth, he rolled up his sleeves and called for someone to boil water, or you offered a victim hot coffee. Only the great Groucho Marx broke this pattern. After being knocked flat, presumably out for the count, he suddenly sat up in the midst of the crouching figures trying to help him and said, "Force brandy on me" and then, as suddenly, collapsed again.) But alas, ours is a teetotaling navy. They could offer us no brandy, nor accept our beer, and there was no way in the world that they could hand us coffee over the submerged bulk of her hull which lay between us and their narrow deck. Finally, in mutual frustration, we parted, they to return to their secret exercises away from the sight of man, and we to the exhausting job of getting the mast, rigging, and sails back aboard, securing them, lashing up a jury rig, and making our way home to Westport, Connecticut, there to wait long weeks for a new mast ordered from the Pigeon Brothers.

But this unhappy incident aside, I had tasted my first blood. I could never be satisfied with a bland diet. I would be spicing the recipe from now on. Even while *Figaro II* was being built, I knew that lurking behind my restiveness to see her finished was the impatience to get at changes. She was built by Hinckley of Southwest Harbor, Maine, his version of an Owens Cutter. The original Owens Cutters, designed by Chuck Owens, were superlight hulls held together by chewing gum and a prayer. I remember sitting in the cockpit of Bobby Coulson's aging cutter, *Finn MacCoul,* one pleasant afternoon, chatting, sipping a beer while at anchor when a slight flutter of breeze ruffled through his rigging. A light shower of aluminum screwheads, nuts, and washers hit the deck. Bobby took another sip of beer, gave a friendly look at his masthead, and then just as pleasantly said, "That keeps happening all the time, but I think there are still enough left in the mast to hold it together."

Henry Hinckley would have none of this; he insisted on a solid boat. She came out yards heavier than any one of the originals. Naturally in light airs I had trouble with the lighter boats of equal size. So that fall we sailed her back to Maine, and, in keeping with my plans, Henry put on a bowsprit and added a mizzenmast. Next year we won all three days of the Off-Sounding Series, going away, and made a fourth in the Bermuda Race.

Since the race to Sweden I have built a new *Figaro IV* and now a *Figaro 5.* I have learned a little more about boats in the ensuing years—the operative word is "little." The sophistication of my changes have far outstripped the sum of my acquired knowledge. But men have been known to build a life-style around the problems of squaring the circle, determining the sex of angels, or solving chess problems. I had a great-uncle who gave up a career as a school principal to devote his life to playing chess, living on hand-outs. He may have attained the title of Master, I am not sure, of Grand Master, yet he seemed to live in an aura of peace and serenity. I also knew a man who owned a glorious collection of Bach recordings which he played in rigid rotation and kept an account, in ledger form, of the progressive deterioration of the surfaces. In any case, my own enthusiasm has kept me happy, poor, and sometimes victorious. A description of the changes in *Figaro IV* and 5 are complicated, even awe-inspiring, but do not properly belong to this tale. Enough that every sign shows that my changes to *Figaro III* have drawn a prize in the lottery.

16

WE are in midvoyage, having come approximately 1,500 miles along our track. The circled dot on the chart is roughly halfway between the start and the finish, but we can hardly warm to the idea that it is all downhill from here. There are enough long and difficult miles left to cool that notion. Nevertheless, the midway point has its psychological compensations. There is something to having come halfway and to being still nearly in one piece. In some circumstances this part of a voyage can be dreary, what with unrelenting discomfort, the attrition from the war of the inanimate object against man, and the everlasting sameness. All of this can corrode the fine edge of morale in a racing crew.

Human beings are fast adapters—that's why they are No. 1 (or does that place belong to the ants?). Men can exist at the equator or the poles by merely changing clothes and diet. You can shoot humans into the pitiless cold of weightless space, and given the proper equipment, they will still function and perform. They can and will do this if properly motivated. But let the motivation slacken, and they grow listless and perfunctory. Constant adversity can make you fighting mad or make you think, "Oh, to hell with it." By some magic, we on *Figaro* have retained our edge even though the *merde* has been hitting the fan right from the start. We have suffered adversities, certainly not in silence, but in spite of all the Goddamnit's and frustrated "why us-es?" we have worked our way past them. We have learned to adjust to new duties and new time schedules for body functions. For a man accustomed to visiting the head regularly after his second cup of coffee and first cigarette every morning of the year, an ocean voyage in a small boat can be very disrupting. When you think about it, you realize that most bodily things are organized around your sleeping. Here on board, sleeping times are organized on an every-other-day schedule and in two periods of the twenty-four hours rather than a man's customary one. We work at odd hours and are faced with an endless repetition of duties, normally a stultifying process, although in some respects this particular repetition has its good points. Even the alarums and excursions, the threats from weather, lose their menace with repetition. But here we are halfway, a little beaten and bent although still going strong. We have become adapted to our topsy-turvy world, and the miles-to-go entered in the log each day take on new meaning.

Part of the adaptation process is learning to take weather vagaries in stride. We sail under a big weather system which within itself holds smaller weather cells in a complex series of patterns. The overall trend and wind direction persists, but it changes when a smaller cell stumbles over us. Then we are in a fast series of squalls, rain, threats of knockdowns, and general hell. It makes for constant sail changes. One moment we are racing along in a strong southwesterly, the sheets and guys taut, the seams of the spinnaker and the staysails straining, the main and mizzen eased and pulling, and *Figaro* going all out toward the northwest corner of Scotland. Then the wind shifts to the southeast. Translated into weather phenomenon, it means something unpleasant and un-Lochinvarish is coming toward us out of the west. Our required course is 70°. To hold it, we must change sails. Down come the spinnaker and staysails, and, depending on the wind force, up goes the No. 3 Genoa or No. 2 or No. 3 jib top over a foresail. The easy sailing is gone.

176

Gone is the gliding rush forward, replaced by a smash and a bang as a gradually building sea makes hash of the leftover wave pattern from the departed southwester. Now one no longer rolls easily from side to side in his bunk; instead one submits to the flapjack treatment, being tossed on a cold, damp griddle. And on deck one no longer watches the long curling wave tops roll past as you toboggan downhill. Instead, the wind drives salt spray diagonally across the deck. It stings faces and hands and rattles against oilskins like winter sleet driven in anger against a windowpane. Then the rains come, a blinding deluge which no matter how much you try to keep out, finds its way inside your oilskins, down your neck, and over your chest in freezing tracings like an icy-fingered cardiologist mapping your chest to see how much of this you can stand.

You endure the treatment for hours until this, too, passes, and the bluster drops in the back side of this local front, trough, or what have you. You now submit to the rigors of the boundary layer, not much wind but a roiled sea, the crossed patterns of the southeaster just gone and the southwester that was. The helmsman chooses a path with great difficulty, trying to pick a route through the roil which will keep the boat moving somewhere toward our objective while minimizing the rolling and plunging. Then, with an abandon equal to its first reversal, the wind comes in from the northwest. Once more the scramble, down with the jibs, and once again into the breech go the spinnaker and staysails. Everything done to the satisfaction of the watch captain, you settle down to wait for the next sail changes.

It is demanding work for a small crew. Each watch tries, if possible, to complete the job without calling for help from the other watch. That lot are in their bunks, with luck asleep—a precious commodity not to be splintered. Besides, with your own good example set, you expect them to honor your sack time with the same deference. Steve and Cleody, and Bucky and Bruce in the other, carry the brunt of the changes. After all, they are the respective Indians of their watch; all others are chiefs of one sort or another. So these young'uns do the lugging, hauling, snapping on, hoisting, and winching. It is difficult work—the sails are wet and heavy. If they have not been left on the stay, stretched out, and tied to the rail, they must be heaved up from below, stretched out on deck, hanks to the fore, the clew aft ready to take the sheets. The pistol hanks are stiff with salt, and fingertips become bruised and aching with the strain of opening. The jib halyard bounces all over the place, whipping around the headstay or, if let out too much, incredibly finding a home behind the spreaders. Often when changes are made at night, the jib and spinnaker halyard take to making cat's cradles, way up high near the tip of the mast where the trouble cannot be seen and one must rely on instinct to unravel the mess. Finally, everything squared away, one man on the winch, the other keeping the halyard taut, the sail goes up the stay, is sheeted home, and we are at speed again. The young-'uns come dragging back to the cockpit, drooping and tired, all sense of fun departed. The last watch had a bad time. Now they are below trying to recoup and recharge their batteries. May they enjoy the sleep of the just, and may flights of nymphs attend their rest.

Sleep! What a taken-for-granted word and pampered life-function this is on land. Viewed from what we sleep upon it is difficult to conceive that people ashore have any trouble sleeping. When we remember how we, too, once could luxuriate in beds fashioned to our whim while surrounded by all the goodies of a reasonable existence, not sleeping now seems a perversity. The world we left behind is filled with beds—hard beds, soft ones, beds that come in assorted widths and colors—single, double, queen, or king size—waterbeds, feather beds, beds made cool and smooth by crisp, clean sheets, beds made warm and comforting by a soft, companionate rump alongside, or one that stands in monastic isolation in a room of its own, beds in which you lull yourself by reading, listening to music, or for those far gone, looking at the late late show. Such are the furniture and accouterments of sleep ashore.

But what does *Figaro* provide for the wooing of Nepenthe? Within this 1⅛-inch mahogany and cedar shell, which so precariously holds out the blustering North Atlantic, are six berths. To describe these in the derogatory manner they deserve, I can simply call them plywood shelves topped with three inches of foam-rubber mattress. They are not quite as uninviting as the fakir's bed of nails; still they could bring complaints from Zeno or any other card-carrying Stoic.

They provide one kind of sleeping when the boat is going downwind, relatively erect or slowly rolling. Then you brace and wedge yourself against the alternating pull of gravity. You manage to pack yourself in like a fragile specimen being transported to safety. Each man's sleeping style and berth gives rise to a different intricate solution. Going upwind in a seaway is an agony of another sort. The luck of the draw gives you either a weather or leeward berth. In the weather berth you are kept from falling out by a bunk board. *Figaro III* has wooden bunk boards (a barbarity I have given up in my later boats). These are as harsh and ungiving as a tight shoe pressing the corn of a little toe. At a 25° angle of keel, the unupholstered side takes almost as much of your weight as the mattress.

Since none of us is equipped with the forbearance of a Saint Simon Stylite or his ability to draw holy ecstasy out of discomfort, we must take other measures. One such is to draw out the mattress so that it slides over the harsh restrainers. That technique has a narrow edge of efficiency; any considerable lessening of the heel angle at a given moment plunges you into a disconcerting puddle in the hard and wet wooden V made up of the wooden top of your pallet and the side of the boat below the upholstered pad. It forms a natural basin to collect the run-off of condensation. Overlapping the mattress is a hopeless method when making regular tacks, for then you must get out of your berth and rebuild at the first call of ready-about or you tumble to the cabin sole as reward for indolence. Some settle for improvised layers of anything spare between their complaining side and the indifferent bunk board or else forget the whole thing and put up and shut up.

It is impossible to keep the damp out of the bunks. The inside of a boat is as natural a condenser as a bootlegger's still, if blessed with a gamier aroma at times. Respiration, cooking vapors, the alcohol flame of the stove itself, all contribute moisture which condenses on the sides (called a ceiling in a boat!) and the overhead. All of these surfaces have contact with the North Atlantic and the air above it. The mean temperature is in the fifties. The bedsheets become as charged with damp as though they had been hung out in a fog. You can add to this subtle distillation the direct drips and splashes that find their way through the skylight, and other deck leaks of mysterious origin. We can do little to overcome this discomfort except to warm the damp with our body heat.

Monk alone attacks the problem of drips and leaks forthrightly. Betty, through her own bitter experiences in return voyages from Bermuda, knowing the damp at first hand, has provided us with large clear-plastic sheets to be improvised in some unspecified defense against wetness. Monk looked at these folded packets long and hard. Finally he took one and, spreading it over his bunk, crept directly beneath it. Since Monk's personal thermostat has, as you have been told, a setting unlike that of any other man, he wears nothing under his clear bedsheet. His manly distinctions are on view. He does not respond to any remarks which liken his cellophane-wrapped figure to the various cuts of meat one finds within film-covered cardboard trays at a supermarket self-service counter. But when I, musing aloud, say I have never seen anyone sleeping inside a condom before, he takes umbrage at the implication of the associated symbol. He lets his normal good nature surface again only when I admit to its being a gratuitous image and assure him that my astonishment was wholly relegated to the size of the prophylactic. I had been wondering whether this one would be stamped medium or large size in Brobdingnag.

180

Very tall men enjoy their own private sufferings on my boats—men like Don Jones, Bill Burnham, Frank Crawford, and Bobby Symonette. Tom Young and Bob McCullough who stand well above the upper reaches of six feet, pay special dues. When these men stretch out their length, they seem to keep spreading like a ladle full of flapjack batter in a pan. My bunks are 6 feet 4 inches, a reasonable length for most men, but these sufferers of giantism are lucky if they get away with just touching the bottom and the top. More likely they sleep with a permanent crick in their necks or search for a berth in which they can dangle their feet over the end. This last is a cold exercise but obviously to be preferred by some. Unhappily, for those tall in the saddle, *Figaro* must seem like that inn run by Procrustes.

I am normally sympathetic to their situation, but at moments when their complaints become noisome, I am almost moved to repeat a line of that acerbic architect and social critic Frank Lloyd Wright. It was told me by John Huston, the lanky movie director. Frank Lloyd Wright, as sufficient unto himself as Jehovah in his many-splendored paradises, had come to visit and comment on the house John had had built for himself and the gracefully tall and lovely Lesley Huston, his wife at that time. Wright, more than ever his abrasive self, finished a slandering critique with, "Besides, this living room is too high; it lacks human scale." John, his creative patience worn to its nub, looked down at Wright's very modest height and drawing up his own majestic stature said, "Perhaps we view human scale differently—I am a much taller man." Wright, barely waiting to whisk away a crumb of canapé, replied, "Any man who grows to more than five feet seven inches is a weed."

At my height of 5 feet 10½ inches I am comfortable, unshaken by Mr. Wright, and my 6-foot-4-inch bunks suit me fine.

One time I did not feel sorry at all. We were racing to Bermuda in *Figaro II,* a smaller boat and much weighted with stores and gear. Don Jones and Frank Crawford, both great quaffers of beer in the centuries-old tradition of Anglo-Saxons, made a surreptitious count of the beer stores. Obviously dissatisfied but not daring to make an open comment, they casually strolled off the dock and returned shortly before we went to cast off. Don Jones held a case of beer under his arm. I blew my charge, saying they could put no more weight aboard; besides, there was no more room. Don, who had gone through the American management courses on interpersonal relationships, replied in his most reasonable and honeyed voice, "Sure there is, Skipper; let me take care of that." Suddenly the Captain William Bligh buried inside me was unleashed. "OK, you bastards," I yelled, "you want the beer; it stays in the bunk with you. You are on opposite watches and the beer doesn't get opened until the ship's stores are gone." They took this as a huge joke, which made me madder, but as I remember they took turns sleeping with a case of Rheingold damn near all the way to Bermuda and seemed to gather comfort from its malty promise. How they managed it escapes memory.

The Simple Island Boy gets around his length-bed-ratio problem with ease; I always imagine by some previously worked out Euclidean theorem. But then Bobby is an ingenious nest builder and defender. When he has built the nest to suit his needs, he instructs, trains, and harries his bunkmates into its proper employment and preservation. His alternate bunk warmer is Bucky, a most tractable and unsecret sharer. They share a bunk in the forward cabin. This is the zone of the free fall and the hard ride when on the wind. It is assigned to them because it is almost long enough for Bobby and because of his and Bucky's durability and iron stomachs. In the course of solving the storage problems of his personal gear, Bobby tapes his boxes of Havana cigars to the overhead as being the handiest and driest place on the boat. Bucky does not smoke, and in hard weather, the mere presence of these cigars, their real or imagined perfume, is a challenge to his normally peaceful stomach. In spite of his plaints, Bobby is adamant, assuring him that it is a perfume to which, like oysters, he will grow accustomed—even better, learn to smoke and enjoy them. Bucky blanches at the mere suggestion but carries on manfully. He has not been educated by Dominican friars for naught. Each mile we sail is a mile nearer paradise for him, truly a Pilgrim's Progress—that is, if penance still retains its old market value and has not depreciated.

In space-talk nomenclature, habitability functions, such as sleeping, eating, etc., are dignified with category titles called life-support. Their performance in space is attended by so much difficulty that they deserve the dignity. Since working in this field I now recognize that these same simple habitual acts, when taken from land to sea in a small boat, deserve a category of their own, something with struggle and irritation in it. As an instance, consider getting dressed while the boat is pounding ahead on the wind.

It is 0200, dark and raining. You are awakened into a world you were never meant to inhabit. Your every fiber is screaming for you to keep to your bed. But a duty stronger than all of your nerve ends makes you rise. Besides, another man is panting to get into this same gyrating nest. Once on your feet, you find it difficult to stand without support or bracing. The business of lifting a leg and thrusting it into trousers calls for a nicely timed gymnastic act; that is, if you can get it through at first go. If not, the gymnastic act converts into a turn of free-style wrestling. Your clothes are still damp from the last wearing, but you suppress the shudders and drag on this solidified mass of clam chowder. Oilskins seem to be lined wih minuscule teeth and claws that cling, grab, and clamp into every microscopic protrusion they pass. The business of sheathing oneself in a waterproof layer is an exhausting task, sometimes requiring aid from a mate to screw a garment away from its sticking point. Sea boots present a very special problem. They seem possessed of a balky spirit, are as recalcitrant and skittish as a grass-fed horse in the morning and as unwilling to be entered as the Sabine maidens. They offer up a fight with no visible reward for winning in sight other than that the task is over. The toe of a sea boot responds to a magnetic urgency which is out of phase with the direction of one's foot.

Finally you are dressed; half the strength restored since the last watch is spent, and still a whole watch to go. You swallow a cup of something hot. A man of the watch about to come off has boiled up water and put out various instants—coffee, tea, cocoa, bouillion, even cold beer for the unreconstructed. He helps you to your choice, all of the time not too subtly inviting you to step out into the brisk, invigorating air, so good for your health, so that he can go to bed. You go up on deck to be met by the raillery of the hooded and huddled lucky bastards about to go off, leaving you to all that rain and slop. You respond in kind but halfheartedly; after all, it is they who are bound for bed. When they leave, you patrol the deck to acquaint yourself with how things are left. Despite the fact that you received a full description from the off-going watch, you must see for yourself. Then your watch settles into it, sails are trimmed, the speedometer checked. You are trying to get more out of her than the friends and strangers who just left. After all, aren't you the go-fast watch? A little later you just settle for talk.

These late watches are a time for intimate talk unless the weather is so bad that we retreat into individual silences. It is in these periods that reminiscences, life histories, and charms of former loves are drawn out of the dark of one's insides. Perhaps it is just intimate conversation. Perhaps the isolation and darkness of the sea acts as a large confessional booth, and these chosen companions offer a limited amount of absolution. Perhaps they simply provide the charm of interested listeners. But one cannot discount the opportunity for an audible survey of one's life. For the most astounding confessions come out at this time, as though in this recounting one tries to learn a lesson, unhappily coming too late, or to convince oneself of an inevitability not visible at the time of making a choice. At one time or another there comes a compelling need to answer the unanswerable question, "Why are we here?" (into life rather than on the sea). It is as compelling to answer the easier one, "How did it happen?"

This night the muted conversation (so as not to wake the sleepers in Zion) is of the most importance. It is with Cleody and Steve and concerns their futures and possible careers. It is not the first such conversation. This has been a serial discussion. Hidden behind a casual air is a questing urgency, for they keep returning to the subject, however devious the opening gambit. In earlier conversations I tried to discover any predilections or predispositions on their part but could not discern any. They were waiting for revelation or guidance and kept their own ideas (if any) closely guarded. It had also become clear in the earlier conversations that they felt themselves being harassed into making an early commitment. They could not identify the forces bringing these pressures to bear (this was the beginning of the decade in which *the system* was identified as the ogre of our time). I pointed out that this pressure was one of the obscene diseases of our goal-oriented time. Besides, the adulation of youth is part of the current mystique, worse than it had been in my own time, by now having entered the very fabric of our society. An artist, unless a vetted master, must be a young artist. Even corporations have made youth the soul of their personnel directives. It is as though a man stops living after thirty-five.

The exemplars—Schubert, Shelley, Keats, Mozart, et al., are dangled before us. The early years of the creators are drilled into our consciousness, even though Bach, Beethoven, Wagner grew in power and profundity as they grew older and Brahms wrote his first symphony at forty, not having felt ready before. Shakespeare, Goethe, Michelangelo never stopped growing, and no one would ever know what the genius of Mozart would have done had he been able to survive past thirty-five years of life.

(In the last years of his life, among many less consequential works—cantatas, songs, concert pieces—he wrote the opera *Magic Flute*. The year before he had written *Così fan tutte*, a piano concerto, a string quartet, the motet *Ave Verum,* and was working on his own Requiem in D with his last breath. I can make this catalog because I once cherished it as encouragement for my own fleeting youth. One should always use gods and heroes as his archetypes.)

On the other hand, it is true that Sir Isaac Newton wrote the *Principia,* invented the calculus, and laid down the basis for the laws of dynamics and universal gravitation by the age of twenty-six and that he then wrote on for fifty-eight years more, millions of words, mostly clap-trap, about occultism, alchemy, and mysticism. But then Sir Isaac lived all of his eighty-four years as a virgin, going to his God unfulfilled by anything but arithmetic. According to his own witchcraft, all of that repression and "gism" must have backed up into his brain. "I gather that you two boys," I said to them, "will avoid this trauma, at least if I make any sense of your conversation.

"Certainly the earlier one decides the sooner he can get on with his job. But remember this, accident plays a great role in every man's life. I don't believe in the book of your life being written beforehand and kept in a library upstairs, nor is it like a novel in which a life plan is set down at a tender age on page three and proceeds inexorably to a denouement. There still are heavenly crap rollers or, better yet, just plain human accidents. Therefore the most important thing is to expose yourself to a maximum of experience and opportunities."

Our conversation had come once again to architecture—my own starting point and a continuing interest to them. I have been stressing its psychological rewards, a matter of greater importance than material benefit. They came back to it constantly but each time expressed their fear of mathematics which they presume to be its central discipline. I tell them this may have been so once, but now it is nonsense. Whatever you are told to believe, it comes down to having enough math to pass the courses and the examination for license. If it were not for the existence of engineers and handbooks which have predigested formulas all worked out, half the architects in the world, those honored and those practicing in the light of one brief candle, would be reduced to their true callings, as greeting card salesmen or do-it-yourself plastic toy demonstrators.

I tell them that architecture has entered a climatic gee-whiz phase. An amalgam of avant-garde, building surface decorators, critics, curators, and photographers, supported by corporate identity programs. A great originator, Louis Sullivan, once said, "Form follows function." Le Corbusier shifted to "Function follows form." With Mies van der Rohe it came out, "Form follows the function of the steel armature." And now various expressionists have begun to express every airshaft and pipe chase as an element needing tons of concrete, flying out in ways to challenge gravity and to announce the vague presence of some pipe or shaft all for the sweet uses of creating an interesting form and shadow. Buried are the needs and functions of the humans for which this collection of shafts, chases, and walls presumably are intended. There is a school of architects who join every crusade against Fascism except in the kind of building they erect. In this they are despotic as to the structure they impose on people.

Carême's prophetic words have become doubly true. Architecture is indeed a confection, using up almost as many words as bricks.

But take heart, boys, it is a noble art. By the time you are ready this style too will go. It is the nature of things now. All is fashion. Each generation must destroy the one before it. Let's hope you can look forward to a more reasonable future, to understand a human use for a structure, to explore it by linear means and in dimension for spatial relationships, then to build it so it will stand, to be occupied and enjoyed by the people for whom it is intended, not simply for magazine layouts and fashion backgrounds and great for critics who have a living of their own to make.

In order to give them further assurances and to help destroy their inhibitions and urge them to courageously seek experience, I find myself telling them the history of my own

187

career, how accident working on suppressed and inarticulated desires came out to the end it did—good, bad or indifferent. At least it brought me to this point of time and place out in the Atlantic.

Unavoidably the foibles of my career had become a compressed story of my life because of the presence of Cleody. He has heard it in bits and snatches, never as a continuous sequence and never specifically pointed at him before. He may have built another kind of jigsaw picture with the pieces as he heard them. Now perhaps the story of my own fits and starts, or hesitations and changes of directions, may make his own assumed walls, those to be breached and scaled, seem less formidable.

I have set down most of the selfless reasons for telling that story, but was that entirely the case? Sometimes, in the midst of all the goodies, one sniffs out a taint of failure, a clean miss of original targets and hopes, perhaps not a miss but certainly a sidetracking. Was this story still one more reassurance for me? I assuredly wanted to come off well to Cleody. A man's son is a most important judge. So I did not make myself come out too badly. Still, with all that, my earnest concern was that he not be frightened away from seemingly difficult choices. I believed then and I believe now, granting that some men are more gifted than others, that men owe more to accident than they care to admit.

Night watches are long; we have plenty of time. I start when I was twelve.

That's when the first terrible accident in a man's life happened to me. My mother died. At this point my father, his world shattered, became a working model for the Job of his time. He lost his wife, his money, his grip on his business, and we lost his constant presence in the family circle, which consisted of my two sisters, my grandmother, and myself. He would show up from time to time on an increasingly irregular schedule leaving behind barely enough money to keep the home now carried on by our maternal grandmother. How that magnificent woman kept us together and functioning is a monument to the strength and nobility of women and to the survival of humankind in an urban society. We were thrown suddenly from a sheltered and cultured life into a bare-bones existence. My mother was a brilliant musician with a circle of equally cultured people around her.

I had been a bright student, but desire for learning degenerated so that by the time I was launched in high school I had become a champion truant. In despair my grandmother asked her brother, a master lithographer, to take me on as an apprentice. As soon as I could legally be removed from school he did so. Now, perversely, the easy opportunities removed, I became eager for the education so casually scorned before. I always had been a voracious reader; now the character of my reading deepened and I returned to high school at night and, from there, went on to New York University, Washington Square, also at night, while still working on the lithographic skills.

Social life in these years was barely existent and my escape from dreary repetition lay in listening to music, drawing, and reading, wherein I lived a fanciful vicarious existence. I lived a heroic life in books. The heroes were artists, musicians, scientists, who achieved the pinnacle after a life of struggle or rebellion. Jean Christophe, Beethoven, Martin Eden, Jack London, Dr. Martin Arrowsmith, Byron—the real and invented became a single reality. Now I knew I wanted a life of creativity. But what kind, how? The nearest opportunity while continuing to support myself and contribute to the family exchequer seemed to be in becoming a lithographic artist. I needed to improve my drawing skills. At this time New York University ran a night school in architecture in midtown New York. They gave courses in drawing and watercolor painting. It was easy enough to switch some courses from Washington Square.

Then the second great accident, the magical meetings that change a life. One evening I was in the drawing class, drawing, as I remember, in charcoal from a plaster bust of Lorenzo the Magnificent. I had fussed with the lighting to dramatize the great Medici's broken nose and crooked mouth. I heard a boisterous voice from the architectural *atelier* across the corridor. I looked into the room. There I saw a short, dark, and handsome man who was passing among his students like a happy Jeremiah. He was exhorting all, smoking endless cigarettes, drinking whiskey from paper cups, and creating general havoc. I watched as he picked up tubes of tempera and watercolor (yellow ochre, Naple's yellow, and raw sienna, to provide a warm base for a rendering, if I remember correctly). He then smeared this mixture with both hands across a tightly inked drawing, obliterating with each slashing stroke, weeks of careful work, at the same time exhorting his students to loosen up their minds. He was Lloyd Morgan, a marvelous man, an indifferent architect, and a great teacher. If it is a teacher's purpose to set a fire that will never go out, to instill a desire to learn to excel, to enlarge one's vision, then Lloyd Morgan was the greatest teacher I ever met. I cannot accurately isolate a major truth he taught me. Yet I have been consciously and subconsciously grateful to him every day of my life since. He was the epitome and promise of everything I had been reading.

Soon I quit a relatively well-paying job at lithography, worked out an understanding with my father about noncontribution to the family needs, enrolled in New York University's night school of architecture and took a job in an architect's office as an office boy for $15 a week.

The next three years were a blur of dedication and nonsleeping. In the office from nine to five and in Lloyd's atelier from six to one or two A.M. During this period, under Lloyd's urging, I took courses in other studies, especially sculpture and painting, to enlarge my capacities. I suffered for six months as a student of Arshile Gorky who had just become hung up on Wassily Kandinsky. Gorky made my life miserable by singling me out as an architect. Waving desparingly at his other students, he called them "shmearers," but I, as an architect, would have some concept of form and the unities. He then refused to let me paint so that I would be unspoiled and kept me drawing from plaster casts of cubes, pyramids, and globes, at the same time sitting by my side while wonders I did not perform. He showed and explained plates and books of Kandinsky's work, waiting for his magic to overwhelm mine. His explanations always seemed highly metaphysical at a time when I sought logic. Finally, by mutual agreement, I quit, unreconstructed, unregenerated, and untaught.

But through all this period my growing ambition was to go to Paris to study, a desire inflamed by my reading and fanned into a roaring blaze by Lloyd Morgan who had gone to the École des Beaux-Arts. One glorious day I won a pair of scholarships in competition, one to Fontainebleau and the other to Paris. It was another great accident. Fontainebleau was a start, a stop on the way to Paris, as exciting as it had been for D'Artagnan, another kind of artist. My father promptly borrowed my scholarship money. He would double it for me and leave some over for himself as well. All I got out of the scholarships was my steamship ticket to LeHavre and a few drinks on the boat. My discoveries began then. Wine, women, and song, as the saying goes, all took their turns, but mostly I found that architecture as taught in France had little place in my realities. I found myself avoiding the architecture classes and painting instead. At this time I helped a painter student render frescoes in the approved Renaissance style in a nearby church, mixing plaster, troweling on a new wet coat for painting in the morning, and cutting out the hardened unpainted portions each night. It was a brief period of excitement— painting in a Renaissance media has all sorts of associated romantic suggestions. The balance of this time was monumentally dull. Everything would change when I got to Paris.

But nothing did. The École des Beaux-Arts had been founded by Cardinal Richelieu (D'Artagnan's great enemy). The heart of the school still belonged to Giovanni Lorenzo Bernini and, as is said now, "I couldn't relate." I gave up on architecture, putting in enough appearances at the Atelier Laloux and as a *Negre* in the loge of the Prix de Rome *logiste* Jean Labatut to maintain the sham of interest. As far as I was concerned I had become a painter. Now I went through a period of great privation, always hungry, at times without lodging, sponging from friends. I was still spiritually supported by the idea that this was in the Grand Pattern. Out of this suffering would come greatness. Didn't every biography and story stand as silent witness? Even when I was reduced to a nadir of existence, it was like Rimbaud, but I was still a "clean-cut American boy," so if there was no poetry, there were no drugs or a homosexual Verlaine in pursuit either.

I came back to America broke during the last agonies of the Depression. There was little work for architects. I held several different jobs. The most fun and most enlightening job at this time was with Elsie de Wolfe, the leading decorator in the world at the time. I was household architect for this remarkable woman. Through her I came in contact with a new order of woman. That side of my education was filling out nicely.

I came to the place in which I am now president by taking a job which seemed to offer everything—a reasonable salary, at least enough to get by on, for working three days a week. This left four days in which to paint. This was another accident, for I was soon working six and seven days a week and painting when I could. Which brings me to now, the desire still there, to a degree unfulfilled. A part-time architect, a part-time painter, a full-time industrial designer, and a one-time bum with a yacht. A career shaped by accident working on underlying desire and once as uncertain and searching as both of you are now.

There was nothing left to say except to answer a few questions about Paris, which had nothing to do with architecture.

Steve went on to study architecture. Cleody, after a baccalaureate in liberal arts, went on to study architecture, then unceremoniously quit and turned up at the Wharton School at the University of Pennsylvania. He now seems exuberantly happy, pursuing a career in the development of planned communities. He is deep in modular and systems approaches to building. Perhaps his infant son Colman will be an architect or a painter or . . . I am still a one-time bum with a yacht.

I am no Scheherazade. The weather gods are not lulled by my tear-stained tale. They may even be wrought up by this casual turning of one's back to their awesome might. After all, what does the inquiring into our own puny life mean to them? We are ringing all the weather changes tonight. They are giving us the full treatment. Having turned petulant, they give us a taste of every dreg they can shake out of their nasty bag. Our log bristles with unbelievable changes. At one moment the watch scrambles forward to lower the spinnaker because of a lack of wind. A drifter is set in its place. Then the wind booms in from the northwest so suddenly that it catches our main aback because of the many go-fast strings attached. Reluctantly the other watch is called to help straighten us out in a hurry. The spinnaker is reset and the wind builds up to 25 knots. Then it starts to clock and continues to slowly move forward until it becomes foolhardy to carry the chute. It is replaced with the No. 1 Genoa until that sail begins to scoop up the bow wave. We lift the foot clear with the fore halyard set in the midfoot cringle. But as the wind continues to move ahead we find ourselves on the wind. The No. 1 is taken off because we are on the verge of being overpowered. The No. 3 Genoa is set in its place. One gets the feeling that we are being tested for something.

We thrash ahead with the combination of No. 3, main and struck mizzen, into a moonlit night when, for an indecent reason known only to themselves, the gods of wind and wave becloud the moon and turn on a fog and drizzle. The wind goes light and we struggle to move along.

In what remains of the lonely hours of the night, while huddling under a waterproof hood and thinking of all those lovely fleshpots recalled in the telling of the past, you are suddenly startled by a steamer's foghorn to starboard. What the hell! What's anybody doing out on a night like this? We turn on all of our lights and make sure of our radar reflector. What a joke! We must turn up as a blip so small as to be confused with an impairment in the radar screen, especially when the watchers on board the larger ship, dulled by looking at nothing ahead and expecting nothing, pass you off as a bit of electronic hash. After all they never saw the *Andrea Doria*, and she had a hell of a lot bigger rating than us. However, despite their petulant behavior, we trust in the gods but nevertheless prepare to repel boarders.

We never see the steamer. She may have been near; at least she sounded so. But we are busy with another series of sail changes and pause only moments to look around.

Through all their miseries the crew remain miraculously ardent and good-tempered. It should be a cause of wonderment, but it's not. You expect this kind of response; you feel that way yourself. It is why you came.

I keep looking at Steve and Cleody to see if a new incandescence lights up their faces. I cannot see past their scraggly beards. Perhaps it is there, underneath.

17

THERE is nothing like rain running down your neck or the frustrated hope of finding comfort in a damp berth to take over the forefront of your thinking. Because such experiences are constant affronts to one's instinctive yearning for comfort and security the tendency in any immediate re-telling is to dwell upon the hardships, but it would take a great deal more than these modest discomforts to disguise the wonderment in sailing across the ocean.

I have crossed several times, either cruising or racing. Each passage offered its own mixed bag of miseries as well as delights. Each passage has its own memories of acute discomfort and of moments when the dormant tickle of fear threatened to crawl to the surface; times when you ask yourself, "What the hell am I doing out here?" But even as you ask, you know, given the opportunity, you will do it again. That is the wonderment.

People habituated to air-conditioning, electric blankets, and tight dry roofs may look askance at the ocean racer as a sort of cross between a nature-freak and a punching bag. Since parlor games never go out of style, he can in some exotic version of twenty questions—animal, vegetable, or mineral—be cast into a variety of role-playing parts. One could start with a late-blooming hermit, for instance (except that he plays it as a groupie), a man getting away from it all. In this role, he holds one reluctant foot in this century, but his old-fashioned, original or unoriginal sin-laden soul longs for a harsh desert cave where he can shrive the flesh to his heart's content in an attempt to rediscover the spiritual delights of St. Anthony, St. Jerome, or in the ultimate plunge to a fierce Elysium, that of Manicheus himself.

On the other hand, he could be indulging no greater severity than that of being a hopeless romantic, a happier Captain Ahab, yelling into the wind through a beautifully engraved eighteenth-century speaking trumpet, trying to shout down the sociological and technological truths of his own time.

Or again, the irreverent if puzzled landsman can put our man down as definitely kinky and think the whole enterprise a bit of practicing, elegant masochism—nothing nasty, mind you, just a guy who gets his kicks from being used hard.

There is probably a featherweight of truth in each role. There is a certain spirituality, but it is not necessarily religious. The awareness of His Oceanic Omnipotence and that of his cohorts is not so much a retreat from reason as the evocation of a romantic fancy, the same touch of fantasy that has this sailor carry a handsome, meticulously crafted, nineteenth-century chronometer on board at the same time as he listens to an electronic time signal over the radio. There is an undoubted relish for the mysteries. As for masochism, I have heard too many satisfied purrs over the pleasures of a warm dry bunk, a tasty meal, an easy sun-warmed day, to take that idea seriously. It is too simplistic. In our crew we are as worldly as befits our various ages and all are comfort-loving. Yet having hard times when at sea is part of the total experience. It comes with the table d'hôte special of the day.

In ocean racing one finds something less and something more than the essence compressed into George Mallory's reply "Because it is there" to the question "Why mountaineering?" Another British mountaineer, Leo Amery, has described that dedication "as a form of worship as well as a sport" (for a nation of self-advertised stiff upper lips, the English are prone to break through their emotional barriers in the presence of flowers, certain small animals, mountains, etc.). Part of the mountain mystique, nay even the language, casts the climber in the role of "conqueror" after an "assault." He lays his life on the line in a mysterious and strenuous *auto-da-fé*. In crossing an ocean, there is nothing left to conquer. It has been going on for thousands of years in rafts, canoes, and ocean liners. An ocean racer does not grant the possibility of failure, only of not winning. He knows he will make it; he will survive.

But how many places and times in this misshapen existence can you live in a one-to-one relationship with nature, sometimes its master, sometimes its pawn? Where else can you be aware of your contribution and immediately recognize its effect in a joint performance? How wonderful to escape for a time, a faceless part in a bewildering system which more often moves laterally rather than forward, toward goals which are difficult to identify or defend. How bloody marvelous to be engaged with the uncertain certainties of a single antagonist, the sea. You know its shape and size, and, however immense it is, you are involved with only a small part at a time, which in itself has neither passion nor memory, and which implies no domino effect. What is done is done and over with; there are no third person carry-overs. For the several weeks of a passage you are concentrated on clearly defined duties in the presence of a clear purpose. You no longer punch at a bag of feathers.

Out here you leave behind a discordance over which you have no control, a fabric of affairs in which events rather than reason lead. For a time the sense of loss over an art no longer attuned is appeased. Gone is the loneliness in thinking that you alone in all the world believe that what was once an evocation of emotion and beauty is now flatulent or wallowing in an esoteria verging on put-on, the personal property of dealers in gobbledygook. The loss of one kind of beauty is propitiated. You now live and work in the presence of an elemental beauty which is consciously shared with your fellows.

Best of all you are away from everything which diminishes

the knowledge that you are that glorious thing, a human creature. Once again, Pico's man, your physical self, vibrates to the environment. A magnificent animal, *numero uno*, though not as strong as an elephant, swift as a cheetah, or as sharp-eyed as an eagle, yet you have enough of each ability to survive and surpass. You hover somewhere between groveling before the gods and mocking them, but you have been granted the privilege of laughter. And though not given the exotic vocal chords of the mynah bird or the sweetness of the thrush, you have learned to make poetry and songs of thanksgiving for the existence of places and occasions where you can feel enlarged at the core of your being.

The miseries are there, but as part of this lovely game they act as a sort of litmus in proving out and serve as an album for later years.

Edgard du Prey, in the middle of a night watch, once said, "Bill, there are two things to put in the bank—money and the memory of such a night." The memory bank is just as important as the other. No matter how general the experience, being men, each one responds in a manner tuned to his personality and at a given moment. He can voice irritation, be stoically silent, ruefully witty, or turn on an antic hilarity. The remarks, reactions, and recriminations pass through the boat like a cloud's shadow racing across the face of the sea. In such a close community everything said and done is important. The more memorable words or happenings stamp an occasion indelibly.

On the day, for instance, when in my capacity as official taster of the bilge, I sampled the contents of that foul reservoir and found it all salty, hardly a hint of brackishness to indicate a continuing freshwater leak, I shouted, "That's great! It's all salt water!"

That calm Parliamentarian, Symonette, ceremoniously puffing a Montecristo ("to get rid of the taste in my mouth," he would have assured me) paused long enough to remark—"This is the only boat in which I have sailed where it was an occasion for rejoicing to find she was leaking, where we are given the choice of death by drowning as opposed to dying of thirst."

No reply can be equal to such Socratic logic except perhaps a proper quotation from an Epistle to the Corinthians or something of equal gravity.

Or what can be equal to the memory of Monk staggering back from the bow where he had gone to take a morning sun line. He is balls naked, his body wet with spray, a spate of drops still dribble from the matted chest hair, pressed under the plastic bag shielding the sextant slung around his neck. Naturally he has removed all his clothing before going forward to take his shot of the pale sun hiding behind the Genoa jib. "It stands to reason, man. Hell, you can dry your body with a towel, but clothing—once wet, where can you dry them?" He can't be bothered with oilskins; he won't be on deck that long.

The air temperature hovers somewhere in the upper fifties. With every dip of the bow the spray must have hit him like an icy needle shower after a sauna. He pauses at the break of the cockpit before going below. "Capting," he says, "it is beautiful. She plows into the seas like something alive. I recommend the bow in the morning as a place to fuel up with inspiration for the rest of the day."

You only smile acknowledgment, suppressing as best you can the sympathetic shivers that threaten to rack your frame.

And the rapid turn of mood in our irreverent young, who should, in their proper turn, clean up after a meal, but find it difficult in some weather to discharge their duties below without discharging the meal as well.

Then, that kindly old Viking Knud, out of the largeness of his heart, offers to clean up in their stead. They are meek with gratitude. Then Knud, in search of the detergent, asks for AIYAX. The squeamishness and gratitude drop from them with the rapidity shown by various beneficiaries of the Marshall Plan. These ungrateful youths fasten on the *Y* sound of the Scandinavian *J* as though this were the mother lode of all Anglo-Saxon wit and word play. They bandy words and phrases about; each new invention, less graceful than the last, keeps them doubled in spastic laughter, much to the annoyance of their older, kindlier, and more literate companions. Knud himself is lost in puzzlement.

I know how it feels to be hung with something you have said, and the merriment that follows, which surpasses understanding. My own words have been turned against me, each time attended by general glee and the faraway music of hautboys and rebecs. One must understand that a mean and subterranean game goes on aboard *Figaro*. It is the quiet rebellion against the privileges of office, my own office to be precise. The captain of the *Figaro* is awarded every honor, but his comfort is always fraught with peril. There is an open season on that.

On occasion while steering, my mind lost in lofty thoughts, I have inadvertently stuck *Figaro*'s nose into a big green one. At such a time, the boat feels as though I had jolted her into a passing water spout. She scoops half the ocean over her deck. Those below are jostled and sprayed by a flume of drippings which come through the sieve that serves us as a skylight. I have explained these steering aberrations (too few really to require more inventive consideration) as having encountered "a rogue sea." Who are they to doubt my truth?

But as surely as pride and arrogance goeth before a fall, so did I goeth and fall, a most ungracefully real one, out of the head, or toilet, to call it as it is. Bruce was steering at the time with the wind out of the northeast. *Figaro*, plunging in a mean sea, shook us around like ice cubes in a cocktail shaker and in a temperature almost as warm. The liquids in me, condensed by and subjected to that cruel shaking, cried for release. This had been a growing awareness, a building pressure which I tried to turn off by thinking good things. But biological hydraulics could no longer be denied. Reluctantly I left the spare comfort of my berth, clad in long johns and socks, and struggled in the violently tilted cabin, going uphill, to the head. Grasping both jambs, I pulled myself through the doorway and closed the door after me just before falling out. Somehow I managed to wedge myself into this cock-eyed *cabinet privé*, our own little Tower of Pisa, where gravity runs aslant. I was engrossed in directing a flow diagonally through the air into a canted receptacle below, a matter of rather fine discrimination, when Bruce hit a brick wall. *Figaro* had been behaving like the live model for Rimbaud's *"Le Bateau Ivre,"* but you could accommodate to a rhythm of sorts. Between being so occupied with marksmanship, trying to keep myself erect and adjusting to a rhythm, I could no more stop my fall than arrest the passage of a comet. I exploded through the door, keeping myself well in hand, and crashed into the locker opposite in that narrow passage. I hit it in the best blocking-back style with my head and shoulders, but with that all style ceased. I crumpled to the sole and lay stunned, my head ringing, St. Catherine wheels whirling behind my eyes. A great silence descended. The captain of the *Figaro,* clad in baggy long johns lay sprawled on his cabin sole, sprawled like a drunken Noah—he has been ingloriously tossed from his own W.C. No one moved or spoke for an eternity of seconds. I was the first to break the hush. I tried to yell which, with the strength I could spare, came out more like the last despairing gasp of a man done in by his onetime friends, "YOU BASTARDS."

Bruce, still steering, said, "Sorry about that, Captain—it was a rogue sea."

Was that a snort of laughter or some new ringing in my ears?

On another occasion the fates (and the crew) were unbelievably able to reach me in my bunk, to make a shambles of what had been coziness, and then use my own words to turn aside wrath. I was snuggling in the torpor of half-sleep, just having wakened and wishing mightily to be back in that dream. This time Cleody was helmsman, and from what I could put together from their half-heard, faraway voices, that watch was still playing the despicable game of trying to catch a shipmate unawares, to fill his boots or get water down his neck. My indignation was only half-hearted—I was too sleepy; besides, we were sailing off in a quartering sea. Assuredly nothing could happen to spoil the peace of this afternoon. I would speak to them later.

Then by some freak of timing *Figaro,* being rolled to leeward at the moment of meeting a wave, took on a boarding sea which came roaring up the waterway, hit the cabin house like a breaker hitting a cliff, broke high in the air, poured over the cabin house, and shot down the companionway. Most incredibly it found me in my bunk some distance from the opening. It came over me like a firehose. The shock was indescribable. The gasp which normally comes with a sudden cold immersion was choked off by water in my nose and mouth. I coughed and sputtered. I could hardly grasp what had happened, but that spreading wet and cold was not long in making itself known. All peace and contentment gave way to rage. I crawled from the berth, mad as a wet captain, shouting my wrath, trying in some way to release the outrage which flooded my being only to hear my first-born, Cleody, my son, carrier of my name, the staff and rod to comfort me in my declining years, shouting, "I GET A THOUSAND POINTS—I GET A THOUSAND POINTS."

I felt miserable. I faced the need to change the bedclothes as well as my own, but dry it as best I could that berth would be wet for a long time. Before I retreated into soggy and defeated silence, I said with measured bitterness, "You miserable skunks."

Symonette, the kind of man you keep in the bow of the whaleboat to twist the killing harpoon, asked, "Are you unhappy, my captain?" And then, most despicably, even once again (perhaps trying to turn some of my wrath on to himself and away from his young watch-mates who needed as much help as baby vipers), added, "We are only trying to comply with your orders, Captain, sailing her to the point of discomfort."

I cannot remember my exact reply. It was not "Fiddlesticks."

Miseries at sea come in all shapes and sizes and from a

variety of sources. So far a great deal of ghoulish humor has been at my expense. But my time will come. It always does. The wheel turns relentlessly. Once, when racing in another latitude, I had mine back after putting up with a few quiet tricks. It started badly. Of all things I was wakened by a flying fish in my bunk. They said it came in through the open port—which later, after repeated swearings on a stack of Bibles, I took to be the truth, but not at that moment because of the merriment. Perhaps I am obsessively suspicious. The wet flapping of a fish waking you from a sound sleep scares the hell out of you and you respond accordingly. When I appeared not to be laughing as much as they and I suggested that they return to their watch duties, the pleasure flattened some. By themselves, they continued to milk the incident for whatever fun they could find in recalling it. It even beat throwing stinkbombs in the movies. It was then I could dispose of the fish, burying scales, etc., in their little heaps of clothing, sweaters, and shirts not needed in the warm night. A flying fish is very soft-fleshed and fragile. It is warm in the Gulf Stream air and the fish loses its virtues rapidly once out of its medium. In that lack of state of grace it gives out cloying and mighty stinks.

My time will come. It always does.

But no matter the miseries and superficial indignities; they drip away even as the last of the rain and squalls pass on ahead. You go on deck in answer to a call to come up and see the sunset and find the sky shot with orange reds, blue pinks, violets, and purple in the most improbable combinations—nature imitating J. M. W. Turner. You see great flaming rays of sunlight pouring through gaps in the dark pileups of clouds. They seem to be searching out blessedness as in a Rembrandt etching. And then at the last moment the sun slips out from under the masking menace of the low-hanging clouds; you see it go down clear. The sea in the west turns a red-gold as you turn to those near and say, "We will have a good day tomorrow." They nod sagely, few words are spoken. There is nothing much to say. But you will know this to be the best of all possible worlds, and each man alongside would have been a fit companion in the fellowship of the *Argo*.

18

BUCKY says I bring a degree of reverence to our undertaking. It is not because, as captain, I hold services, say grace, or maintain an outward air of piety. It is because I sing Bach while steering. When I say "sing" I am stretching the sweet uses of the verb. But lest one think my choice of the master is simply a Baroque tic that breaks out any time I steer, let me tell you that I was a spear-carrying type of member of two different choruses, each of which performed the *Passion According to St. John,* and that I tried a lick with a pick-up madrigal group. With unusual charity and forbearance my composer brother-in-law, John Colman, says that while my voice may not have quality it does increase the volume and texture of a group. It cannot be all bad, as witness the response from Bucky. His opinion must be tempered, however, since he suffers from the want of redeeming features in his shipmates. As a young man who once considered a life within the Benedictine Order, he is acutely aware of the scatological bent to our conversation and of the endless seminars on comparative studies in female anatomy. He is silently disapproving. But I do not use Bach as a censor. With all else that he is, Bach is music to steer by.

True, no one should sing or talk when sailing close on the wind. So it is while reaching or running that we dare a try at the pleasure generally reserved for the shower bath.

Admittedly I am a Bach freak. But it is an inoffensive addiction, if unusual in helmsmen. (In a theater set piece the man at the wheel, a baritone, sings a sad chantey while a chorus of one hundred male voices and the London Philharmonic come on strong behind him.) Singing chanteys, however, is not conducive to good steering. I know only one man who can do both at the same time but he's a tenor. The trouble with chanteys is words. How can a man concentrate on steering when he is trying to remember what happened next to the Maid of Amsterdam after "I put my hand upon her thigh/She said young man you've gone too high." Sooner or later, in trying to catch up with the rhyme scheme, he loses timing with the boat.

Nothing, to my mind, can stand up against a full-throated rendition in *la la's* of the "Double Violin Concerto" or "Jesu Joy of Man's Desiring," to give you a range. (In the concerto and canata you do all parts.) Nothing can capture the surge and drive and the potential for emotional release, when—at the wheel, driving downwind in a following sea—you, having made a subconscious choice from the Breitkopf and Hartel and the BVI Catalogs, are giving full voice to your joy. Somewhere in the back of your head an orchestra is accompanying you. The open sea is a greater invitation to song than any shower stall.

It cannot simply be my special taste or hardening of the esthetic arteries, but it is impossible to think of any future generation of helmsmen singing Anton Webern or Karlheinz Stockhausen to the rhythmic accompaniment of the open sea. And imagine setting up a serial row in an equally imaginary music stand in front of the wheel.

None of my shipmates follow me in my choice of steering music. For that matter, we have only two modest singers other than myself aboard. Monk is a word man and has an incredible vocabulary of folksongs and poetry, but in his case the words diminish the importance of the music. (I also notice his steering becomes erratic when he is in the middle of a spate of locution.) Knud's songs run to Scandinavian folksongs and English chanteys. Not only has the crew avoided my lead in edifying choice, but, other than Bucky, they have treated my execution of a difficult passage with impassive silence. I can put this down either to awe in the presence of consummate artistry or to the fact that since I own the boat, all sorts of painful quirks are condoned.

No matter the device used in serving a trick at the wheel, the miles to go are running out rapidly under us.

The miles go by and life aboard goes on. It is filled with small details, unimportant decisions, yet each is given importance because it is what makes up a day. For instance, at times the judgment of a minor league Solomon is required. We have been using our captured water to free containers and make room for a new supply. The water in our surviving tank is a reserve. Bruce decides to test some of our early captured reserve which has been stored forward. He finds "Old Circus Tent" too strong for his delicate palate even when mixed with Tang. He therefore helps himself to the ship's main, now emergency, supply. When I protest, he asks, "Why not use the main supply now and save the new stuff for emergency?"

Monks wants to know, "Where were you when we thought of abandoning the race altogether, much less making a choice of vintage?"

I ask myself, "Why not?" There is logic in his request. Against that is my instinct to conserve everything against any possible happening. I tell him, "I will think about it."

The restless barograph is going down again. The clouds are moving toward the southwest, indicating a low-pressure cell to the south coming our way. Not another! Sail changes by now are a matter of rote, going on before your eyes without due stress or importance, like scenery being shifted in a Chinese theater by black-robed figures while the play goes on! Only here we are actors and stagehands both.

The evening period of radio monitoring reveals a sad and dramatic bit of news. A boat has been dismasted (later identified as *Drumbeat*, Max Aitken's 60-footer). She is going into St. John's, Newfoundland, under jury rig and power. When I find out who it is I am unhappy for Johnny Coote, her navigator and No. 2 man, and Gerald Potter the sailing master in this voyage. Captain Coote—a bright and happy black-haired, blue-eyed submarine captain who has given up the depth to sail the surface of the sea—and Major Potter—still as lean, straight, and tall as a guardsman should be, who has given up horses for boats—are my good friends and boon companions, and I know they have been looking forward to this race. I will miss them in Sweden, if, in fact, we make Sweden ourselves.

In this same monitoring exchange I tell the other boats I will hold to my first decision about reporting position in latitude and longitude. Despite the objections of Dick Nye and myself at the time the idea was first broached, those not wishing to participate were asked to delay the final decision until some time at sea in order to discover whether we would change our minds. I have not. No one asked us to take an oath not to listen at the times other boats were reporting positions, but I feel honor-bound not to listen to the regular position broadcasts. We will listen to the monitoring periods; that will be a safety measure in case anyone gets in trouble. We will maintain radio silence, that is, we will not transmit unless in trouble.

We must have gone well during the night. With morning light we see *Palawan* to leeward. We've caught her! When she sees us a spate of sail changes take place aboard her. She begins to drop to leeward, not necessarily moving ahead. By 1030 she has disappeared to leeward or faded in the changing light.

This is a morning when everyone gets religion. Busy work by all hands—Bucky overhauled the fireplace, brought out the fuel, and laid a fire. Bruce put the smokehead on the chimney stack. The fire started, I watch like a hawk against choking and smoldering. The comfort one draws from the fire is offset by the threat of death by asphyxiation. Bruce washes pots and pans and Bucky sweeps up in the cabin and then starts sewing on the shredded mizzen staysail, a seemingly hopeless job, but Bucky goes at sewing in the Confucius manner, "A sewing of a thousand miles begins with a single stitch."

Bruce goes to work drilling out the remains of a broken screw in the port dorade. We have been taking drips through that ventilator. He believes that a bolt and nut can be sent through the soft metal collar to seal off the offending leak.

Cleody and Steve, not to be outdone before the break of the watch, hoist Reardon to the masthead to inspect all fittings. When he goes below, they replace all of the unemployed halyards with messengers, inspect them for chafe and meathooks, make necessary repairs and send them up again in their respective blocks.

It is a good day all around. We have a warming and drying fire in the fireplace, the cabin is clean, the bilges pumped and sponged dry, and the barograph is rising again. The low-pressure area to our south has moved ahead into the southeast and the wind consequently swung back into the northwest.

During the late afternoon kaffeeklatsch, the Reuters of the ocean blue, *Connie,* reports sighting a yellow spinnaker, later identified as *Hamburg,* a larger boat!

And before dark another unidentified sail is sighted ahead and to leeward. It is dropping aft and to leeward.

The next few days are filled with more undramatic detail. We eat a splendid meal of corned brisket of beef topped off with apple pie and cheddar cheese.

It rains and the wind goes ahead.

The rain stops, it brightens, and the wind moves aft.

We test the port tank and find six inches of water.

The wind goes ahead and we have trouble with the draft of the chimney and choking smoke in the cabin.

We have only 878 miles left to Ronaldsay.

Monk gets a fleeting sun-sight.

The clocks are advanced to No. 1 Zone Time.

The bilges are pumped dry.

Beards begin to flourish, no longer looking like dirty smudges. Each sprouts differently, but all are fingered with the same gravity.

Rain, and the chute comes down.

The sun is out again—Genoa down, chute up.

Miles to Ronaldsay, 620—miles to date, 2,323—course now, 075°.

Bastille Day

0430 A jet plane passes over us on a course of 070°.

0745 Strike No. 1 Genoa to repair cloth tearing at clew from strain on seams. Set Yankee over Genoa staysail.

Monk gets a morning sun-line. When you are heading east, the morning sun is always behind the headsail. Monk describes this morning's acrobatics in the log as "Balancing on pulpit—clinging to headstay—legs wrapped around pulpit—bow wave splashing spray on sextant mirrors—sun a dancing ball on a gyrating horizon." Oh for the life of a small-boat navigator.

It is a beautiful sunny day, like the Bastille days I remember as a student in France. My memory is jogged back to my student days because of the talks with Cleody and Steve about a life and career in architecture. They are quietly thrashing out ideas of a future in the course of these conversations while my own mind is quickened with memories of my student days. Perhaps owing to my presently acute condition of celibacy the two Bastille days I remember best inevitably centered on two girls who never met or had anything in common except that they were both very pretty. As I look backward in an enlarged album of remembrances and with an added decade of experience, these are still the nicest kinds of memories. Vivent Les Girls of France!

I met the first in my earliest months in France. She was a dark-haired beauty, vibrant, alive, and full-fleshed, the kind that struggles with a mustache in the late, married years. But then she was the most beautiful waitress in our school commons at Fontainebleau where I spent a few months. She had the most apt if improbable name as far as I was concerned — Mademoiselle France (no relation to Anatole). Indecently, I have forgotten her forename. I was inevitably drawn to such vibrant beauty and by some miracle she to me. But I was young, shy, and inexperienced and settled for looking and longing, a sighing Werther long after Goethe finished with him. She, even then showing the traits of strong peasant stock which is ever the bedrock of French pragmatism, evinced her practicality by having herself transferred to the table I shared with my friends. In the face of such a romantic stratagem, they did what they could with advice and consultation and the furnishing of several carefully drilled French phrases to advance my anticipated seduction of our beauty. They acted as a sort of corporate Cyrano de Bergerac. I did very little to gain entrance to this paradise, largely because I spoke no French and she no English, a barrier I thought, perhaps ridiculously, to be insurmountable. I know that experts advise the best way to learn a language is by taking a native to bed, a sort of daily double of rewards. But like the Hungarian recipe for an omelet which begins "First you steal two eggs," in order to start learning you need first to get the native between the covers. During the stalemated interim while I sharpened my French and my courage, she showed me many kindnesses, such as larger servings and a second dessert.

On the Fourth of July our group, an American Bohemian enclave entirely surrounded by solid French bourgeoisie, decided we would hold a mint julep party as a display of patriotism with one of the most American of American libations. Our choice was also guided by the fact that Luke Dent, a southerner in our group, had hoarded several bottles of Kentucky sour mash bourbon. Our beauty helped by getting us mint and ice. So that when Bastille day came along I could do no less than invite her to be my guest at a reception given by the *maire* in honor of the big-spending Americans.

The mayor's party was held in the courtyard of the Town Hall, a stiff and lifeless mixture of architecture in earlier and ignobler syles. Alternated French and American flags hung limply from widows around the perimeter. Mild refreshments were served and a discordant band tried their hand at American dance music. We sat at metal tables, under umbrellas, like the terrace of a zoo cafeteria. At decent intervals we got up to dance (a foxtrot!). Most tables held boisterous groups whose self-engendered noise tended to erase the lack of charm in the ambiance. Mademoiselle and I sat alone, for my friends, ever thoughtful, considered this the best way I could close in for the kill. It was a protracted agony. We could not communicate except when we danced when I would whisper blandishments into her ear in English and she would ask me in French what I had just said. The rest of the time I just sat, while she chattered in alien tongues or kept quiet, too. My mortification drew out. I was a man with lockjaw present at a feast; then even that frustration vanished. I can recognize how sexuality could run high when the crew of the *Bounty* hit the beach in Tahiti in spite of a lack of a common language. There was nothing bourgeois about the local society. They were not oppressed by a Calvinist ethic or the surveillance of the confessional. Besides, both parties were stripped to the waist and numerous clumps of bushes offered cover to the lack of communicating. But in this arid, paved, wasteland of nineteenth-century architectural taste, I felt far removed from Fletcher Christian or even the more naïve Rodolfo and Mimi. I wanted nothing so much as to be in my room with a good book. I finally inveigled some of my French-speaking friends to join us. They started making passes of their own, but at least the first agony abated.

But this turn did not suit my mademoiselle. She had other ideas. She invited me to join her at a French celebration. I could not plead illness or an urgent call from the President, and so in fear and trembling I went with her to a part of the town I never knew before. There the party spread from inside a café out onto the street, which I dimly remember as a small square or a sudden widening in a narrow thoroughfare. Sprightly music came from a tinny piano, an accordion, a violin, a trumpet, and a snare drum. I was warmly greeted as mademoiselle's American friend (rich, of course) although I did not think myself very popular with the younger blades who quite properly had their own idea about the proper employment of mademoiselle's attention, person, and charms. But in the mood of the day I was accepted, spoke English volubly, to which they nodded and smiled; they spoke French, to which I nodded and smiled, and I had a joyous time. I no longer felt estranged but danced with many girls and women who perhaps were their mothers, ate what was offered, and drank red wine like mother's milk. I could pay nothing, I was a guest. The party went on into the night when, slightly fuddled with drink and overwhelmed with love for my fellowman, I found myself walking mademoiselle home and all that love for humankind now concentrated on her being.

Everyone kissed everyone at the party. It was nothing, therefore, for the two of us to stop under the deep shadows of the plane trees, full and bursting with leaves and promise, to embrace and to kiss. But now it was no longer a passing, friendly gesture. My blood ran hotter and faster, and ardency, ever ready, quickened. We would even lean in the shade of an old stone wall (covered with posters and warnings to post no bills) where we would kiss and I could press my hungering body against her warm, soft, heavenly self and even on two occasions place my hand on the cloth which shielded and strangled her intoxicating breasts like a cuirass, keeping them safe from invasion of impure intention. All other attempts to discover her mysteries and delights by tactile explorations were politely and firmly repelled. Nevertheless I almost trembled with the intoxicating belief that before long paradise would be open to me. I took the polite rejections as a matter of form and style. Overriding this was the knowledge that she was French, and, after all, everyone knew what French girls were like. Anyone who had ever read a book had that idea drummed into his mind. It was just a case of waiting for the right time, the right button to be pushed, the right moment to ask her to come to your room (if you could figure out how to say it). That was the trouble—how do you get to put the question when you don't know the words.

Finally we reached her door and the dream ended with a bang. Now I was permitted to kiss her cheek, just one time and, at that, once over lightly, followed by a single shake of the hands. Somehow she made me understand by subtle gesture that protective ogres might be on the watch, perhaps a father and a battalion of brothers all armed with 12-gauge shotguns. She went inside and I home to an empty room, sad and aching from the lovers' complaint.

The next day in the dining hall we had slipped back from our intimacy. I could find no way to recapture the momentum or further my campaign. Perhaps she needed a long and formal courtship as prelude to any decision. Perhaps she had more conservative ideas about our future. Certainly I needed to know more of her language. In two weeks she shifted to another table. She left behind a promise unfulfilled, a memorable Bastille Day, and a question to which I never will find an answer. Did she, with age, grow a mustache?

The other Bastille Day memory concerned another sort of idyll and an American girl. She, too, had dark hair, but in her case it provided a dramatic frame for very white skin and a pair of arresting pale blue-green eyes. She was a druid priestess whose forebears had somehow found their way to America, away from the worship of oak-tree gods and into the solidity of the Episcopalian church. She was slight, sensitive, and seemingly overwhelmed by the attention she drew. Naturally I had fallen helplessly and secretly in love. I had difficulty in advancing my suit because she drew male courtship like a queen bee, and I was so poverty-stricken I found it difficult to arrange occasions for us to be alone. She also seemed to be frightened by any direct frontal attack of a would-be swain.

I had scraped, saved, and borrowed for this particular Bastille Day and had arranged long in advance that we would spend the day together. It was another beautiful day in the full flush of summer. I packed a picnic which we carried on the train to Pontoise where I rented a rowing boat. The idea was for an idyllic day in the country, drifting on the river and looking at the scenes made holy by the impressionist painters. I knew the area well, for I went there regularly to paint in an attempt to capture for myself some of the magic they found. (Perhaps they had used it all up.) But now my trips served me well. I could point out "This is the place Pissarro stood," and then whip out the appropriate postcard-size replica. She was flatteringly impressed and I positively aglow. But there was more to the day than just my ego gratification and her education. There is magic in recapturing the sense of place known heretofore only in a famous painting. The enjoyment of both the place and the painting is enriched. There was also the enjoyment of each other, known to each other before in circumstances other than this gorgeous day. We lolled in the boat in a fantasy, I like a cavalier gentleman and she the object of my adoration. Slowly, gradually, we were drawn together until I could hold her, softly, tenderly, then blissfully, to kiss her lips, aware of her delicacy, and translate the trembling of her mouth to the gentle fluttering of butterfly wings. This deliberate, delicate growth of intimacy added unbelievably to my delight. A pattern of love was slowly unfolding.

We returned to Paris and dined at a small restaurant not far from the Place St. Michel. These were the days when Paris was more than a collection of great restaurants, museums, and the Crazy Horse saloon. It had temporarily invaded our bloodstream. Wandering on the left bank in a long curve homeward to the Ile de la Cité where she lived, we came upon another café-indoor-outdoor-Bastille-Day celebration. It was so full and riotous that we joined it uninvited and in that melee, convinced we would be unnoticed. We were happy in each other's arms dancing, alone together in the multitude. Our very isolation among the many increased the awareness of ourselves. Adam and Eve, the only two of their species in a swarming Eden. Our kissing now held a mixture of restrained longing along with the pervading tenderness. I was blindly happy, but she became uneasy, aware suddenly of having drawn notice. Many of the noisy celebrants, well into drink, made preliminary gestures of cutting in. She was frightened at the prospect. I could give no assurance of holding them off. After all, weren't we cutting in on their party? Common courtesy required a willingness to share.

We escaped unscathed, the longing which hovered at the point of ignition all day had now burst into flame. We walked slowly until we reached the left-hand quay of the Ile de la Cité. She clung to me in reaction to her fright and in response to her own feelings. Great old trees overhung the wall over the Seine. We stopped often to kiss; my hands now roamed over her sweet body as free as twin lovers—they were no longer restrained to hesitant gropings. Then I lost all my self-discipline when I felt her blindly search for me. We both knew we must find a place. We went to hers, mine was a hovel. On the way I suffered all the mastering impatience described by the irrepressible Lady Sarah Churchill, First Duchess of Marlborough, who in her diary telling of her duke's visit home from a long campaign wrote, "My Lord on returning pleasured me thrice without removing his boots."

But I still knew my beloved was a virginal priestess, a sensitive creature easily frightened by a rampaging stud, and I wore no boots. The moment of finding oneself and one's love to be suddenly behind a closed door for the first time is momentous, even disconcerting. You either fly immediately into a blind passion or move tremulously, perhaps awkwardly, toward the moment of oneness. I approached her with tenderness and even then was careful not to scare the frightened colt. I was deep in the fantasy of myself as the all-powerful male, gently bringing the virginal flower to full bloom of delight. I was lost in this role until she evinced signs of wanting an important role for herself. I gave ground, not unwillingly, slowly surrendering my tender male dominance to the exotic arts of Thais and Lola Montez. Then my pleasure almost gave way to chagrin. This was no virginal flower. She was a full-blooded and knowledgeable tigress. Over and above my surprise, like an iron thread running through the golden gossamer web of my delight, was the bewildering question, "Where and how did she learn all this?" I never knew what she thought about, not then or later. But it had been a magical Bastille Day and a night when the sky showed the distant flash of fireworks and the summer air carried the faraway strain of the Marseillaise, the perfect ending for a perfect day.

She went home to America soon after and married. I never saw her again, but she left behind a dim memory of her hauntingly sensitive face and the eternal wondering of what thoughts flashed through her husband's mind on their first night together and what he thought of later.

But this Bastille Day at sea is a far cry from those two days a long time ago. All they share in common is the weather. And on this one I have time and opportunity to remember and enjoy. I don't know what my shipmates are thinking. Some haven't had time to gather many memories. In any case, despite the garrulousness, these are private areas of thought no one ever exposes. Men, no matter how dedicatedly communal, must still be very private creatures.

We settle for a dinner as a mark of our celebration—no dancing, no *amour,* only a little red wine. And with the understanding that this is an international recognition, I cross the Pyrenees, so to speak, and make a *"Paella Figaro"* out of chicken, crab meat, rice, saffron, etc. It is topped off with a cherry pie. The navigator offers a B&B to the young and we, the elders, settle for Courvoisier brandy, coffee, and Dunhill cigars offered by Symonette.

The night closes out with a late star fix, a latitude of 56° 38′ N and 15° 41′ W. We have 433 miles to Ronaldsay. Our base course to North Rona in the Hebrides is .081°.

19

JULY 15. Once upon a time, I am told, a water dowser doing his stuff over a chart spread out in his New York office, found water in Bermuda! Hosannah! I believe! I believe! Ever since Gutenberg, printed paper has been putting out spells. We have just been electrified by a change of charts. The boat is charged with expectancy. We have left off navigating on the sparsely detailed North Atlantic Pilot Chart—a great sheet of white paper filled with semi-cabalistic symbols—wind roses, current diagrams, abstractions about the incidence of gales, the vast depths of the ocean floor, and only the barest outlines of the land. The only way one can place himself on that sort of chart is in relation to a set of lines ruled on the paper. They are an intricate abstraction called the coordinates of latitude and longitude, in themselves a clever invention of man having no place in the natural order of things. Now we are using a chart with a stirring title, "The Western Sea Approaches to the British Isles." How's that for something with a ring of history to it? In addition to the title, it shows a well-defined coast line with place names that hang on the edge of your romantic subconscious—the Outer Hebrides, the Butt of Lewis, Uig. Reason can argue that this is still the Atlantic—a mere change of names alters nothing; in sailing off one piece of paper onto another we have not departed. But the waters feel different—these are British waters, Britannia's waves.

We start a new day at 0300 hours by pumping these very waters from our bilges. The leak is slow but persistent, like a postnasal drip. We should be putting ourselves into the mood for a landfall on St. Kilda, but we are too busy with things here. The wind is a volatile strumpet blowing up noisily or becoming apathetic with indifference. Right now it churns the sea and we scramble to shorten sail by putting a reef in the mainsail. The boat rides easier and we settle down on course, hoping to doze while awaiting our turns at the wheel. Then the wind, exhausted or made languid through its own antics, drops out. We shake the reef out of the main, replace the jibtop with the No. 1 Genoa. But there is insufficient wind to hold the boat steady. The heave of the leftover sea sets *Figaro* rolling in an unholy motion. It is enough to take the starch out of heroes.

My view of history and these waters becomes less epic. I can even denigrate heroes. I choose to imagine Sir Francis Drake at such a time in these conditions. He will have taken to his cabin, hung up his sword, replaced his sea boots, doublet, and hose with a long flannel nightgown, and sought solace in his bed. After all, these are liberties which well-established swash-bucklers can indulge in. His reputation is made, he has nothing to lose. It is merely an eccentric indulgence. But my grip on command is less secure. I am burdened by the need to set an example. I must demonstrate an imperviousness to the little agonies, else it is only owning the boat which gives me the right to be captain, a hollow basis. But with the burdens of office goes a certain amount of bolstering privilege. My rank entitles me to a choice of roost from which to exhibit my impassivity (if I can beat someone else to it). I am lucky and get to choose the leeward corner under the dodger. If one hopes to keep his innards quiescent in this, topsides is the place to be, some quiet place to stare out at the horizon and think clean thoughts.

Rockall! At 1000 hours the navigator assures us we are over Rockall; not near it mind you, but over it. We see nothing. It is a secret he shares with the god of navigators. Rockall is a rocky spindle thrusting up from the ocean floor off the west coast of

Scotland. It is not another sunken Atlantis. I never met anyone who has ever seen it, but then my friendship with west coast Scots fishermen is limited. I do, however, know a few yachtsmen who are willing to swear they sailed right over it. I have seen photographs which purport to represent this upthrusting extension of land. It is a lean, jagged spindle, altogether frightening. In any case, with or without a solid mass to organize the composition, this is a bitter stretch of seascape. The weather is fashioned to suit—high winds, jumping seas, and misery.

A slashing rhymester among us (whose handwriting bears an extraordinary resemblance to my own) has set it down in underlined caps on a water spattered page in the log:

ROCKALL,

FUCKALL,

GALE, RAINS, AND SQUALL.

The weather has settled in. If it is to be lousy, it should be consistently lousy. At least we are moving in the right direction.

I spoke too soon. The wind is all over the lot, first up, then down, then nowhere. A pattern like this surely has more to it than simply to act as a goad to our impatience. Something is brewing!

2200 hours, 10 P.M. and twilight is just closing in. We are wallowing in a falling wind and in the falling dark. Northern latitudes make for a long day, especially one such as this. The day coming to an end has been frustrating, the kind that makes men overreach and put their whole stack into the pot for a desperate throw. Monk's safety valve has red-lined; he can't keep his sense of outrage bottled up any longer. He addresses the gods!

Some could call it an incantation, some a challenge thrown in the teeth of the gods. I call it hubris and few men walk away unscathed from its practice. These he so addresses are no clerks or orderlies of a bureaucracy whose teeth have been drawn!

These are no lowly miscreants but the powers themselves. How far can you push them?

I put his words down to the best of my memory. Naturally we made no record what with being aghast at his daring and waiting for the thunderbolt to fall. After all, anything that happens to him, happens to us.

He began calmly enough, walking up to the windward rail with a brandy bottle and a glass in his hands. His voice was gentle, respectful, if somewhat declamatory. The pitch and intensity changed as he became caught up in the rapture of his own speech. The incantation went something like this:

"Oh great gods of the Western Approaches to the British Isles, we on the yawl *Figaro* racing to Sweden salute you. We salute your cousins on Olympus and in the cave of the winds, with special salutations to Poseidon and his brother, Zeus. We hail all demigods, minions, and cohorts, and not to forget all you pretty lady goddesses. If we have forgotten anyone among you, we ask your majesties, in your nobleness, to forgive us. We have had a trying day.

"Oh hear us, you gracious ones, hear your people on *Figaro!* We offer this libation to you [pours three fingers of brandy into the glass and tosses the contents into the sea]. We ask that you look kindly upon us your servants who have been put to sore trial on your heaving bosom. We know that it is the way of Olympians to put to the greatest trial those whom they love best, a kind of chosen people syndrome that you godhead folks swap around. But, as your omnipotences must know, we are in a race and time is running short; it is time for you to make your move.

"We ask that you stop crapping around and provide us and us alone with one of your finest breezes to take us all the way to the finish. We ask this in view of our long and loving acknowledgment of your existence when other people thrash around in Zen Buddhism and other excesses and apostasies of faith. We ask your lordships to show us this kindness and to sow consternation in the vessels of our enemies amongst whom you will find a rare collection of Presbyterians, Christian Scientists, and Golfers. The time, oh great Poseidon, has come to show your hand, to put up or get lost.

"If you do as we ask, oh great earth shaker, we will raise our children to recognize your name, and on coming in victoriously, we will make the proper celebrations. We will pour champagne into you until you are as drunk as we.

"But mind you, our patience wears thin. We are fed up with the way we are being treated. All day we have been putting up with your shit and we are goddamn tired of it. It is now 2200 hours. Now hear this you meatheads. We give you until 2300 hours to come up with a favorable breeze. If you do deliver, we in turn will do what we can to preserve your everlasting glory. But if you don't, we will join in the calumny on your names. You will not only have lost your last dues-paying members, but we will stand in the rigging and piss on your face while calling you has-beens for all the world to hear. Do you hear us, you meatheads? 2300 hours GMT."

A voice in the darkness, more than a little shaken: "Jesus, Monk, don't you think you're putting it a little strong?"

"You've got to be firm with these meatheads or they crap all over you" is all he will say.

I wait for the Thunderbolt, the Tidal Wave, hoping that the gods will recognize this as a sort of misbegotten rapture for which they are in part responsible. The gods do not further harm those whose minds they have robbed; they leave them stricken with glossolalia.

The wind somes in at 2245. It is from the SSW and we make course nicely. Monk winds his watch and goes to sleep. It was all in a day's work. On deck there is still a hangover of unease.

July 16. LAND HO! At 0945 an obscuring squall lifts and we see the first outcroppings of Europe, a sentinel outpost stuck out into the Atlantic. Steve Matson, our own private eagle-eye, wins the standing prize of two pieces of eight or a peanut butter sandwich by espying two islands, two points on the starboard bow. Monk announces them as the outermost of the Outer Hebrides, St. Kilda and Boreray. We presume he is right. Congratulations are in order. We congratulate Steve; he can hardly unstick his tongue from his peanut-butter-strewn palate to reply. We congratulate our chief blind mouse. He found his way to here and is properly modest. We congratulate the gallant captain. We made it with no one drowning or dying of thirst. He is more grateful than the rest and proposes a drink at an ungodly hour what with matins scarcely gone.

The toast downed, Knud disappears below, roots around in his locker and returns to the deck wearing a tam-'o-shanter. The color is an assault to the senses. He has prepared well for this trip. He sings one of Burns' Highland songs in lilting Scandinavian English. Monk and I join him. The air is figuratively redolent with heather and kippered herring.

It is just as well we had our toast early; it promises to be a rouser of a day. At 0200, when all sensible folk are asleep, the wind decided to move into a new quarter, from the SSW to the SSE and increased. Down came the tender-seamed bluetop and in its place the unshapely Raymond tied to us with a heavy spinnaker sheet. Whitecaps grew larger. Before dawn the spinnaker came down and the Genoa took over the foredeck.

At 0700 a cheerful and matter-of-fact voice over BBC forecast SE winds, strong, possibly increasing by evening to gale, for the region of the Hebrides and West Scotland. It is our Saturday special. The cheerful attitude of BBC, spelling out gloom and doom, once left a resounding mark on me I will never forget. During a Fastnet Race which began in awful conditions and got steadily worse, the BBC weathercaster, giving the last shipping forecast of the night, outdid himself. He was probably comforting himself by an electric fire while he promised us winds of 60 miles an hour from ahead and then, finally conscious of us—the sailing idiots, abroad on this indecent night—closed his accounting of horrors-to-come with, "Good sailing, chaps."

Our sharply falling barometer confirms the forecast, heavy weather nearby and rapidly approaching. We wonder again at Monk's address and special request. Are they mad at us, affronted by hubris? Is this only for us? How wide is the circle?

At 1400 hours we get a fix which puts us at 58°33′ N, 08°33′ W—miles sailed to date 2,775.5—miles to Ronaldsay, 201—base course to Sule Skerry now is 085°—138 miles away. The Northmen voyagers left their appellation Skerry or Sgier all along the northern water track. There are Skerries in the Baltic outside of Stockholm and here in the storm-churned waters north of Scotland.

The weather is deteriorating. If that implies it was good, now getting bad, I should clear the misconception. It was lousy. It is getting lousier. We wait to see it at its lousiest. The wind attacks in the manner of outriding skirmishers expectant of large reinforcement. It blows with a slapdash urgency, snatching at anything it can steal or destroy. Cascades of water are thrown over the foredeck, shooting up spray which whips aft, stinging the hands and faces of those who unhappily must face it. Solid pellets of water hit one's oilskins like the sound of gravel thrown up by a spinning auto tire.

Steve and Cleody are struggling at the stemhead. They are trying to unhank the No. 1 jib top, which, for reasons that will never become clear, was left on the stay and lashed to the rail at the time of setting the No. 2 jib top. Perhaps there was the forlorn hope that this sudden blowup would soon pass through and we could reset it, but that is not how it turned out. Instead the wind-driven water kept working on the sail ties until the bunt of the sail came loose and began to wash up and down in the waterway and shake in the wind. Where it would have been easy to take it off before, now it is a tough job.

Cleody is squatting in the bow working on the hanks. He squats to keep from going overboard. The water breaking over the bow breaks over him as well. From time to time he grabs at the stay to keep from being washed or tossed aft. Steve is kneeling, holding onto anything, especially the sail which he recovers yard by yard as Cleody unfastens the hanks. Steve must also keep the body of the sail from going into the drink where it will tear itself as the rush of water pulls at it. It is slow work. The barrels of the pistol hanks are salt-encrusted and open with difficulty. Cleody's fingers are tender from constant soaking and he must stop from time to time to wipe salt from his eyes. The job finally is done. The sail, heavy with salt water, is stowed and they come aft for a rest, whereupon we decide to put a second reef into the main.

Bruce and Bucky are relentlessly torn from their bunks like babes from their mother's wombs, but their howls are short-lived. There is work to do as soon as they can dress and get into their oilskins. Their cries may be silenced but not their conversation, which, as they get into their gear, largely concerns the inabilities of the watch on deck to do anything for themselves except steal sacktime.

While easing down the main in order to put in the second reef, we find the three top slides near the head have come adrift. I suppose in one way we are lucky that we discovered it now while it is still light. In a short while it will be dark and the condition might have gone unnoticed. If we had not discovered it, the wind could work on the remaining slides until it ripped them off with a swoosh like an impatient *amoureux* tearing off a set of fly buttons or lighting off a string of firecrackers. (One can dream perhaps even at the gates of hell.)

As we are taking it down, the main hangs upon the mast. We cannot move it without danger of inflicting damage. Bucky gets into the bosun chair and goes aloft on a spinnaker halyard. We keep a down-haul line fairly taut, but he takes bumps all the way up. Once level with the point of hangup he finds that the track is working loose from the mast at a butt joint in its fastening. He steers the main slides past this point and we get it down. Knud, now awakened or at least out of bed, and Bucky start working on it immediately. Screwdrivers and screws are sent aloft in a bucket and Bucky repairs the track. It is mean work. He takes a buffeting when he must use both hands for the work; it is bad enough when you can hold on. He must use his feet to fend off. But the work gets done; good man, that Bucky. He doesn't feel at his best on his return to deck, but a little spell of sitting and gasping puts him right again. He is able to join in raising the main which by the way went up with a single reef. By the time it was ready to go we felt that one reef was all we needed.

The whole operation took twenty-six minutes. We did not seem to lose much speed while the main was down.

By midnight the barometer stopped going down. Has it bottomed out? Is this the center of the low? It would seem so, for suddenly there is no wind—none at all! That's the way the wind behaves in the eye of a low! I can't believe this is all there is to it. I suspect that it is a cell within a larger system. OR! Is this something that Monk's audience has sent our way? Have they chosen us as their patsies, a new group of Flying Dutch-men doomed to sail eternally in a circle of stinking weather some few miles wide? The mere suggestion of the thought is unsettling, and, for that matter, what is happening to the old fox, Dick Nye, in all this. He is my most special competition. Is he getting a free ride somewhere?

Thus endeth the day of our landfall. No banners, no bugles, not even a fair sight of the land. Just crap, from the skies, the waves, and overwrought imaginations. Not that we believe any of the things we talk about or think of, but then—how can you be sure?

20

DIES Irae! Perhaps too grim a label even for this grim Sunday, July 17. But then, Scotland, among less terrifying capes and heads, includes a Cape Wrath on its North Coast and this vexed mass seems to be spreading its influence to the whole coastal area, the off-lying islands, and the gray seas that break against its cliffs. From this you will infer that the weather is miserable and you will be right. This Sunday is clearly not to be our day of rest. The Lord Jehovah set a reasonable pattern when, after looking about him on the sixth day and finding it good, He rested on the seventh. The trade unions since have improved on the Lord's planned week. But we are too long out of Eden, out of reach of the benign influence of the American Federation of Labor and Congress of Industrial Organizations, and our little boat has a long way to go before we can sleep.

I suppose that one should expect rugged weather in these parts and shrug it off. If you look at the track charts of the weather systems which, originating in the northwestern regions of the North American continent, travel down across Canada and the United States and then wander eastward across the Atlantic, you will see that most of the tracks eventually pass through this region. The same holds true for the dreaded hurricanes that originate in the Caribbean and tear up the coast of the United States before starting across. And the cyclonic weather that comes out of Iceland pretty regularly crosses here as well. All of these, I presume, are pushed up to these regions by the northern edges of the Bermuda and Azores highs. It all sounds routine, if unreasonable, but we are fed up with it. Our atavistic yearnings, traced in evolutionary descent, put us closer to the ape in the sun-warmed treetops than to the penguin or polar bear on an ice floe. But the show must go on and so must we.

As close after midnight as it possibly could, the wind returned. It was a signal for the day ahead. The idea that we had been sought out for destruction by a local cell is verified. That smaller conniption is wandering ahead of the main body. What is happening is still somewhere behind us. We are on the wind and in a mean sea. We go through a series of sail area reductions, milking each range of wind speeds for the most we can get out of them. Again I am reminded that if we were cruising we would have said "To hell with it" and dropped to what we presumed would be our ultimate reduction. But in racing you give ground (or sail) reluctantly. By 0300 we are down to the No. 2 jib top over a working staysail. We have tucked a reef in the mizzen.

It has been an up-and-down night. Not only has *Figaro* been climbing one watery hill after another only to climb down the other side, but we have gone from berth to deck regularly for sail changes. One such climactic clamber came at Steve Matson's excited call, "What the hell, there's an island on the wrong side." This certainly is not in the same league of calls as "0130 and all's well" or "good night, sweet Prince." It requires urgent response.

He knew the side was wrong because Monk had penciled a course, when the wind was free, which would lay us abeam of North Ronaldsay, having cleared all rocky obstructions along the way. Now we had an island where no island ought to be.

Monk had charged out on deck, lightly clad, as is usual when he is in a hurry. In fact he was in his sleeping costume, skivvies—a shining white Siegfried among the Nibelungen in that black night. We are all somewhat disturbed. Navigation at sea is such a nebulous assurance for everyone but the navigator. Out on the open sea you take his word for it. What the hell! What have you got to lose? There's nothing out there to hit. If he puts you ahead by 10 miles on Monday, he will take it all back by Wednesday. But on a rock-strewn coast! We impatiently wait for his pronouncement. Nothing will hurry him. We wait for the shock of impact, the grinding sound of the keel against rocks, of splintered planking, of the mast going over the side. He gives it his earnest and naked attention. After profound study of the island, our log and chart, he just as profoundly announced it as *Sula Sgier* and then asked what the hell we were doing there.

The watch captain in a time-honored ploy replied with another question, "What does that mean to our course—what do we do now?"

Monk, refusing to be put aside once he has an armlock on a piece of one-up, says, "It just means that you meatheads can't steer a course." Then turning to me, he says conversationally, "If you don't mind, Capting, I will slip below and put on a few clothes. It's a mount cool up here."

"But what do we do now?" the watch captain persisted in a tone that clearly indicated what he thought of navigators who take a vessel in among the rocks.

"Do? Why carry on—there's no sweat."

He turns and goes below and we marvel once again at his general feistyness and private central heating system. To paraphrase Oliver Goldsmith, "and still they gaz'd, and still the wonder grew, that one small frame could keep from turning blue."

What happened was absurdly clear. As the wind headed, and in that sea it became increasingly difficult to hold her on course without going dead on the wind, *Figaro* had to be given her head and let drive, else we would have been on course but going absolutely nowhere. We may now have a problem clearing North Rona.

At about 0330 hours North Rona begins to come clear. Soon it can be plainly seen, a hulking black mass, defined in an equally black sea by the almost luminescent white smothers of waves, like boiling shaving cream, that break high against its bold and pitiless cliffs. Each smash sends solid sheets of spray even higher into the air. A few lights glitter on top, feral eyes waiting to see if we make it.

It is questionable whether we can clear the eastern edge of the rocks on the starboard tack. Knud is at the wheel steering with a fine concentration. He speaks to me softly so no one else will hear. "Skipper, we ought to consider tacking."

I am reluctant to do so. "Stick with this tack as long as we can, Knud," I say, "we may get a lift to help us past." We've still to get over North Ronaldsay. Once past North Rona, we can let up. Any southing I make now will be thrown-away distance if we get a lift. I would like to hold until the last possible moment. We are very close to course now.

"I don't like the look of the water between here and the island. There may be rocks just below the surface," he says.

I am now caught up in the spell of my own bravado. I tell him, "In this state of sea we would see any rock that could trouble us. The seas would be breaking white over them."

"Maybe you are right," says he, going back to his fine job of steering. But not for long. Soon he looks at me again and, this time speaking more firmly but still kindly, he says, "Skipper, I don't like this, I have an uneasy feeling. I will go with you anywhere you take me. I will not take you where I do not want to go. Would you please steer."

"Come on, Knud," I am trying to cajole him into staying on as helmsman, not that I mind steering, but in this instance I am as worried as he is and would rather indulge my worries ad libitum than share them with the concentration of steering. "Come on, we may get a lift at any moment."

"The tendence," he replies, "is just the other way."

There is nothing left for me to do but steer.

He is right. When the wind puffs harder it comes from

farther ahead. I hold on as long as I dare. Tonight, for this sinner, there is no lift. We go over on the other tack. The ocean is mean as we go over and smacks us with a big one to show us it is still looking. I kept watching for an easy sea on which to make our flop, but at the last moment it turned ornery. This and the clatter and shaking of the sails and their hardware as we passed through the eye of the wind—a clatter which shook the whole boat and seemed to threaten our continued existence—made it a memorable tack. Once settled on the port tack I turn to Knud and say, "I surrender!" Then I hand over the wheel and go to the corner under the dodger to brood over my hurts.

"My God!" I suddenly think. "Do you suppose that Dick Nye went by Rona without requiring a tack. That's generally his way, the— " It is a black and miserable night, a breeding place for miserable thoughts.

We had no way of knowing, but we had been living on easy street until now. We thought things had been bad, but in reality all of that running and reaching, with just a modicum of sailing on the wind, had softened us up. Now we were on the wind for fair, 30 to 35 knots of it, a sea to match and we were not liking it at all. Even *Figaro* is complaining. When falling off the top of a big one into the hole behind she sends out alarming creaks. Life has suddenly turned grim. There's no longer any thought of special meals or happenings. Just getting through the day seems job enough. Simply putting on or taking off clothes becomes a long-drawn-out agony. Pulling on boots and oilskins in a leaping canted cabin is more exhausting than changing sails. Our cabin is no longer a haven. Comfort and discomfort are relative. Knud, for instance, finds that underwear he rejected one and one half weeks ago as too "damp" is now delightfully "dry" by comparison with what he is wearing.

In the faint light of predawn we see a rare sight, a touch of Moby Dick in the night. A large sea animal jumps clear of the water. It is positively not the Loch Ness Monster strayed, but a *killer whale,* so identified by those on board who claim to know such things. It is a very great fish (or mammal?) to leap so high. One is set to musing. What larger, more terrifying monster could have been chasing him? Perhaps this was some wild courtship dance in which he displayed his might to a coy and delicate female below. Indeed, this may have been a coy and delicate female (I never noticed) playing "catch me if you can" with a still larger and ardent male, lunging at her from behind his rock office below. Or simply a big fish filled with good spirits and goatish glee, kicking up his heels on a day that suits him to a tee. It sets one to wondering. Rare and separate indeed are the creatures that inhabit this earth.

As the day gets along things go a little better. The glass seems to have bottomed out and the sun gives every evidence of trying for a breakthrough. Our noon position by Dead Reckoning puts North Ronaldsay 62 miles away. Distance sailed to-date 2,917.5. We are at 59°27′ N, not far away, over the northern horizon, is the Arctic Circle, a chilling thought.

The wind is whipping in at a cold 35 knots. The waves are just beginning to throw their tops. We sit in the cockpit and talk of other ships and other long splices. For a while all of our attention and invention is spent on comparison of techniques for performing natural functions in the head in a jumping sea. A valuable seminar is run, during which time the individual ways to contend at differing angles of heel on port and starboard tacks are exchanged. But after a while this subject loses its general fascination.

We fall back into individual silences. The brooding atmosphere that hangs in the air settles around the boat once more. It is as though the whole region consisted of a special brew held in an invisible retort, leeching out an ancient bitterness. Our hopes for improving weather are dashed. *The glass is falling again.*

These are embattled waters. Men have been struggling with the elements and one another here for millennia. But unlike the sunny littoral bordering the Mediterranean, rich in antiquity and archaeological ruins, there is a scant recorded history to set down, the comings and goings of the many peoples who have traversed these troubled regions. The same waters quickly close over our keel track, leaving no trace, exactly as it has done for ages. But recorded or not, these waters were traveled, the rocky islands settled by a succeeding and ever-changing line of sea adventurers. Signs crop up from time to time to show that some Neolithic Kilroy was here.

These islands and reefs, threatening to pick our bones white, have caught and held or destroyed other and earlier voyagers. In some dark prehistory non-fur-bearing animals who proved to be somewhat like ourselves must have crossed the ocean from west to east exactly as we are doing now. But with what a difference. Borne on the prevailing westerlies, caught up in currents. Slim evidence indicates that ancient Eskimos came in skin boats and archaic Indians in bark canoes. As late as the sixteenth and early seventeenth centuries such large boats were still seen by mariners fishing between Newfoundland and Greenland.

We sail by these islands thinking them harsh and forbidding, but early men had an urgency to explore and settle, even here. The Neolithic wanderers, the voyagers from the east, found their way into these islands. They could not benefit from the westerlies but had other advantages, a stepping-stone series of islands stretching from the northern forests of Europe through the Shetlands, Faeroes, and Orkneys and reaching west to Iceland, Greenland, and Vinland.

These very islands were settled by seagoing races, so dim in antiquity that they were gone before the civilizations as we know them were formed in the Mediterranean. The men who took their places were intrepid voyagers in their own right. Celts from Ireland, Picts from Scotland. Of these, too, only fragments of history remain.

We sail with carefully constructed charts, but the infant science of geography took first notice of these islands starting in about the fourth century A.D. when Pytheas, a Greek mathematician, astronomer, and geographer, set out from Massilia (Marseilles), sailed out through the Pillars of Hercules (Gibraltar), and, turning north, found his way to a Scottish port. There he learned of islands to the north and west. He ventured on, a great act of courage in itself, and found a great mysterious land. He named it Thule (Iceland). It had already been given a name by the voyagers of the northern waters, but their name for the island is lost in time.

During the fifth to seventh centuries, these seemingly forbidding waters, sewn with dragons' teeth reefs, racing tidal currents, and vexed by gales, became a busy commercial waterway. A bustling Celtic and Pictic maritime industry traded with northern Europe far into the Baltic. These were the Phoenicians of the north, trading but making no large settlements.

All this came to a halt in the seventh century when the Northmen, spurred on by troubles in their own lands, began the scourge of Europe. These were the terrible Vikings, incredible voyagers and cruel fighters. It is the shadow of their one-time presence which we on *Figaro* feel most. By the ninth century the Viking terror lay over most of the European littoral. Their terror reached around as far as Sicily. The auburn hair and pale eyes of some northern Spanish beauties are a result of their genes. These men, curiously, were settlers as well. Many of their raids originated from these very islands along which we sail. No one knows what happened to the earlier inhabitants.

Something of this dark and troubled aura transmits itself to us as the afternoon wears on. We cannot put a name to the sensation, but the feeling of foreboding is just as real as if we could identify it. I decide that we are approaching a nadir of morale, a bad time so near the finish. Hoping to break the spell, I say, "What the hell, we may as well go for broke as the way we are. Let's sail for *total discomfort;* let's take out the reef and up the jib by one. The wind is getting lighter." With work to do and the reminder that we are still racing, the atmosphere lightens somewhat.

And then the sort of accident upon which no one can count puts our morale safely over the top. We have been followed continuously by two birds across the Atlantic. They are either the same or the relays have been subtly changed. Now one of them, after considerable time and study, is choosing his man and, his alimentary canal being richly stuffed with our biodegradable offerings, lets go a rich cargo of guano all over Steve Matson, the target for today. He, the chosen one, is suitably indignant, but his shock and chagrin just makes us laugh the more. Perhaps the rude, unsympathetic humor of the Vikings is infectious even after being long dormant. Perhaps it is the normal and not so lovable qualities within us that make us respond to Steve's plight in this way. Laughter, we are told, often rises from the demeaning of one's fellowman, hence the clowns, dwarfs, and pratfalls.

By and large we are decent men, yet here our hearts are lightened by a simple indignity visited upon one of our fellows. Is this the way the great planner wanted it to be? Dr. Freud, where are you?

Night closes around us, holding its terrors in abeyance. We are governed by only one thought, "Let's get on with it." But that thought is on the back burner of the mind. Right now we want nothing so much as sleep. It is not easy to come by. We are hard on the wind which blows in and out and we respond to it like automatons, changing sails to suit. We tack every two hours to take the Orkneys close abeam.

At 2230 we pass Brough Head. It looms 120 feet high at the head of the Brough of Birsey. It is our first landmark in the Orkneys on an island with the curious name of Mainland. We tack offshore once more. One way or another we will crawl or crash our way around these blasted islands.

21

MONK wakes me at 0130 hours, seemingly my first deep sleep in days. I come out complaining bitterly at being disturbed, muttering, "What's wrong now?" He cheerfully assures me nothing's amiss. I assure him that waking me is amiss enough, but he pays no attention. "Capting," he says, "you've got to come on deck and see this. It's a rare sight, right out of Sir Walter Scott. It's magnificent."

"I hae me doots," I think but pull on some clothes and make my way up the companionway. The deck watch looks the way I feel, huddled like mourners at an Eskimo wake. They sit in a driving mist looking worn and forlorn, wishing they were any place but on this deck, just so long as it is dry and warm. But impervious to it all, there stands a great black presence. High up, towering 260 feet in the air is a brilliant, unblinking white light, brilliant and aglow as an ingot of molten iron held in a crane's tongs in the dark fastness of a foundry. It sits on top of the sheer black bulk of Noup Head. We seem close enough to ram it although I am assured it is three-quarters of a mile off. This is my first close encounter with the Highlands of Scotland in its most northerly thrust into the sea. It is more an impression than a full view. Its bulk is almost absorbed into the night. Only the light at the top defines its dimension, but actually seen or its outline suggested, it is an inspiring sight. Monk's romantic comparison is more Robert Louis Stevenson than Sir

Walter Scott, or better yet more Richard Wagner than either. This is a perch from which Valkyries hurl themselves into a battle to pick up the bodies and souls of fallen warriors.

The mist is thick and, against the halo of the light, is seen as myriads of independent droplets. The size, weight, scale of that silent black mass seen against the misty foreground intensifies the brooding quality of the region. It symbolizes everything that lies behind it, the wild Highland landscape, no tame thing to be pulled about and arranged on a piece of canvas to suit the academic rules of composition, triangulation, and perspective. Even though it is all blacked out, I can, in my mind's eye, see the craggy landscape over which Rob Roy, Alan Breck, and David Balfour wandered.

I thank Monk for waking me and tell him I would not have missed this glimpse of Scotland for worlds. Snuggling in the blanket, however, I find myself being lulled to sleep by romantic visions much softer and more inviting than the craggy landscapes to the south and involved in adventures far more enticing than the lost cause of Bonnie Prince Charlie.

At 0400 we encounter a heavy sea from ahead. All the signs are that of a strong tide bucking into a head wind. We must have a strong current running under us, favorable for the moment, it would seem. We dig out the current charts for the waters around the British Isles, a most complicated set of arrows and annotations. *But, for Christ's Sake, there is no Reed's or Brown's Almanac!!!* The charts are an exercise in futility. They all refer to the time of High Water at Dover. That is the magical datum. *And the daily tables for the times of High Water at Dover are in the Almanacs!!!* We have been given the coded message holding one of the treasured secrets of the universe, but they have forgotten to tell us where to find the code books. An impotent and scary examination of the charts shows that the current in these regions gets up to 5 knots and, on the easterly side of some of these islands, can run northward for as many as nine hours continuously. How's that for little green apples!

There is not a Goddamned thing to do about it. We can't call Mike Richey at the Royal Society of Navigation. He is on board *Anitra*. The low surface visibility cuts out a chance for local observation and interpretation. Those not personally involved in the oversight can stand on their silent high and mighty. The ranks of the Just are full and strong. But for Monk and myself, neither the earth, sky, or sea provides a hiding place. We are the horses' asses for all to see, to take measure and make note of, he for making the omission and I for not checking it. To give our shipmates their due—the problem once announced and commented upon is not dwelt upon. After all, what end would that serve? It is our first telling failure directly attributable to carelessness and bad preparation. What a time for it to emerge. Up until now all setbacks have been accidents, and we met them to the best of our abilities and preparedness. But there is no excuse for this. We will be lucky to come out of it alive and well, much less as winners.

And then to hammer the point home, the gods of this region (obviously more exercised over Monk's cavalier remarks than we first thought likely) reverse the switch, the wind maker dies down and the fog machine starts making haze at full speed.

Just before the fog closes down the navigation department, Monk constructs an estimated position based on our D.R. and a single sun-line taken with a very wan sun and a feathery horizon. This bit of hocus-pocus he claims puts us at L 59°27′5 N and 2° 120′ W. We choose 119° as a base course into the North Sea. The wind is dropping more and more. All reefs have been taken out of the main, and with the No. 1 Genoa we are moving forward at slightly over 5 knots.

In the middle of a thick gray morning we sail into a disturbed sea. The surface is covered with strange, agitated waves, triangular eruptions roughly one foot to eighteen inches in height. These rear up vertically as though stirred by a great machine. Occasional flat areas show as spreading swirls, the kind created by the upwelling of subsurface currents. It is an ugly surface made more so by the fact that we cannot see for any distance, only that area immediately near the boat. When we encounter one of the swirls, we come on it suddenly and are in it at the same moment. You can feel it in the boat. It is then that impossible ideas like a descent into the maelstrom become an almost reality. There is nothing more horrifying than to come onto an area of disturbed water in an otherwise normal sea, especially when you cannot see for any distance than that immediately around you. Monsters! Maelstroms! And malevolence!

The air is filled with a strange chuckling sound. It issues out of the waves. I have seen and heard such a phenomenon before. The race at the end of Long Island Sound at maximum current and the inshore end of Portland Bill look something like this and give off somewhat the same sound. Here it seems louder and stronger and we don't know where we are. I have always heard that sound from the sea in onomatopoeia saying, "Gonna getcha, gonna getcha." I don't like it. No one is going to get me! I may not know where we are, but I know one thing: *We are sure as hell in a tidal raceway going to beat all hell one way or another. And toward what?*

I plunge below to look at the chart and search the area close to our last penciled estimated position. Glaring at me from the chart is a dreadful kind of name. Along with the sight and sounds above, this seems to be the most likely place. Small wavy lines printed on the chart indicate stronger than normal currents. This must be it! *The Bore at Mull Head. What the hell is a Bore?* It must be the ultimate maelstrom—the one that eats ships with the casual ease of swallowing tea biscuits. It is not as though we were casually standing off at a safe distance looking at the chart and one of nature's curious phenomena like a bunch of bloody tourists. We are in it! In this place seemingly right out of Edgar Allan Poe, a writhing horror is waiting to engulf us or dash us against the black cliffs.

I shout up, "For Christ's sake, let's get the hell out of here. Take her on the offshore tack."

We hold our breaths. *Figaro* tacks sluggishly in that agitated sea and strangely lethargic wind. The swirls almost stop her going through the eye of the wind. Then she slowly gathers headway. It is a long time before we breathe easily. The surface of the sea has gone back to a normally bad pattern. Not seeing probably made it bad. *But for Christ's sake! Who thought up that name? The Bore!*

We stay in the bumps for what seems ages but finally sail into slightly smoother water. There still is a rolling head sea, indicating a strong tide, and the wind continues to drop. We are in Long Island Sound racing conditions or—*Horrors!*—is this to be a repeat of the Bay of Biscay. In 1957 we sailed like hell for weeks only to enter the limits of that normally uproarious body of water and found ourselves in a one-and-one-half-day calm, sat helplessly, and watched Blunt White in *White Mist* sail up to us. Dick Nye, it turned out, sailed into Santander, the finish. Calms never seem to catch him, at least when I am racing against him.

Dick Nye—he is beginning to oppress my waking thoughts. He is my special friend and *bête noire* at sea. We have been racing against each other for years and have been placing a bet on each race. Dick is one of the half-horse, half-alligator breed that opens frontiers, builds empires, and wins races. His collection of silver is such that the open silver market and the U.S. Mint keep careful tabs on his movements and intentions. He is the only man I know who, on taking a new boat out on its builder's trials, accidentally got mixed up with a number of boats straining to get somewhere. When Dick finished the trials for the day and came back to his dock deep in discussion with the builder, he found an awards committee waiting for him, to give him a splendid new cup. He had won a race that very afternoon.

Dick and I have a bet on this race. It is a multiple bet, a sort of daily double. It started with a $50 bet each on the Bermuda Race and on this the Transatlantic. Neither of us won the race to Bermuda, but I beat him, which provided some solace. Seeing him on the Royal Bermuda Yacht Club lawn the afternoon of our finish, I approached him, drink in hand, feeling no pain and asked if by some chance he happened to have my fifty bucks. He shifted his drink to the other hand, made some vague passes in the air with his cigar, and suggested that the whole idea of payment was ridiculous, a temporary exchange, since he was bound to win the Transatlantic. "Why don't we just let it stand and the winner of the T.A. will get double or nothing." I was enough sheets over to agree to anything and we went on to other things.

The next day he, equipped with a fresh drink and cigar, allowed as how we were letting our commercial instincts destroy something that was essentially a gentleman's sport. I agreed that such was the case, but nevertheless the fact remained that I had won fifty bucks. He reached into his pocket, produced a $50 bill, gave it to me, and said, "We are square now. What say the losing skipper buys a dinner in Marstrand for both crews and their wives and friends." I agreed, always one to sustain the gentlemanly over the crassly commercial and material. And so, here we are, seemingly being diddled by the fates, and Dick's crews are known for their gregarious instincts—their friends and appetites are legion.

At noon by D.R. we establish our position at L 59°30′ N– LAT. 1°53′ W. Our day's run after so many splendid days is only 78 miles. Is that horrible Spanish pattern about to repeat? Go like hell for most of the way and then get screwed at the finish? Is this lack of air being served out to us alone or is it a general pattern? Someone on board may not be living right. Our miles-sailed-to-date (along the course, not through the water) is 2,995.5 miles. Through the water we can challenge the Flying Dutchman for miles sailed.

We have entertainment on BBC to lighten the day. Shortly after noon, over the home service, we hear a fond and loving portrait of Postgate, the Latinist, by Raymond, his son. It is a rare man indeed to deserve such a loving son. We hear a superb picture of a Victorian gentleman and scholar. At times I am overwhelmed by an Englishman's use of his own language. It is prose poetry in the bardic tradition. This is such an occasion.

1300. We now are sure of where we are—*a fix!* L59° 31′ N–LAT. 1° 52′ W. We are heading into the North Sea on a base course of 120°.

As a welcoming committee when we sail into the new body of water, porpoises greet us, coming close aboard on both sides of the bow. Paired comets, they leave white trails in the gray-green water as they race alongside. At home, every time we see a porpoise we say it is a sign of easterly weather. But, with the coming of these visitors, the wind swings behind. We put up our painfully stitched together blue-top spinnaker and it promptly comes apart. It comes down and in its place the shapeless Raymond goes up. The sewing of the blue-top begins again. We are a bunch of sad-sack Penelopes putting in the stitches, but the gods take them out. Someone or something is working hard to keep us out of the marital bed with the goddess Victory. The idea of being one of Victory's suitors is enough to warm a man on the northern sea reaches.

We never see North Ronaldsay. After we had looked at the name for so long on the chart, the place had taken on an importance out of context with its size—it had become a station on our way up our watery Calvary, a marker on our road to Mecca. And now we don't see it at all. The passing is flatulent; there is no joy in Mudville; we even suspect our passing at all. Men need signs and symbols; abstract acknowledgments are not enough. At 1645 hours the navigation department issues a new bulletin. We are at L59° 27′N–LAT. 1° 27′W. We have sailed more than 3,000 miles from Bermuda—3,010 miles to be exact. We are sailing a required course of 120°.

The wind plays games. We finish stitching the stitching on the blue-top and put it up in place of the Raymond, but the wind pipes up and we dare not carry it. Back goes the Raymond. Soon the wind is too much for the Raymond. So down that comes and the White bulletproof goes up in its place. We no longer think about such changes anymore. We just make them; Pavlov has won.

At 2230 hours the wind goes light again. Too much we think for fragile blue-top which had found its way up again, so we finish the day with the Raymond.

Tuesday, July 19.

Nothing extraordinary takes place during the dark of this new day except that the wind pipes up and comes slightly ahead. We go back to the White chute. In taking down the Raymond, we discover a tear on a seam. It is *Figaro*'s luck! Bad in the sense of tearing, good in that it is an early discovery before real harm could set in. Steve starts sewing before major damage is incurred.

Our young are aging too fast on this journey. Crossing the ocean is like opening a bottle of wine and letting it stand before drinking. It matures and comes into its own rapidly in the last hours. At 0240 Monk is steering and asks Cleody to trim the spinnaker pole. Cleody's comment, "Tell me when you go through the course again." He is logged for impertinence and fined one day's pay. You don't crap around with senior officers. A whole boat's discipline is at stake!

Sail Ho! At dawn light, we see and are overtaking a dark-hulled, masthead yawl—who? Conjecture runs wild, *Germania?* She should be in by now. *Hamburg?* Could be. *Anitra?* Could be. Deductive and inductive reasonings are publicly vented and weighed.

Evidences

1. Men are seen, presumably pissing to windward! German.
2. A green beer bottle is passed—Carlsberg?—St. Pauli Girl?
3. Carrying a mizzen staysail on the wind—German.
4. Seems strapped in carrying heavy canvas—German.
5. We are not in a position to judge the reason for a stain on mainsail or color of schmutz on deck. The idea persists that this is *Hamburg*—larger than us, naturally.

As the morning deepens the wind comes ahead and goes light. We take down our No. 1 Genoa and put up a big light reacher. We gain 0.3 knots.

246

1200 hours. Radio Fix L 58°22′N—LAT. 2°36′E. Day's run, 157 miles. Miles to finish 2170. Miles-to-date, 3,150.

1200 hours. (*Hamburg?—Anitra?*) bears 60°.

1300 hours. (*Hamburg?—Anitra?*) bears 52°.

1400 hours. (*Anitra?—Hamburg?*) bears 47°.

It is *Anitra!* An almost sister hull! She gives us time!

1500 hours. We have Stavanger clear on consol—34 dots.

1600 hours. *Anitra* bears 42°. We are eating her up. She takes a long gamble and makes her course to cut close to the south coast of Norway. That is the shortest course, a straight shot at Skagen lightship, our finish. But the south coast of Norway is normally a light air zone and has a west flowing current. We refuse to be sucked into the gamble. We hold off to make an intercept of the coast off Jutland in Denmark. We hope the winds are better there, and we should find an east flowing current.

1800 Stavanger consol—45 dashes.

2000 hours—Stavanger consol—44 dots. DR L 57°58′ N–LAT. 3°56′E.

Base course to point off Hanstholm 110°.

We feel all charged up; the finish is just 176 miles away. We have come 3,237 miles and *Figaro* is at speed—never dropping below 8 knots, going as high as 8.5.

Figaro smells water—the proper bit of it at last.

22

THE early morning hours of Wednesday, July 20, are spent raising and lowering the White bulletproof and the No. 1 Genoa, one or the other as the wind stunts about. We are in the Skagerrak, a fairway from Ore Sound and the Baltic into the North Sea and the Atlantic. We see the lights of steamers to port and starboard.

As a relief from sewing spinnakers, we now are sewing the No. 1 Genoa. It is all because of a stupid accident. Because of chafe to sheets when on a long board, it is our practice to shift to the handy billy to hold the Genoa firm once the sail has been sheeted to its proper trim (now I use wire sheets). While we were making the shift this time, the open hook of the handy billy snagged the tabling of the Genoa leech, and the strain tore it up for several feet with the quickness of a stripper's zipper. Now we are putting the tabling together again. There is no rest for *Figaro*'s sewing circle.

We really are going now. *Figaro* acts like a cavalry mount in the charge of the light brigade. She is caught up in the final charge. So are we all. The speedo hangs around 8.8 knots, but when it drops for a half hour's period to 8.3 knots, the helmsman who must make the entry feels and acts like a traitor to the general weal. We now expect to do over 8.5. What a difference from a few days ago when anything over 5.5 knots was treated with loud cries of excitement.

At 0800 Steve Matson, beloved by birds and gifted with the eyesight of their king, sees Norway on our port beam.

Now that we are nearing the finish, our curiosity gets the best of us. The die is cast, we may as well know the worst. We turn on the radio to hear what we can. Who is doing what to whom, who finished, and when? We first turn on the telephone receiver to the talk between ships. Lo and behold there they are, just where we left them days ago—*Palawan* and *Constellation* are still at it. They have had a long-distance visit all the way across. That's interesting enough. BUT most astoundingly it turns out *THEY ARE ALL BEHIND US, THE WHOLE BLOOMING LOT, EVERYONE WITH WHOM WE KEPT COMPANY FOR DAYS!*

A shot of electricity goes through us. If we were carrying a high charge before, we must now run the danger of having a high arc jump from backside to backside. We diddle with the sails to see if we can squeeze another ounce of speed from them. *Figaro* hears the news and, for one hour, does over 9 knots.

We feel that lunch cannot be treated as an ordinary affair. The signs and portents gather. It may be farfetched, but even hearing the Sailor's Dance from the ballet, the "Red Poppy," we take as being meant for us. The gay music is a fitting accompaniment for our rising spirits. I give a demonstration of a Cossack dance while sitting in the cockpit, after which I call for a drink before lunch, after which Knud cooks something vaguely Swedish but of the first taste. We settle down to grind out the remaining miles.

At 1830 Knud turns on a news program from Stockholm. Suddenly he freezes to attention and then says, "Yeesus!" Something wonderful or something terrible has happened. We try to read his face to interpret what he is hearing. It is good. His is not the mask of tragedy. The corners of his mouth point up to the happy heavens. His face shines out like the bright white neon sign of a diner when seen on a dark night, gleaming on a road wet with rain, and you are hungry and tired of driving. We gather around waiting for him to give us a translation from the Swedish.

This is the gist. A cargo ship belonging to the Clipper Ship Line (incidentally belonging to Sven Hansen's father) has reported *Anitra* south of Norway and moving well. She is expected to finish at the line off Skagen Light Vessel before midnight tonight. In that case, the announcer says, she will have saved her time on everyone who finished before her. No one behind seems in position to challenge her win. Sweden is jubilant—a Swedish racer is going to win the King's Gold Cup.

We are beside ourselves—"jubilant" is hardly the word. He means us, we are going to win! *Anitra* must be behind us. She can't have worked out ahead. We passed her and have been going like a train of cars since. That steamboat captain is just making Brownie points with his owner, a powerful man in Sweden. In any case he can't have seen us; we are holding well down to the south.

My God! Think of it, we are up there, in the running. If that announcer is right and the wind holds, we've got the monster man, Dick Nye, right in the bag! And *Anitra!* We've always had trouble with her. Only last year she won the Fastnet Race, Europe's premier ocean race. *Anitra* is one hell of a boat. When Sven saw my *Figaro,* he fell in love with her and had Olin Stephens do him a keel version. She was built in Sweden by Bengt Plym, one of the premier builders of the world. Finished bright (varnished, not painted), each plank is matched and she is finished like a violin. Sven operates the New York branch of the Clipper Lines. He is a good friend and a smart competitor on the water.

I pound Knud on the back. "It is the custom," I say, "going back thousands of years to reward the messenger who brings good news. Let's open a bottle of wine. The Swede who is going to win the Gold Cup is you, Knud."

"Let's not," I am advised. "It still sounds too good to be true. After all, she could have lucked in. She had less distance to sail and the captain of the cargo ship said she is moving well. Remember what happened in the Bermuda Race the year the

Bermuda radio announcer was naming *Figaro* the winner just as *Finisterre,* for whom we had been waiting for over nine hours, came in with twelve minutes to spare?"

"OK, fellas, we'll keep it down. But Goddamnit this time *Anitra owes us time* and she is behind us." I feel sure of this, but then—I have been disappointed so many times before.

1950 *Sail Ho!* Would you believe it? Just like the sea stories by G. A. Henty I read as a boy—*Sail Ho!* There's *Anitra* right in our wake. We can see the blue-top spinnaker. She is hull down, which puts her a minimum of three miles behind. She probably found the going light on the other side and crossed over, which put her right in our tack. The Simple Island Boy sighted her first, in the setting sun. His announcement was calm considering the excitement and bubbling jubilation that followed.

Can this really be? Is the golden finger of fate finally going to goose us with joy? Even the idea of it is overwhelming. Delight and joy run through us with the pleasantest of shivers. Everyone is beautiful, everyone is a sparkling wit. Anything at all can set us laughing—what a feeling. No pleasure that will grow out of this race can match this particular kind of sustained delight. It is drawn out for a long time; you are almost sure, and yet the slight measure of uncertainty lurking in the background feeds the anticipation of the climax to come.

The final action today is being played out in the best tradition of classical drama. The unities are being observed; the action is taking place in a single day. There is an inevitability to the outcome and a most fortuitous use of messengers even if in our case these have been electronic. Racine and Corneille must be smiling down from their special heaven if Conrad is not; but what care we? We just hope that the faceless messenger speaking government-approved Swedish on Stockholm radio knew what the hell he was talking about. It is all so dramatically right (especially the part written for us). The boats behind are well behind and those in front not in front enough. It that guy is right, we've got Class A and B in our hot little hands right now. What a gorgeous feeling. *Goddamnit, this is why we came! To feel this exultation, now, not when you get a prize. The feeling is over by then, but now, when you are still on the boat and in company with all who shared the woes and are now sharing the win. Nothing that comes out of a needle or bottle can top this.* That son of a gun on the Stockholm radio had better be right.

Our spirit is infectious. The wind catches it and blows up a bit. We take down the mizzen sail in order to make *Figaro*'s handling easier, to give us the most control. Why take chances now and blow the whole kaboodle?

At 2000 Hirshels Light is aft of the beam to starboard. The distance to the finish is 26 miles.

At 2040 Skagen Light Vessel is visible, 1 point on the starboard bow.

At 2050 the wreck light is visible on the starboard bow.

At 2155 the wreck light and Skagen Light Vessel bear 10° apart on a course of 083°.

At 2220 the wreck light is abeam close at hand to starboard. It is 4.7 miles to the finish.

Roaring in to the finish, we are hailed by a large sailing schooner.

"Ahoy, *Anitra,*" she calls out to us, followed by a spate of Swedish. Then a bright searchlight snaps on, picking us out. This is followed by voiced consternation. The schooner is *Cinderella,* a yacht training vessel used by the steamship company belonging to Sven Hansen's father to train cadets. They have been lured out to hail Sven's victory by the same reports which unwittingly gave us such a boost. Having expected *Anitra,* a sister yawl, our silhouette made them sure it was Sven's victory. But when the light went on, their joy went out. *Anitra* is bright-hulled. We are white. Their light snapped off. A cruel spear had plunged into a once happy heart.

Knud goes to the rail and hails the schooner, calling Einer Hansen by name. He gently tells him *Anitra* is about a half hour behind. "We are *Figaro.*"

A voice answers. "Well done, *Figaro,* congratulations," and a scattering of applause. They sail off into the dark with their burden of sadness and we concentrate on finishing.

We cross the finish at 22.52—19 hours GMT. Standing at the wheel, I hail the light vessel, "This is *Figaro.*" A voice calls back. "Well done, *Figaro.*" I ask, "What time did *Carina* finish?" He takes a while to look it up while we round up. In a while he calls the time. We have beaten her, but good. I lean over the wheel and call out to the crew, those on deck and those below in their bunks, "It's pheasant under glass for every man."

No one can sleep. That was OK while we were racing and had to keep up our strength and efficiency, but that's all over now. Monk sets a course for Marstrand. Skagen LV is at the corner of Denmark where the Kattegat begins. It is where you can turn down Oresund for Copenhagen. But Marstrand is in Sweden, across the water near Gothenburg, about 26 miles away. We open a bottle of champagne. It is warm and fizzles all over the place. We have taken champagne along on several big races hoping for some such occasion. I never thought I would like warm champagne.

We reconstruct the watches. I give the youth brigade the deck and another bottle of champagne. They use most of it, shaking it and making it fizz over one another like a seltzer bottle. Loud and often rude sounds come from above, but we, the veterans below, could not care less. I bring out a bottle of Cognac and Bobby breaks out the Havanas. Everyone lights up and toasts the race, ourselves, and *Figaro*. Before long we have a good solid fug below. It is so thick it dims the lights and you can almost feel its texture between thumb and forefinger. Before we arrive off Marstrand we are well into a second bottle and feeling no pain and strangely undrunk. We were drunk when we started at Skagen Light Vessel and have been slowly drinking ourselves sober.

As a matter of fact, this is only an introduction into a stretched-out week of waiting until the smallest boat in our race finished. (He happened to be Bobby Lowein in *Danegeld* who had becalmed in a severe case of Harry Flatters!) During this time we were drowned in skoals and salutations. Happily no one beat our time. We won the race, class and overall and from the middle of the fleet, the hardest way to do it. We received the King of Sweden's Gold Cup but not from Gustav of Sweden. He, being an archaeologist, was at Oxford University receiving a degree. But Olav of Norway is a sailor. He stood in for his neighbor king and gave us our prize. Our hobnobbing with royalty did not stop with that. The Swedish princesses, very pretty girls, came into the harbor in a beat-up powerboat and tied up alongside of us. It was the year of the very short shorts and of bikinis, and our boys always found extra deck work when the princesses were sunbathing.

There is something excessively fascinating about a stretch of royal thigh.

But that was all later. That morning when we sailed into Marstrand, shortly after dawn, the world was full of enchantment—fresh and lovely. The town was dominated by a medieval stone castle, flags flew from everything, and the harbor was graced by a square-rigger, all yards braced (she had been converted to a hostel). We sailed in as knights errant. We had come a long way to find our Grail. And there before us we saw *Carina*. She was backed against a quay. We backed alongside her, tied ourselves to her and to the quay, and cut the engine. We had arrived in the land of the blond sprites and trolls.

Then I saw Dick. He was weaving slightly, the effect of seeing us no doubt. He held a drink and waved a cigar vaguely at us. But draped around him was one of Sweden's finest products, a long-legged beauty with long flaxen hair and breasts that sprang like the twin arrows of Artemis. She was also a little tipsy. It had been a long night of celebration going from boat to boat, probably having started with S. Huey Long.

Dick, looking over her shoulder at me, said to her, "Now there is a real American millionaire and a prince of a fellow."

She looked toward me, undraped herself from around Richard, and with light fairy step climbed over *Carina*'s rail and then over *Figaro*'s. She draped herself around me, her arms enfolding me and placed a kiss full on my lips. This prince slowly felt himself turning into a frog.

For the mathematically minded: We came in with twenty gallons of water! Dick swore his dinner cost $400.